Homo Oeconomicus

Volume 27, Number 4 (2011)

ACCEDO

Accedo Verlagsgesellschaft, München

Band 75
der Schriftenreihe des
"Munich Institute of Integrated Studies"
Gesellschaft für integrierte Studien (GIS)
(Reihenkürzel 0049)

Homo Oeconomicus 27(4)
www.homooeconomicus.org
Cover: Katharina Kohl
Photomaterial: Detlef Reiß
The electronic archive of Homo Oeconomicus
is retrievable via www.gbi.de

Gnesener Str. 1, D-81929 München, Germany
www.accedoverlag.de, accedoverlag@web.de
Fax: +49 89 929 4109

Printed and bound by Books on Demand GmbH, Norderstedt

ISBN 978-3-89265-075-1
ISSN 0943-0180

Homo Oeconomicus
Volume 27, Number 4 (2011)

EURAS Yearbook of Standardization, Volume 6
edited by Manfed J. Holler and John Hudson

Homo Oeconomicus 27(4): 395–417 (2011)

www.accedoverlag.de

An Alternative Explanation of Parties' Extreme Positioning: A Spatial Model Analysis under the "Second Degree Preference" Hypothesis

Achillefs Papageorgiou
University of Tampere, Department of Political Science and International Relations, School of Management, Tampere, Finland (Author for Correspondence)
(eMail: Achillefs.Papageorgiou@uta.fi)

Ioannis Papageorgiou
Université de Toulouse, Institute de Mathématiques de Toulouse, France
(eMail: ioannis.papageorgiou@math.univ-toulouse.fr)

Abstract This study draws heavily on Adams' (1998, 2001a,b) *biased model* of voting. The main objective is to offer an alternative explanation of parties' placement in positions more extreme than the positions of their party identifiers. To explain parties' extreme positioning we put forward the heuristic term of "the second degree preference." According to this term, if two parties present the same policy issue position inside the partisan constituency of a third party, the latter's identifiers will prefer the party that used to be the closest to them prior to any relocation. A spatial analysis shows that under the assumption of the "second degree preference" the party at the edge has a strategic advantage to articulate a position that is further away from the position of the bulk of his partisans.

Keywords biased model of voting, spatial models, deterministic voting, party identification, three-party competition

1. Introduction

Scholars have used spatial models, among others, to solve voting paradoxes (Nurmi and Saari 2009, Nurmi 2009), fathom the power of institutions (Napel and Widgrén 2004, Steunenberg et al. 1999, Shepsle and Weingast 1981, Poole 2005), locate parties' core positions (Saari 2009) etc. Having the work of Downs (1957) as a starting point, the spatial models have been mostly linked with the scholarly work that deals with party competition on a single or more dimensions of policy issue competition (e.g. Stokes 1963,

ISBN 978-3-89265-075-1 ISSN 0943-0180

logic and can be empirically tested in a three-party system when the basic assumptions are met[2].

The study develops as follows. Section 2 presents Adams' (1998, 2001a,b) *partisan model* and discusses the two schools of voting that Adams' model reconciles: The Michigan school of voting and the rational school as expressed by Downs' proximity or spatial theory. Section 3 displays the main assumptions of our stylized example and introduces the heuristic concept of the "second degree preference." The section that follows presents a spatial analysis of our stylized example differentiating among two sub-cases. In the first case, the party in the middle stays inside his[3] partisan constituency while in the second case he relocates inside the partisan constituency of the party to his right. In this second case, the heuristic concept of the "second degree preference" is introduced. Section 5 discusses the restrictions of the stylized example presented. Lastly, section 6 presents avenues for further research.

2. Partisan model of voting

Adams' early work as presented in his two articles (1998, 2001a) and book (2001b) is divided into two parts. In the first part, Adams (1998, 2001a,b) sets the foundations of his *partisan model* at a theoretical level. Through a stylized example Adams (1998, 2001a,b) shows that "in multiparty elections parties have electoral incentives to appeal on policy grounds to voters biased towards them for nonpolicy reasons" (2001b: 21). In the second part, Adams tests his arguments empirically by the means of a simulation analysis.

Adams' (1998, 2001a,b) *partisan model* is founded on the argument that voting is deterministic. The term deterministic voting denotes a situation where parties can accurately predict the voters' choices (Coughlin 1992). Put differently, deterministic voting does "not allow for *error* by voters" (Poole 2005: 8).

Adams (1998, 2001a,b) reconciles two different thoughts on voting: the Michigan school of voting, as expressed through the concept of party identification, and the rational school of Anthony Downs, as became famous through his classic book "An Economic Theory of Democracy." The Michigan school of voting took its name after the university to which the authors of *The American Voter* were affiliated. The Michigan school of voting professes that voters usually cast a ballot for the party of identifica-

[2] We discuss this point at section 5.

[3] We adopt the convention of referring to the party as "he" and to the voter as "she."

tion. Party identification is a psychological tie that voters have towards a party and is defined as "the sense of personal attachment which the individual feels toward the [partisan] group of *her* choice" (Campbell et al. 1954: 89). Party identification is not synonymous to either voting behavior or political ideology. As Blais (2001) and his colleagues put it:

> [P]artisans are partisan because they think they are partisan. They are not necessarily partisan because they vote like a partisan or think like a partisan, or register as a partisan, or because someone else thinks they are a partisan. In a strict sense, they are not even partisan because they like one party more than another. Partisanship as party identification is entirely a matter of self-definition (Blais et al. 2001: 6).

By arguing that party identification is not synonymous to voting record, it is clear that a person who consistently votes for the same party does not necessarily identify with this party. In other words, although there is a high likelihood that someone who always votes for the same party also identifies with this party, nevertheless one's voting record does not suffice as exact information on his party ID; this is because a voter may vote for the same party for reasons other than being an identifier of the party. In its positive context the fact that voting behavior and party identification are not synonymous means that a voter's party identification does not cease to exist when the voter casts a ballot for a party other than the party with which she feels the closest to.

Contrary to the Michigan school, the Downsian school of voting, as expressed through the proximity or spatial theory, holds that voters make up their minds purely on the premise of rational grounds. According to proximity theory, voters invariably cast their ballot for the party that stands the closest to their ideal policy issue position (Downs 1957). A strong assumption of the spatial theory of voting is that:

> The positions the candidates announce prior to an election will be the positions they subsequently enact once in office. Since voters typically have preferences defined over policy outcomes and not over electoral announcement per se, but their only information at the time of voting consist of these announcements per se, the equivalence of announced position and policy outcome appears to be one of analytical tractability at the expense of realism (Banks 1990: 311).

Another basic assumption of the spatial theory is that voters' and parties' preferences can be demonstrated as points in the policy space. The space may consist of one or more dimensions depending on the number of issues. When there is a single issue, the space is one-dimensional; when the policy issues are two the space is defined by two dimensions and so on.

Assuming a competition in pairs, one can calculate the gains for each party upon finding the cut-point between their policy issue positions. The cut-point stands for the position that is equidistant from the policy positions of two contestants. All voters whose ideal policy issue position is identical to the cut-point will be indifferent towards the two parties. All voters to the left of the cut-point will vote for the leftmost party, while all those to the right of the cut-point for the rival. As Berger et al. (2000) have shown, during competition in pairs each party can get more votes by moving the cut-point closer to the other party's position. The most famous articulation of the spatial theory of voting is the median voter theorem (MVT). According to MVT if voters are distributed normally, the winner of the elections will be the party that will occupy a position in the middle of the distribution[4]. If neither of the two parties occupies the median, the winner of the elections will be the party positioned closest to the middle of the distribution.

Adams' (1998, 2001a,b) uses components of both above-mentioned schools to present his *partisan model* of voting. According to the *partisan model* the utility of the voter can be given by the following deterministic model:

$$U_i(\theta)=b_\theta-(x_i-x_\theta)^2$$

b_θ equals a constant if voter i identifies with party θ and zero otherwise; $(x_i-x_\theta)^2$ measures the policy issue distance of voter i's position (x_i) from party θ's position (x_θ). So b_θ represents the component of party identification, while $(x_i-x_\theta)^2$ stands for the proximity or spatial component. The negative sign in front of the quadratic function denotes that utility decreases with distance. When the voter presents a position identical to the party of choice, i.e. when $x_i=x_\theta$ the voter's utility reaches maximum[5] and equals the degree of her partisan attachment. For the purposes of the analysis, party identification is assumed to have the same effect for all voters, a postulation that has been used before regarding the effect of party identification in Finland (Papageorgiou 2010a), Britain (Adams 2001a), Norway (Adams and Merrill 1999) and France (Adams and Merrill 2000).

---

[4] Here, we refer to a very simple version of MVT. For instance, Shepsle (1991) and Palfrey (1984) consider the case where there are more than two candidates; Plott (1967) considers the case where there is more than one dimension of competition; Alesina (1988) considers the case where parties are policy seeking; Aragones and Palfrey (2002) consider the case where one candidate enjoys an advantage over the other.

[5] As $\partial^2 U_i(\theta)/\partial x_\theta^2 = -2 < 0$, $U_i(\theta)$ is strictly concave and symmetric to x_θ. $U_i(\theta)$ is also symmetric to x_i because $\partial U_i(\theta)/\partial x_\theta = 0 \Leftrightarrow x_i=x_\theta$, with a unique maximum $\max_{x_i} U_i(\theta)=U_i(\theta)\big|_{x_i=x_\theta}=b_\theta$.

According to equation (1) party identification and policy issue preferences influence party choice but not one another.[6] The former postulation has been criticized by authors who have argued that party identification is related, among others, to perceptions of parties' positions (Clarke and Stewart 1985). The postulation is, however, in compliance with the argument that party identification is an exogenous determinant of the party choice (Campbell et al. 1960) that remains stable and unaffected by short-term forces (Green and Palmquist 1990).

To gain further insights on party competition under Adams' (1998, 2001a,b) *partisan model*, consider a situation in which parties λ and κ are positioned to the left and to the right of party θ, respectively ($x_\lambda < x_\theta$ and $x_\kappa > x_\theta$). Also, assume that voters identify only with one party, e.g. party θ (so $b_\theta > 0$ and $b_\lambda = b_\kappa = 0$) and that party λ and κ want to siphon off θ's partisans. θ's, λ's, and κ's utilities are given below:

$$U_i(\theta) = b_\theta - (x_i - x_\theta)^2$$

$$U_i(\lambda) = -(x_i - x_\lambda)^2 \text{ and}$$

$$U_i(\kappa) = -(x_i - x_\kappa)^2$$

For λ to attract support from θ's partisans, λ should present a position for which the utility differential of λ over θ is positive or

$$U_i(\lambda) - U_i(\theta) > 0 \Rightarrow -(x_i - x_\lambda)^2 - b_\theta + (x_i - x_\theta)^2 > 0$$

As Adams has shown[7], when party λ proposes the voter's ideal policy, that is when $x_\lambda = x_i$, θ's partisans will defect to λ when

$$-b_\theta + (x_i - x_\theta)^2 > 0 \Rightarrow |x_i - x_\theta| > b_\theta^{1/2}$$

[6] The discussion on whether party identification is endogenous or exogenous to policy preferences has spanned half a century. Scholars such as Franklin (1984), Fiorina (1981) and Markus and Converse (1979), assert that party identification is endogenous to policy evaluations. Others such as Green, Palmquist and Schickler (2002), Schickler and Green (1997) and Miller (1991) counter that party identification is an exogenous characteristic. Such argumentation means that voters do not change their party identification to fit their policy issue beliefs.

[7] For proof see Adams (2001b: 36).

Figure 2 C 's two options

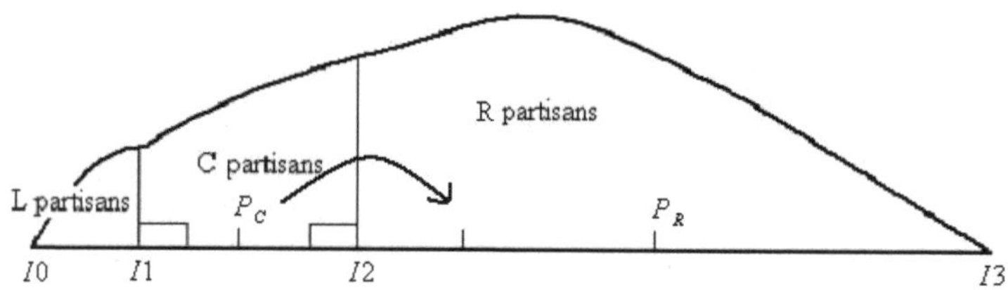

Under II, scenarios are developed for which the heuristic concept of the "second degree preference" applies. The conceptualization of the "second degree preference" does not change the functional logic of voter's utility but supplements it in situations in which two political parties relocate to the same policy issue position as a means of dragging rival party identifiers. According to the "second degree preference" condition when one party relocates to the same policy issue position with another party, rival party identifiers do not perceive the two parties as identical but opt for the party that used to occupy a policy position closer to them prior to any relocation. The "second degree preference" hypothesis makes intuitive logic. A new policy issue position on behalf of a party that voters had associated with a radical different policy issue position compared to their own is not likely to attract a great deal of support. For the ordinal configuration L-C-R, the second "degree preference" hypothesis means that R partisans will prefer C to L when both of them adopt the same position inside R's partisan constituency. Cases I and II are presented in due order.

I. C inside his partisan constituency

Suppose that party R is placed within the boundary of his partisan constituency at $P_R \in (I2+b_R^{1/2}, I3)$. We adopt the convention of symbolizing the votes found in the interval (a,b) with $\langle x,y \rangle$.

With the party R fixed at this position, the following quantities are defined:

When $P_C \in (I2-b_C^{1/2}, I2)$ we define:

$$\text{G1}=\max\left\{\begin{array}{l}\left\langle 2I2-P_R-b_C^{1/2}, I2\right\rangle, \\ \max\limits_{P_C:P_C>2I2-P_R}\left\langle P_C-b_C^{1/2}, \dfrac{P_R^2-b_R-P_C^2}{2(P_R-P_C)}\right\rangle\end{array}\right\}$$

when $P_C \in (I1+b_C^{1/2}, I2-b_C^{1/2})$ we define:

$$G2=\max\left\{\begin{array}{l}\max\limits_{P_C:P_C>2I2-P_R}\left\langle P_C-b_C^{1/2}, \dfrac{P_R^2-b_R-P_C^2}{2(P_R-P_C)}\right\rangle, \\ \max\limits_{P_C:P_C<2I2-P_R}\left\langle P_C-b_C^{1/2}, \dfrac{P_R^2+b_C-P_C^2}{2(P_R-P_C)}\right\rangle, \left\langle 2I2-P_R-b_C^{1/2}, I2\right\rangle\end{array}\right\}$$

and when $P_C \in (I1, I1+b_C^{1/2})$ we define:

$$G3=\max\left\{\begin{array}{l}\max\limits_{P_C:P_C>2I2-P_R}\left\langle I1, \dfrac{P_R^2-b_R-P_C^2}{2(P_R-P_C)}\right\rangle, \\ \max\limits_{P_C:P_C<2I2-P_R}\left\langle I1, \dfrac{P_R^2+b_C-P_C^2}{2(P_R-P_C)}\right\rangle, \left\langle I1, I2\right\rangle\end{array}\right\}$$

Lemma 1 $G1, G2$, and $G3$ are the maximum votes that C can win if he chooses a policy issue position that falls within the intervals $(I1, I1+b_C^{1/2})$, $(I1+b_C^{1/2}, I2-b_C^{1/2})$, and $(I2-b_C^{1/2}, I2)$, respectively (Figure 3). Consequently, if

$$G=\max\langle G1, G2, G3\rangle$$

then G is the maximum number of votes that party C wins if he proposes a policy issue position that is found within the boundary of his partisan constituency.

Figure 3 C*'s policy positions*

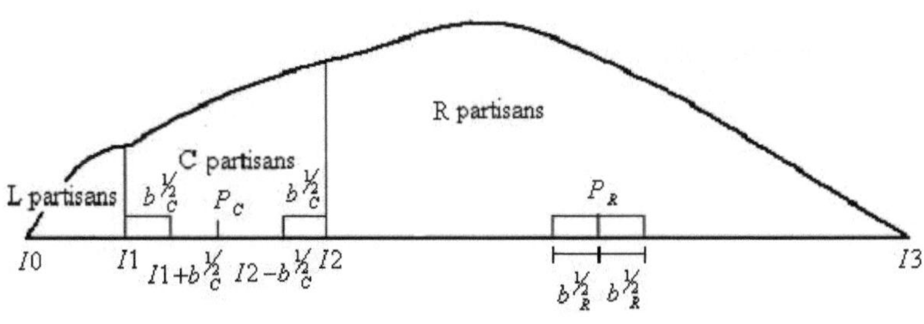

Proof To calculate the voters that C gets when he presents a policy issue position P_C within the constituency of his own party identifiers, it is assumed that voters who vote for C are found in a continuous interval, for example, (A,B). The upper bound B is conditional upon C's distance from party R. The lower bound A depends on party L's distance from party C. The points A and B are the only ones for which

$$U_B(C{:}P_C)=U_B(R{:}P_R) \text{ and } U_A(C{:}P_C)=U_A(L{:}P_L)$$

($U_X(Y{:}P_Y)$: This is to indicate the utility of voter who is at position X when party Y is placed at position P_Y).

Initially, we first determine the upper bound of the interval (A,B). Point B can be inside the constituency of C's partisans or inside the constituency of R's partisans. We distinguish among three sub-cases:

A) First, assume that $I2=\dfrac{P_R+P_C}{2}$

This implies that:

$$I2\text{-}P_C=P_R\text{-}I2 \Rightarrow -(I2\text{-}P_C)^2=-(P_R\text{-}I2)^2 \Rightarrow U_{I2}(C{:}P_C)=U_{I2}(R{:}P_R)$$

Because of the continuity of the interval (A,B), the last relationship means that position $I2$ stands as the "border" between C's and R's voters, and thus $B=I2$.

B) Suppose that $I2>\dfrac{P_R+P_C}{2}$ and that $P_C \in (I1, I2\text{-}b_C^{1/2})$

Then,

$$I2\text{-}P_C>P_R\text{-}I2 \Rightarrow -(I2\text{-}P_C)^2<-(P_R\text{-}I2)^2 \Rightarrow U_{I2}(C{:}P_C)<U_{I2}(R{:}P_R)$$

Therefore, $I2$ will vote for R, which implies that $B<I2$. Because the voter(s) at B are placed within the partisan constituency of C, they identify with C and therefore the following utilities are obtained:

$$U_B(C{:}P_C)=-(P_C\text{-}B)^2+b_C \text{ and } U_B(R{:}P_R)=-(P_R\text{-}B)^2$$

We want:

$$U_B(C{:}P_C)=U_B(R{:}P_R)\Rightarrow -(P_C-B)^2+b_C=-(P_R-B)^2\Rightarrow$$
$$-P_C^2+2P_CB+b_C=-P_R^2+2P_RB\Rightarrow 2(P_R-P_C)B=P_R^2-P_C^2+b_C\Rightarrow$$
$$B=\frac{P_R^2+b_C-P_C^2}{2(P_R-P_C)}$$

Notice that the inequality $I2>\frac{P_R+P_C}{2}$ has a meaning only when $P_C\in(I1,I2-b_C^{1/2})$.

For $P_C\in(I2-b_C^{1/2},I2)$,

$$I2>\frac{P_R+P_C}{2}\Rightarrow I2-P_C\rangle P_R-I2$$

is obtained. It follows that if $P_C\in(I2-b_C^{1/2},I2)$, then P_R should be placed in a distance smaller than $b_R^{1/2}$ from $I2$. This is impossible by definition as $P_R\in(I2+b_R^{1/2},I3)$.

Therefore, $I2>\frac{P_R+P_C}{2}$ cannot hold true for $P_C\in(I2-b_C^{1/2},I2)$.

C) Suppose that $I2<\frac{P_R+P_C}{2}$

Then,

$$I2-P_C<P_R-I2\Rightarrow -(I2-P_C)^2>-(P_R-I2)^2\Rightarrow U_{I2}(C{:}P_C)>U_{I2}(R{:}P_R)$$

Therefore, $I2$ will vote for C, which implies that $B>I2$. Because $B>I2$, it means that the voters who are placed at B identify with party R and therefore,

$$U_B(C{:}P_C)=-(P_C-B)^2 \text{ and } U_B(R{:}P_R)=-(P_R-B)^2+b_R$$

We want:

$$U_B(C{:}P_C)=U_B(R{:}P_R)\Rightarrow -(P_C-B)^2=-(P_R-B)^2+b_R\Rightarrow$$
$$-P_C^2+2P_CB=-P_R^2+2P_RB+b_R\Rightarrow 2(P_R-P_C)B=P_R^2-P_C^2-b_R\Rightarrow$$
$$B=\frac{P_R^2-b_R-P_C^2}{2(P_R-P_C)}$$

To finish the proof it remains to show the lower bound A. Party L does not have a fixed position like R, but he locates according to C's posi-

Lemma 2 showed that when C "squeezes" R, he wins R partisans but he also loses some of his own who defect to party L. What cases a), b), and c) in Lemma 2 argue is that C will "squeeze tightly" R if what he will gain among R's partisans will be bigger compared to what he will lose to L.

As the analysis indicated, C will "squeeze" R if the latter's partisans found in partisan constituencies such as the ones in a) and b) in Lemma 2 outnumber C's partisans. Furthermore, C will "squeeze tightly" party R or, in other words, C will locate at $P_R\text{-}b^{1/2}$ only if the interval $(P_R\text{-}2b^{1/2},P_R\text{-}b^{1/2})$ has sufficiently more partisans than R's "zone of invulnerability" $(P_R\text{-}b^{1/2},P_R)$. If there are not many partisans at $(P_R\text{-}2b^{1/2},P_R\text{-}b^{1/2})$, then C will have no reason to locate at $P_R\text{-}b^{1/2}$. In this case, all partisans found between

$$P_R\text{-}b^{1/2} \text{ and } \frac{P_R^2\text{-}b\text{-}P_C^2}{2(P_R\text{-}P_C)}$$

will vote for R.

Figure 5 Extreme position taking

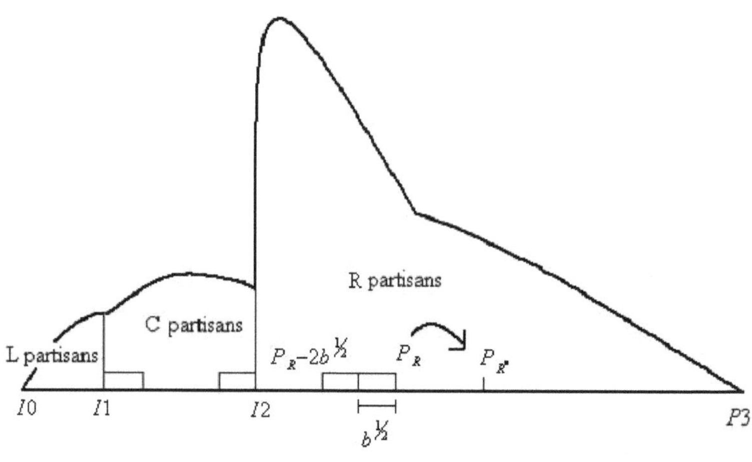

Remark Corollary 1 and Lemma 2 show a surprising finding. If the bulk of R's partisans are near R's fixed position, party R will suffer a bigger partisan defection than if the bulk of his partisans would be further away. Put differently a party will be better off having his party identifiers placed further away on the policy issue dimension than in a close proximity to his position. This finding runs counter to intuitive logic as one would expect that the closest a party is to the bulk of his supporters, the smallest the partisan haemorrhage ensuing from the rival parties' strategic move, will also be. Therefore, for example, for an imaginary distribution as the one illustrated in Figure 5, party R will be better off if he presents a position at P_{R^*} than at P_R.

5. Discussion

This paper aspires to offer an alternative explanation of why parties adopt similar but more extreme policy positions than the positions of the majority of voters who support them for non-policy reasons (Adams and Merrill 1999, Adams et al. 2005). To explain such cases we put forward the heuristic term of the "second degree preference." The concept of the "second degree preference" refers to situations where the identifiers of one party are more sympathetic toward one rival than the other. A spatial analysis indicated that in a three-party competition, the party with the largest partisan constituency is better off when he presents a position that is more extreme than the position of his partisans.

Here we claim to have presented neither a sophisticated theory akin to Adams' (1998, 2001a,b) nor a theory that can be easily tested. As has already been asserted, the stylized example presented is of technical interest and therefore any attempt to apply it to a three-party system would be doomed to meet serious constraints. For example, contrary to the theory, in a real-world tripartite party competition the following holds true:

1. Not all voters identify with political parties.
2. Party identifiers are not distributed at discrete intervals but at intervals that overlap.
3. Although it is more often the case in multiparty systems, even in a tripartite competition parties might leapfrog one another.
4. In real-life elections competition for rival voters is not restricted to sequential parties.

However, on relaxing some of the assumptions one can test the concept of the "second degree preference" by the means of a simulation analysis in a real three-party system. To our view, the British party system could be used as a bed test for our theoretical construction. Consistent to our analysis, this will mean that assuming a left and right dimension the utmost right wing party, the Conservative Party (R in our theory), will be the "rival" party while the Labour Party (C in our theory) and the Liberal Democrats

(L in our theory) will be the "challengers."[10] This seems plausible given indeed the big pull of voters identifying with the Conservatives and their rivalry with the adjacent Labour party. Of course, what makes for the right, middle, or left party in a party competition is pertinent to the dimension of competition, so that different parties at the time can be considered as "rivals" and "challengers."

Adams (1998, 2001a,b) who uses the same assumptions, as the ones employed here, inevitably relaxes most of them when testing his theory in the British party system. For example, Adams in his two publications (2001a,b) relaxes the assumption that the partisans are distributed in separate intervals as this is a postulation that is not supported by the British National Election data of 1987. However, relaxing this postulation is not harmful for the theory as the positions of the British partisans are strongly correlated with the positions of the parties. Also, in his empirical application Adams (2001a,b) merges the party sympathisers with the party identifiers to create a fully biased British electoral as assumed in his theoretical model.

Also, drawing data on the Manifesto Research Group, Adams (2001a: 125) shows that in a party system with a small number of parties such as the British the order of parties' positions do not usually change, an argument that complements the theoretical assumption that was also set here which is that parties do not leapfrog each other.

Although, deterministic models can rarely spot equilibria (Plott 1967, Cox 1990), the fact that this study does not locate Nash equilibrium as Adams shows in his work (1998, 2001a,b) is undoubtedly a serious shortcoming of the present analysis. Acknowledging this weakness, parties in the paper at hand only had one chance to respond to rival parties' strategies and in that sense parties' optimal positions were "one-off" optima.

6. Further implications

In this research note, the use of "party identification" was used for convenience. Instead, any other individual characteristic that biases party choice could be used (e.g. party sympathy or party membership). Furthermore, different characteristics could be merged with the scope of creating a fully biased electoral as the one assumed in these examples (For example, one

---

[10] In out stylized example L's position appears to be further to the left compared to C's position. This is for presentation purposes only. Applying our theoretical construction to the British party system, it is not important if the Liberal Democrat's position is so much to the left of the Labour party's position, as it appears in the example.

could create a biased electorate by adding voters who identify with a party with voters who sympathize with a party or with voters who are members of a party). Also, party identification could be replaced by any other item that casts a "valence-advantage" (Ansolabehere and Snyder 2000, Groseclose 2001, Hollard and Rossignol 2008, Schofield 2003, Schofield and Sened 2005, Schofield and Miller 2007) for one of the contestants (e.g. the party leader's popularity).

Also, one can expand the analysis presented here by allowing for abstention. Although, such an addition would add severely to the analytical complexity, it is work worth showing as usually studies utilizing deterministic functions of voting assume no abstention[11].

In a previous paper (Papageorgiou 2010b), the simulations analysis allowed for the presence of independents. Independents are those voters who do not identify with parties. Bringing the latter block of voters into play, the analysis should consider two voting functions, one for the independents and one for the partisans. To capture the independents' voting behavior the biased model introduced at the outset of the paper will reduce to a proximity model where voting will only depend on the voter's distance from the party[12]. For the rest of the voters, who are biased to a political party, Adams' (1998, 2001a,b) *partisan model* will continue to apply. To reiterate the point, the aim of the present study was to consider the implications that a fully biased electoral would have on party strategies and therefore the presence of independents was not considered here. However, if one allows for independents in the analysis, the results would heavily depend on the amount and distribution of independents along the policy scale. For instance, assuming that they are no unobservable factors that render decisions indeterminate from the parties' perspective and assuming a huge amount of independents found at the centre of the policy issue dimension, party strategies are expected to behave according to the classic Downsian model; parties will move centripetally towards competing for independents, the block of voters whose vote is truly the decisive one for the outcome of the elections.

References

Adams, J. (1998), Partisan Voting and Multiparty Spatial Competition: The Pressure for Responsible Parties, *Journal of Theoretical Politics* 10: 5–31.

---

[11] For an exception see Zakharov (2008)

[12] Since party identification would have no effect on voting, b=0 and so (1) becomes $U_i(\theta)=-(x_i-x_\theta)^2$.

Adams, J. (2001a), A Theory of Spatial Competition with Biased Voters: Party Policies Viewed Temporally and Comparatively, *British Journal of Political Science* 31: 121-158.

Adams, J. (2001b), *Party Competition and Responsible Party Government: A Theory of Spatial Competition Based Upon Insights from Behavioral Research*, The University of Michigan Press.

Adams, J. and Merrill, S. (1999), Modelling Party Strategies and Policy Representation in Multiparty Elections: Why Are Strategies So Extreme?, *American Journal of Political Science* 43: 765-791.

Adams, J. and Merrill, S. (2000), Spatial Models of Candidate Competition and the 1998 French Presidential Election: Are Presidential Candidates Vote-Maximizers?, *Journal of Politics* 62: 729-756.

Adams, J., Merrill, S. and Grofman, B. (2005), *A Unified Theory of Party Competition: A Cross National Analysis Integrating Spatial and Behavioral Factors*, Cambridge: Cambridge University Press.

Alesina, A. (1988), Credibility and Policy Convergence in a Two-Party System with Rational Voters, *American Economic Review* 78: 796-805.

Alvarez, R.M. and Brehm, J. (1995), American Ambivalence Towards Abortion Policy: Development of a Heteroskedastic Probit Model of Competing Values, *American Journal of Political Science* 39: 1055-1082.

Ansolabehere, S. and Snyder, J. (2000), Valence Politics and Equilibrium in Spatial Election Models, *Public Choice* 103: 327-336.

Aragones, E. and Palfrey, T. (2002), Mixed Equilibrium in a Downsian Model with a Favored Candidate, *Journal of Economic Theory* 103: 131-161.

Banks, S.J. (1990), A Model of Electoral Competition with Incomplete Information, *Journal of Economic Theory* 50: 309-325.

Berger, M., Munger, M. and Potthoff, R. (2000), The Downsian Model Predicts Divergence, *Journal of Theoretical Politics* 12: 228-240.

Blais, A., Gidengil, E., Nadeau, R. and Nevitte, N. (2001), Measuring Party Identification: Canada, Britain and the United States, *Political Behaviour* 23: 5-22.

Campbell, A., Gurin, G. and Miller, E.W. (1954), *The Voter Decides*, Evanston, IL: Row, Peterson.

Campbell, A., Converse, E.P., Miller, E.W. and Stokes, D. (1960), *The American Voter*, University of Chicago Press.

Clarke, D.H. and Stewart, C.M. (1985), Short-Term Forces and Partisan Change in Canada, 1974-1980, *Electoral Studies* 4: 15-35.

Clarke, D.H., Kornberg, A. and Wearing, P. (2000), *A Polity on the Edge: Canada and the Politics of Fragmentation*, Broadview Press Ltd.

Clarke, D.H., Kornberg, A. and Scotto, J.T. (2009), *Making Political Choices: Canada and the United States*, University of Toronto Press.

Coughlin, J.P. (1992), *Probabilistic Voting Theory*, Cambridge: Cambridge University Press.

Cox, W.G. (1990), Centripetal and Centrifugal Incentives in Electoral Systems, *American Journal of Political Science* 34: 903-935.

Davis, A.O., Hinich, J.M. and Ordeshook, C.P. (1970), An Expository Development of a Mathematical Model of the Electoral Process, *American Political Science Review* 64: 426-448.

de Palma, A., Hong, G-S. and Thisse, J-F. (1990), Equilibria in Multiparty Competition under Uncertainty, *Social Choice and Welfare* 7: 247-259.

Downs, A. (1957), *An Economic Theory of Democracy*, New York: Harper and Row.

Eaton, B.C. and Lipsey, G.R. (1975), The Principle of Minimum Differentiation Reconsidered: Some New Developments in the Theory of Spatial Competition, *Review of Economic Studies* 42: 27–49.

Enelow, M.J. and Hinich, J.M. (1984), *The Spatial Theory of Voting*, Cambridge: Cambridge University Press.

Endersby, J. and Galatas, S. (1998), British Parties and Spatial Competition: Dimensions of Party Evaluation in the 1992 Election, *Public Choice* 97: 363–382.

Erickson, R. and Romero, D. (1990), Candidate Equilibrium and the Behavioral Model of the Vote, *American Political Science Review* 84: 1103-1126.

Fiorina, P.M. (1981) *Retrospective Voting in American National Elections*, New Haven, CT: Yale University Press.

Franklin, H.C. (1984) Issue Preferences, Socialization, and the Evolution of Party Identification, *American Journal of Political Science* 28: 459-478.

Green, P.D. and Palmquist, B. (1990), Of Artifacts and Partisan Instability, *American Journal of Political Science* 34: 872-902.

Green, P.D., Palmquist, B. and Schickler, E. (2002), *Partisan Hearts and Minds: Political Parties and the Social Identities of Voters*, Yale University Press.

Groseclose, T. (2001), A Model of Candidate Location when one Candidate has a Valence Advantage, *American Journal of Political Science* 45: 862-886.

Hollard, G. and Rossignol, S. (2008), An Alternative Approach to Valence Advantage in Spatial Competition, *Journal of Public Economic Theory* 10: 441-454.

Hug, S. (1995), Third Parties in Equilibrium, *Public Choice* 82: 159–180.

Iversen, T. (1994a), Political Leadership and Representation in West European Democracies, *American Journal of Political Science* 38: 45-74.

Iversen, T. (1994b), The Logics of Electoral Politics: Spatial, Directional, and Mobilization Effects, *Comparative Political Studies* 27: 155-189.

Lin, T., Enelow, M.J. and Dorussen, H. (1999), Equilibrium in Multicandidate Probabilistic Spatial Voting, *Public Choice* 98: 59-82.

Merrill, S. and Adams, J. (2001), Computing Nash equilibria in Probabilistic, Multiparty Spatial Models with Nonpolicy Components, *Political Analysis* 9: 347-361.

Miller, E.W. (1991), Party Identification, Realignment, and Party Voting: Back to the Basics, *American Political Science Review* 85: 557-568.

Markus, B.G. and Converse, E.P. (1979), A Dynamic Simultaneous Equation Model of Electoral Choice, *American Political Science Review* 73: 1055-1070.

Müller, C.W. and Strøm, K. (1999), *Policy, Office, or Votes?: How Political Parties in Western Europe Make Hard Decisions*, Cambridge: Cambridge University Press.

Napel, S. and Widgrén, M. (2004), Power Measurement as Sensitivity Analysis: A Unified Approach, *Journal of Theoretical Politics* 16: 517-538.

Nurmi, H. (2009), *Thin Rationality and Representation of Preferences with Implications to Spatial Voting Models*, Working paper/PCRC University of Turku. Springer.

Nurmi, H. and Saari, D. (2009), *Connections and Implications of the Ostrogorski Paradox for Spatial Voting Models*, Working paper/PCRC University of Turku.

Palfrey, R.T. (1984), Spatial Equilibrium with Entry, *Review of Economic Studies* 51: 139-156.

Papageorgiou, A. (2010a), Finnish Party Positions in 2007: A Matter of Equilibrium or Voters' Projection?, *Electoral Studies* 29: 737-745.

Papageorgiou, A. (2010b), Simulation Analysis of the Effect of Party Identification on Finnish Parties' Optimal Positions, *Scandinavian Political Studies* 33: 224-247.

Plott, R.C. (1967), A Notion of Equilibrium and its Possibility under Majority Rule, *American Economic Review* 57: 786–806.

Poole, T.K. (2005), *Spatial Models of Parliamentary Voting*, Cambridge University Press.

Rabinowitz, G. and Macdonald, S.E. (1989), A Directional Theory of Issue Voting, *American Political Science Review* 83: 93-121.

Saari, G.D. (2009), The Core with Positional Spatial Voting, *Homo Oeconomicus* 26: 501-517.

Schofield, N. (2003), Valence Competition in the Spatial Stochastic Model, *Journal of Theoretical Politics* 15: 371–383.

Schofield, N., Miller, G. (2007), Elections and Activist Coalitions in the United States, *American Journal of Political Science* 51: 518-531.

Schofield, N. and Sened, I. (2005), Modelling the Interaction of Parties, Activists and Voters: Why Is the Political Centre so Empty?, *European Journal of Political Research* 44: 355-390.

Schofield, N., Martin, A., Quinn, K. and Whitford, A. (1998), Multiparty Electoral Competition in the Netherlands and Germany: A Model Based on Multinomial Probit, *Public Choice* 97: 257-293.

Schickler, E. and Green, D. (1997), The Stability of Party Identification in Western Democracies: Results from Eight Panel Surveys, *Comparative Political Studies* 30: 450-483.

Shepsle, A.K. (1991) *Models of Multiparty Electoral Competition*, Harwood Academic Publishers.

Shepsle, A.K. and Weingast, R.B. (1981), Structure-induced Equilibrium and Legislative Choice, *Public Choice* 37: 503-519.

Steuneberg, B., Smidtchen, D. and Koboldt, C. (1999), Strategic Power in the European Union: Evaluating the Distribution of Power in Policy Games, *Journal of Theoretical Politics* 11: 339–366.

Stokes, D. (1963), Spatial Models and Party Competition, *American Political Science Review* 57: 368-377.

Weisberg, F.H. (1980), A Multidimensional Conceptualization of Party Identification, *Political Behavior* 2: 33-60.

Whitten, D.G. and Palmer, D.G. (1996), Heightening Comparativists' Concern for Model Choice: Voting Behavior in Great Britain and the Netherlands, *American Journal of Political Science* 4: 231–260.

Wittman, D. (1973), Parties as Utility Maximizers, *American Political Science Review* 67: 490-498.

Zakharov, V.A. (2008), A Model of Competition with Abstaining Voters, *Mathematical and Computer Modeling* 48: 1527-1553.

Homo Oeconomicus 27(4): 419–442 (2011)

www.accedoverlag.de

Does Central Bank Independence Matter?: An Examination Using the Taylor Rule

Aleksandra Maslowska
Department of Economics and Public Choice Research Centre, University of Turku,
(eMail: aamasl@utu.fi)

Abstract This paper uses an alternative technique to determine if there is a structural break in the history of inflation of a country, which could be related to the introduction of a higher degree of central bank independence. To test this change we use simple interest rules, specifically the Taylor rule. This analysis is based on the data from two countries: Sweden and the United Kingdom. The coefficients in interest for a long-run equilibrium interest rate, an inflation rate and output gap recorded different values (often statistically significantly) in pre- and post-independence periods. However, control tests performed in countries that did not record legislation changes in the time considered showed that a significant break occurred in many world economies, in general, around the years of 1999-2000.

Keywords central bank independence, institution, Taylor rule, inflation, estimation

1. Introduction

Many economists agree that it is preferable to have central bank independence (CBI) from a third party's influence.[1] Several empirical studies showed that low inflation in the country is often accompanied with a high degree of central bank independence. Although a causal relationship has not been explicitly proven, CBI has been accepted as a necessary institution, ever since. The requirements of the Maastricht Treaty imposed on European countries, as well as a debate on the design of the European Central Bank, have kept the idea of CBI relevant until today. This discussion, however,

[1] For example, The Treaty on European Union, chapter 3, article 7, specifies "Neither the ECB nor the national central banks (NCBs), nor any member of their decision-making bodies, are allowed to seek or take instructions from European Community institutions or bodies, from any government of an EU Member State or from any other body."

ISBN 978-3-89265-075-1 ISSN 0943-0180

has been accompanied by several other views underlying that not only is a monetary authority's autonomy unnecessary for price stability, but also insufficient (Hayo and Hefeker 2001).

Our study is motivated by the two main ideas relating to CBI. First, we use an alternative technique to determine if there is a structural break in the history of inflation of the country, which could be related to the introduction of a higher degree of CBI. Many previous studies based their empirical methods on regressions, where an inflation rate is a dependent variable and a CBI measure is explanatory. It is rather difficult to specify what is the right definition of the central bank independence. The inconsistent measure of CBI, and defects in empirical investigations coupled with an autonomous central bank, make it problematic to determine if central bank independence really matters. This paper suggests that these problems can be overcome by using simple interest rules. A proposed method we use may answer the question whether a behaviour a central bank uses to make its policy decisions changes after it gains more autonomy.

Our studies second idea relating to CBI originates from the view that not only can price stability be achieved by influence from other institutions (such as inflation targeting), but it can also be achieved in the total absence of CBI. One such example is Japan, where inflation rates are low but the central bank is far from highly independent. Another case is New Zealand, which proves that inflation targeting is an effective arrangement leading to low inflation, even with a relatively strong role of the government. One may also consider the idea of implementing disinflationary policy by gaining credibility from other institutions in order to pursue this goal as whom in the case of the European Monetary Union, within which its member countries imported credibility from the Bundesbank. Choosing future membership in the European Union has also helped Central and Eastern European Countries achieve a low and stable inflation rate.

The next section describes a theory on central bank independence. It also includes background information on the Taylor rule. Section 3 is an empirical part of this study, and hence includes a description of the data and summarizes the main results. Section 4 concludes the paper's objectives.

2. Theoretical presentation

2.1 On Central Bank independence

The initial spark that caused many researchers to consider the political and economic importance of CBI was the seminal article by Barro and Gordon (1983). Their paper, originating from earlier work of Kydland and Prescott

(1977), describes a central banker as a social welfare maximizer. The public is fully informed about a central bank's control over inflation and output (employment). Monetary authority, however, may have incentives to deviate from its announced target by increasing inflation rate and causing inflationary bias. This deviation from a promise could be avoided if, as Rogoff (1985) suggests, an authority with known preferences about inflation and output is appointed. The Rogoff-conservative central bank has also become a way of describing the central bank independence in theoretical models. This type of conservatism is in accordance with the notion that the central bank's weight in inflation exceeds that of the elected government.

The theoretical and empirical discussion that started in the late 1980s with the work of Bade and Parkin (1988), and continued with the works of Grilli, Masciandaro and Tabellini (1991) and Cukierman, Webb and Neyapti (1992), focused on constructing measures of central bank autonomy and explaining relationships between CBI and the whole economy. The measures' construction methodology have been under severe criticism, especially by Forder (1999, 2005), who points out that many CBI indices have, in fact, a different understanding of what could be the key issue of independence. Brumm (2000) criticizes the measure of *actual* independence (TOR) because it might not consider the possibility of a central bank governor holding the post for a long period (thus giving an impression of a high level of CBI) simply thanks to an agreement with political leaders. In a comparison of two indices - a legal proxy by Cukierman et al. (1992) and Grilli et al. (1991) - Mangano (1998) finds the two indices disagreeing with each other in nearly 60% of all countries included in the area of an attribute concerning the central bank's ability (legal permission) of purchasing government debt in the primary market. Finally, inconsistencies in measures have been underlined by de Haan, Eijffinger and Waller (2005: 175-176). The authors present an example of Poland and opposite directions of the degree of central bank independence calculated for this country when two different measures are used. According to measures of legal independence, prepared by Loungani and Sheets (1997) or Maliszewski (2001), for example, Poland has by far the highest scores among the new European Union member countries. However, when another index of independence is calculated, such as the turnover rate of governors, Poland registers one of the highest values, which in this case means the lowest degree of independence.

Problems with proper CBI proxy and its justification as a solution for central banks continue in empirical studies. The common use of bi-variate models have been widely criticized in the relevant literature. The problem of omitted variables was underlined by Campillo and Miron (1997). Furthermore, de Haan and Sturm (2001) show rather insignificant results from regressions where the CBI is used as a proxy, unless the sample is enriched with high inflation countries.

2.2 On the Taylor rule

An alternative method of empirical investigation used in this study is the Taylor rule (Taylor 1993), which is a simple formula that describes how a central bank's interest rate should respond to changes in the inflation rate and activity levels, given an economy's inflation target and level of potential output. The rule is used ex-post in a descriptive capacity, and provides in this study a view of how a central bank has responded to economic development in the past. The estimated coefficients of the Taylor rule are used to characterize how central banks historically changed policy rates in response to inflation and output gaps developments. A central bank's policy response is additionally determined by the choice of institutions. Therefore, it could be related to the change in the degree of central bank independence.

The well-known Taylor rule directs the central bank to react to deviations of the inflation rate from a target level. It does so without any relation to the absolute level that prices have reached. Such concern with the inflation rate rather than the price level, as Woodford (2003) explains, would seem to characterize policy in all advanced countries in recent years.

Despite its simplicity, the Taylor rule has stimulated much useful research on monetary policy. Clarida et al. (1998), Hetzel (2000) and Orphanides (2003), among others, provide some theoretical discussion on the rule along with some empirical evidence. Clarida et al. (1999) emphasize that "the rule is consistent with the main principles for optimal policy." This means that the rule (1) makes the nominal rate adjust more than one-for-one with inflation rate; (2) makes real rates adjust to engineer inflation back to target and, (3) calls for countercyclical response to demand shocks and accommodation of shocks to potential GDP that do not affect the output gap.

Taylor proposed a feedback policy with a symmetric weight *0.5* given to both inflation and output gaps. Moreover, a constant term, *2*, is also assigned by Taylor to represent a long-run average of the real rate of interest and the same value for the inflation target

$$i_t = r^* + \pi_t + 0.5(\pi_t - \pi^*) + 0.5y_t = (r^* - 0.5\pi^*) + 1.5\pi_t + 0.5y_t \qquad (1)$$

where i_t is the policy interest rate, r^* is the equilibrium real rate, π_t is the rate of inflation, π^* is the inflation target and y is the output gap in period

t. The general form of the Taylor rule, taken from Woodford (2003: 40), for example, and later used in this study can be presented as:

$$i_t = \alpha + \beta_\pi(\pi_t - \pi^*) + \gamma_y y_t \tag{2}$$

where i_t is the policy interest rate and α is the long-run equilibrium interest rate and defined as $\alpha = r^* + \pi^*$. Additionally, β_π and γ_y are coefficients for inflation and output gaps respectively.

The major idea in the Taylor rule (the so-called *Taylor Principle*) assumes that the nominal interest-rate is being adjusted by more than the amount by which inflation exceeds the target. In other words, the coefficient for inflation is expected to exceed the unity, in the case of optimal policy. Therefore, the key lesson drawn from the estimation of this policy reaction function concentrates on analyzing the coefficient for inflation gap.

If one assumes that the coefficient for the inflation gap is smaller than one $\beta_\pi < 1$, that is, on contrary to the Taylor Principle, the expectational difference equation for the inflation rate has an infinity of bounded solutions, so that the equilibrium inflation, in this case, is indeterminate, as in the pure interest-rate control (see Leeper 1991, for example, or Woodford 2003, for the analysis). Coefficients positive but smaller than the unity were recorded in the United States for the period 1960-1979. Taylor (1999) interpreted these as the instability of U.S. inflation and real activity during the 1970s. That is, they indicate passive interest-rate responses.

The Taylor rule has been modified to include various elements of modern central banking. A static relationship such as equation (1) cannot capture the serial correlation present in the data. Therefore, a modification to the rule leads to a dynamic specification. For example, Judd and Rudebusch (1998) estimate the Fed's reaction functions that describe how the fund-rate operating target adjusts in response to changes in an implicit desired level of the fund rate. The *actual* interest rate i_t is partially adjusted to the target, according to the form

$$i_t = \rho i_{t-1} + (1-\rho) i_t^* \tag{3}$$

where ρ is a parameter that measures the degree of interest rate smoothing. This gives the following equation to be estimated:

$$i_t = (1-\rho)\alpha + (1-\rho)\beta_\pi(\pi_t - \pi^*) + (1-\rho)\gamma_y y_t + \rho i_{t-1} + \varepsilon_t \tag{4}$$

where ε is an independent and identically distributed error term. The model with an interest rate smoothing parameter (otherwise called a partial adjustment to the target) eliminates the concern that a simple rule could not capture the tendency of central banks to smooth changes in interest rates. Clarida et al. (1998) explains that the necessity to smoothen interest rates is justified with the fear of disrupting capital markets, loss of credibility from sudden large policy reversal or the need for consensus building to support a policy change.

3. Empirical analysis

Central banks have been chosen for this analysis according to one crucial criterion: the presence of the evolution of the legal system in the area of a central bank's organization and activity. The most prominent examples are the central banks of Sweden and the United Kingdom.[2]

The Riksbank, Sweden's central bank and one of the oldest in the world, has had a considerably high degree of independence for most of its operating time. An introduction of the inflation targeting in January 1993 brought a certain monetary discipline. The subsequent change of the legal act granting the bank a higher degree of independence was its natural consequence. New legislation, which we are interested in, came into force on January 1, 1999. As the monetary authority explains in their report, the new legislation gave "a legal form to the independence that monetary policy already had in practice" (Sveriges Report 1999: 4). It is represented by the shift on monetary policy from the General Council to an Executive Board. Moreover, external communication also improved with the publishing of the minutes from the monetary policy meetings.

The history of the Bank of England has tied the Bank strongly to the HM Treasury and the Government itself. The first modern legal act from 1946 enabled the Treasury to give directions to the bank about monetary policy, which was clearly a part of government policy. After all, it had been the chancellor of exchequer who had been setting interest rates for years. Therefore, the 1996 amendment, crucial for the bank and for our analysis change in its legislation, shifted that major monetary responsibility from the Treasury to the Bank of England. This, and many other alterations of

[2] It is also important to note that many European countries, which adjusted legal acts toward more independent monetary authority, could not be included here due to their membership in the monetary union. In many cases, law amendments were made shortly before their Economic and Monetary Union (EMU) membership, and hence the data series would have been too short for the analysis.

the bank's role, aimed to fulfil the Maastricht Treaty requirements, as well as create a modern style of central banking.

An example of the United States as a control country is added to our analysis. The Federal Reserve System did not record any institutional amendments leading to changes in its independence during the period in question. It is therefore interesting to compare how the central bank of the world leading economy reacted during that twenty year period.

Additionally, for the sake of comparison, one should include several other countries in the analysis, so we include the case of Economic and Monetary Union member states. Figure 1 shows scatter plots of inflation and interest rates in Italy and Portugal, countries with a history of high inflation rates. A breakpoint here is January 1999, when the European Central Bank started to determine common monetary policy and the data was published worldwide. Although these countries are not included in further analysis, it is worthwhile to describe the data.

The period until 1999 is characterized with an obvious disinflationary process. Lower inflation rates in subsequent years can be tied to improvements in degrees of central bank's independence. In Italy, the bank was given fully independent power to set official interest rates in 1992. The Portuguese central bank registered two crucial CBI improvements: the first in 1990, granting greater independence to the board of directors and the second in 1995, when the main mission of the bank was assigned to price stability. These important dates and the data on inflation confirm what many studies empirically showed: a lower inflation rate is correlated with a higher degree of CBI. According to the theory of an optimal currency area, one could consider membership in the euro zone as a loss of monetary policy independence by many European countries. This is observed in the data, where the level of a country-specific inflation rate does not always seem to be as a result of the monetary policy run for that country.

3.1 Data

In his original study, Taylor used the federal funds rate, which was later replicated as the natural choice for the United States. In other papers, which include different samples, the short-term interest rate is represented by an interbank lending rate for overnight loans, or a three-month Treasury bill. Here, representation of this variable differs, depending on the country, but it is always the major monetary policy interest rate. Therefore, in Sweden, the repo rate is the rate of interest at which banks can borrow or deposit funds at the Riksbank for a period of seven days (four first quarters for repo rate is a marginal rate, which stopped being published after introducing repo). In the United Kingdom, the rate is the three-month interbank lending rate, also considered a three-month Treasury bill rate.

Figure 2 Data dispersion

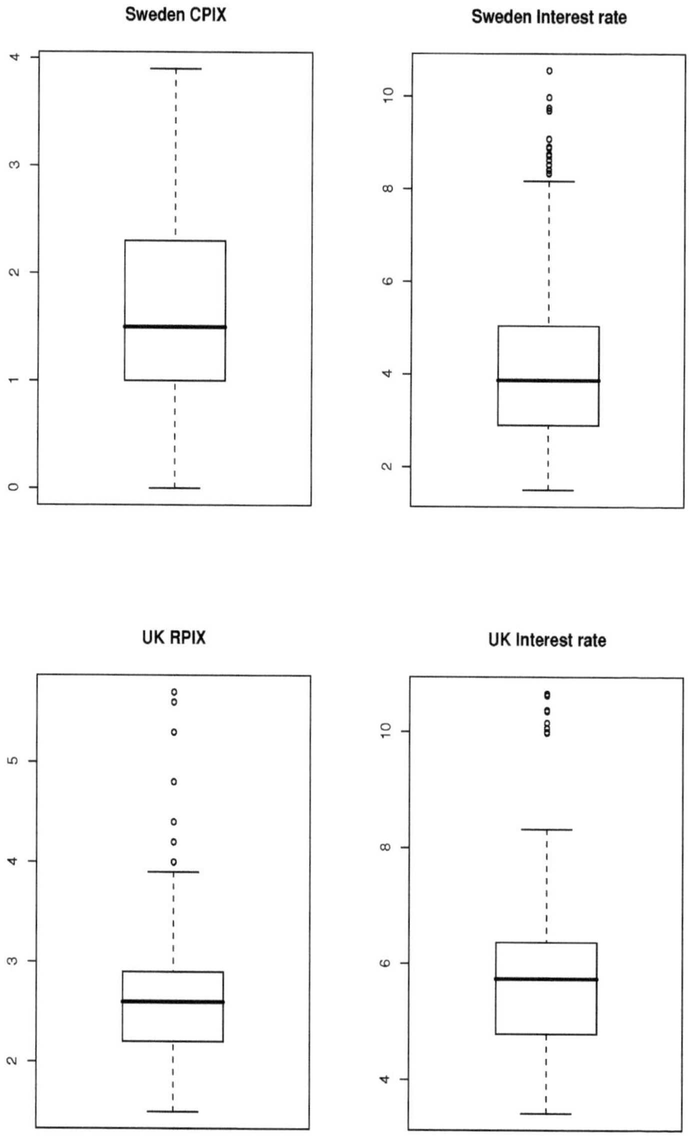

subperiods divided by the date of the legislation change. It is clear that the feature of data for both countries is a large dispersion, lack of symmetry in a frequency distribution with several observations traditionally treated as "outliers" and a large range between the minimal and maximal data point.

A salient feature of economic time series like price indexes or interest rates is inertia, otherwise referred to as sluggishness. This is one cause of the existence of serial correlation, which has been also detected in this data set.[3] Another cause for correlation in this time series is the use of lags in the Taylor rule. In the presence of autocorrelation, the ordinary least square (OLS) estimators are still linear and unbiased, as well as consistent and asymptotically normally distributed. However, they are no longer efficient (see Gujarati, 2003: 454, for example). The implication of this finding for hypothesis testing leads to declaring a coefficient statistically insignificant, even though it may be significant (based on the correct procedure).

The use of OLS estimation is still possible if the standard errors are corrected for autocorrelation. It can be done using the procedure developed by Newey and West (1987). Then, the corrected standard errors are known as HAC (heteroscedasticity- and autocorrelation-consistent). Note that the Newey-West procedure can be used for large samples only. This Taylor rule analysis includes approximately 200 observations, which could be considered rather large. A similar analysis is performed for the United Kingdom. Theoretical justifications of econometric methods are the same as in the case of Sweden. Tests indicate the existence of autocorrelation in residuals, as well as the presence of autoregressive conditional heteroscedasticity.[4]

A conventional proposition suggested while analyzing the kind of policy function considered here is to make an assumption about stationarity of the data (see Clarida et al. 2000). The usual tests (Augmented Dickey-Fuller and Kwiatkowski-Phillips-Schmidt-Shin, for example) were run with the general conclusion that it is hard to find conclusive evidence in favour or against stationarity among investigated variables. However, the Engle and Granger (1987) cointegration test rejects the non-stationarity of the residuals in tests performed for the full sample and subsamples. Furthermore, to cope with the possible non-stationarity of some of the data, the fully modified estimator of Philips and Hansen (1990) has been applied for the Taylor rule in its original form. The fully modified estimation results (not shown) do not differ greatly from the ones obtained using the OLS.

[3] The Breusch-Godfrey test does not reject the null hypothesis of existence of serial correlation with Prob=0,000167.

[4] Checked with Breusch-Godfrey and Arch tests respectively.

3.2 *Breakpoint in time series*

Before any estimation is done, it is necessary to find a breakpoint in the time series, which divides samples into two significantly different subsamples. The breakpoint date is already known, and is based on the schedule of institutional changes in central banks legislation: May 1997 for the United Kingdom and January 1999 for Sweden. The significance of these dates is checked with the Chow breakpoint test (Chow 1960), which analyzes the null hypothesis of no structural break in the sample period. According to this test, the dates of interest clearly divide the sample into two subperiods. In Sweden, the probability of two subsamples being the same is the lowest around January 1999. Several other dates have also been tested. However, January 1999 (1999m1) appears to be the "best" point characterizing the structural break in time series.

Although the date of the Bank of England legislation change seems to confirm the existence of the structural break, the lowest probability that two subsamples are the same has been detected for January 1997. Moreover, none of the dates around May 1997 have proven to significantly differentiate the two periods from each other when the whole period extends to the 1980s that is, including the time before the introduction of inflation targeting. Such a test has been done for the United Kingdom, for example, where the sample before 1992 is clearly different due to a different monetary regime. A Chow test performed for the period of January 1980 to December 2007 with the hypotheses of the existence of three subperiods (1980-1992, 1992-1997 and 1997-2007) indicates the breakpoint only for 1992, and treats the remaining one, from 1992 to 2007 as one unified sample.

As for the Chow test, results were mixed for control countries included in this study such as the United States. Artificially, that is, without any reasonable explanation, a breakpoint date around 1999 was chosen to see if the results obtained for Sweden and the United Kingdom were really driven by changes in their central banks or by other worldwide economic conditions. Although no change in central banks legislation has been recorded, it is possible to detect a structural break in the United States around 2001. However, with the longer period, since 1980, it is the year 1990 that rejects the hypothesis of no structural break. These tests lead to the conclusion of performing two types of tests. First, regression coefficients are calculated for separate subsamples, and second the dummy-variable approach is used to compare two regressions.

An additional test based on unit roots procedure has been applied to detect the existence of a structural break in the data. Among the few available tests, a Zivot and Andrews (1992) test was chosen. This is a sequential test that utilizes the full sample and uses a different dummy variable for each possible break date. The break is selected where the t-statistic from the augmented Dickey-Fuller (ADF) test is at the minimum. Thus, a break is chosen where the evidence is least favourable for the unit root null. Due to low explanatory power of the ADF in the tests performed, a decision is made after a consult with the Kwiatkowski-Phillips-Schmidt-Shin (KPSS) test.

This test gives clear-cut evidence that a structural break took place around January 1999 in Sweden. Therefore, it supports the decision to perform a Taylor rule analysis on the data broken into two subsamples exactly around this date. It is also additional proof that it is acceptable to justify an observed policy change with an institutional modification of the central bank. The unit root tests for structural break failed to confirm that the date of a central bank legislation change, leading to a higher degree of CBI in the United Kingdom, was significant. Based on the described procedure and the data since 1992, January 2001 was more distinctive for the country and its economic policy. However, an ADF test had a small explanatory power, whereas a KPSS test was able to reject the null of stationarity at the 10% level.

3.3 *Diversity of models*

The rule estimated here includes the interest smoothing element suggested by Judd and Rudebusch (1998). The relatively shorter period of analysis causes a smaller number of observations. The use of monthly, instead of quarterly, data multiplies the number of observation by four, allowing for sets of data that include at least 50 observations in one period. The type of monetary policy held in the new millennium, however, characterized with very high interest rate inertia (i.e. small and rare changes in their levels) leads to small correlation between inflation and interest rate. This situation, which perhaps is also a special feature of the monetary policy in the 2000s, caused estimation problems, and had to be dealt with. Several analyses of simple cases, where the current interest rate is explained with a one-month lagged interest rate and inflation rate, show a very strong explanation power of only the lagged interest rate. This preliminary analysis suggests that the second-order partial adjustment model should be used with interest rate lagged at one and two periods as an explanatory variable. The second-order partial adjustment has been also used by Clarida et al. (1998: 1048), who write that it fits the US data significantly better than the first-order model in the sample, from October 1979 to December 1994.

Short periods, leading to a small sample of observations, may cause a problem with estimation results. Moreover, the Chow breakpoint test brings insufficient information needed in this analysis. The dummy variable approach (see Gujarati 1970, for example) covers these problems.

Using a single regression increases the degrees of freedom and hence may improve the relative precision of the estimated parameters, it also indicates which coefficient, intercept or slope is different.

However, remember that every addition of a dummy variable will "consume" one degree of freedom. The model with the dummy variable is of the following form:

$$i_t = \rho_1 i_{-1} + \rho_2 i_{-2} + (1-\rho_1-\rho_2)(TR_t + TR_t{}^*D_T) \tag{5}$$

where TR stands for the Taylor rule and D_T is a time dummy. The whole model estimates values for the whole period first, while the time dummy indicates the change in values of coefficients in the second period, as compared to the first one.

Finally, one more analysis collects all three countries of this study into a panel data examination. Here, again, the dummy variables occur to distinguish, first of all, between countries, but also between subperiods, by including one more time dummy. As expected, including too many dummy variables causes the Durbin-Watson statistics, indicating the presence of autocorrelation in the residuals, to decrease. For example, the panel with only a "country" dummy includes six dummies. The time differentiation makes this number increase to fifteen. Nevertheless, the model for panel data can be represented as:

$$i_t = \rho_1 i_{-1} + \rho_2 i_{-2} + (1-\rho_1-\rho_2)(TR_t + TR_t{}^*D_{country} + TR_t{}^*D_T) \tag{6}$$

One method of allowing for fixed effects (allowing for intercept to differ among individuals) is by again the dummy-variable technique. In this case, tests include either dummies only, to differentiate between countries, or both, countries and the time effect. In order to avoid the dummy-variable trap (i.e. the situation of perfect collinearity), only two dummies are used (for United Kingdom and United States). The intuition behind fixed effects only is that, in case the coefficients are statistically significant, it indicates that Taylor rules are different for each country and for each period.

3.4 *Empirical results*

The first report relates to Sweden and consists of a table presentation of analysis, based on separate pre- and post-independence periods. Such a division of time series has been explained already with the Chow breakpoint test. Additionally, Figure 3 shows scatter plots of inflation and interest rates. Both graphs clearly present different situations - the first period (pre-1999) shows a clear negative relation between the two variables, whereas the post-1999 data are more dispersed.

Table 2 Single regressions and || dummy variable approach for Sweden

Period Variable	Pre-1999	Post-1999	Pre-1999	Post-1999
Interest rate	0,95**	0,98**	0,983***	0,983***
$(\rho_1+\rho_2)$	(0,35)	(0,55)	(0,15)	(0,15)
Inflation	1,95***	0,28	2,42**	-2,15*
(β_π)	(0,36)	(2,98)	(0,88)	(1,25)
Output gap	0,67*	-0,31	1,79**	-2,07*
(γ_y)	(0,34)	(0,71)	(0,89)	(1,12)
Constant	5,89***	3,42**	3,66**	0,05
(α)	(0,64)	(1,12)	(1,49)	(1,6)
Adjusted R^2	0,99	0,98	0,99	
No. Obs.	70	108	178	

Notes: Standard errors in brackets, corrected with Newey-West HAC. Statistical significance at 1, 5, and 10% with ***, **, and * signs.

The first conclusion drawn from Table 2, and the part for single regressions approach, relates to the value of constant α. According to the estimation results, the value of the interest rate is almost two times larger in the pre-independence period than in the period after the legislation change. This strong disinflationary policy is also visible when coefficients for inflation gap are compared. In the pre-independence period, their values are around two - hence, according to the Taylor rule.

The analysis of separate periods does not provide much information needed in this study. Introducing a dummy variable results in variables that now stand for the differential intercept and differential slope coefficients. They indicate how much the slope coefficient of the first period's function differs from the slope coefficient of the second period's function. In the test for Sweden, the differential coefficients are placed in the column for "post-1999" and indicate how much values differ from the first period (hence, they do not indicate the absolute value for the second period). The significance of dummy coefficients differs between the use of contemporaneous and forward-type Taylor rule. Nevertheless, they still indicate that the regressions for the two periods are different.

Setting restrictions for coefficients in the Wald test, it is possible to test the null hypothesis that two coefficients from different periods are the same. For example, constant (α) in period one equals constant in period two (and similarly with other coefficients). The low probability values

Figure 3 Inflation and interest rates in Sweden and the United Kingdom

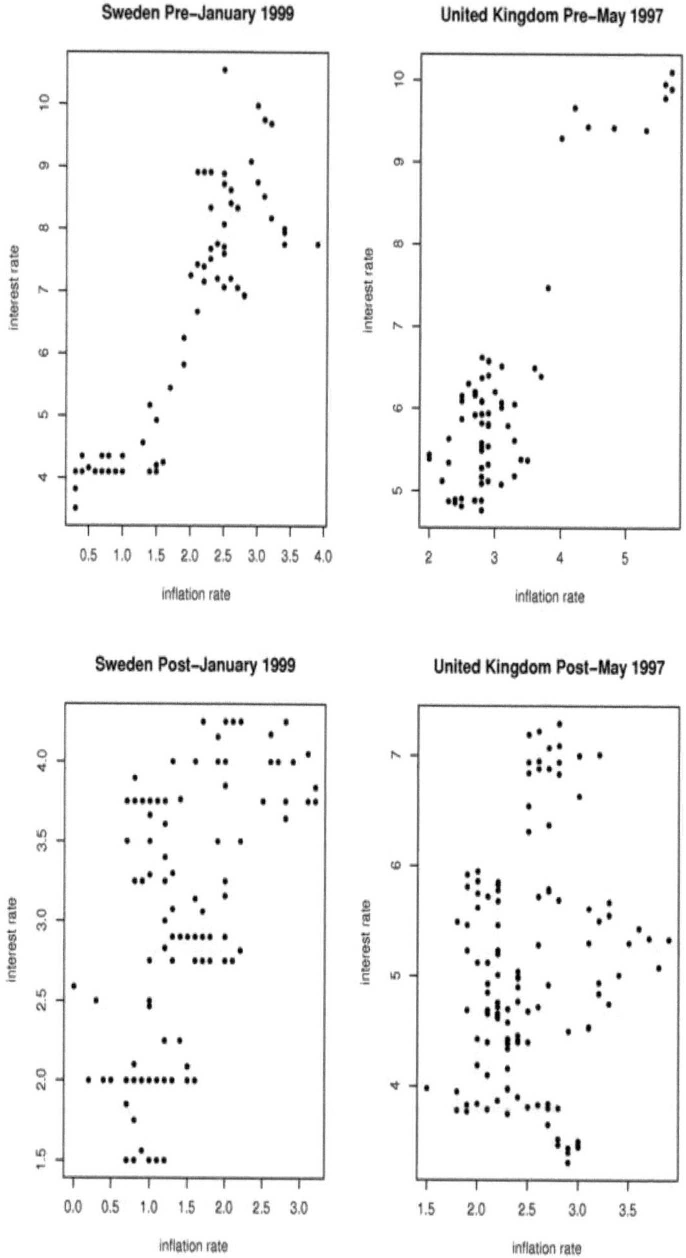

(Prob.=0.000) for constant and inflation rate (both calculated when inflation has 9 observation lead) indicate that the null hypothesis is strongly rejected. For a contemporaneous regression, probability values Prob.=0.02 and Prob.=0.05 for inflation and output gap, respectively, indicate that the null hypothesis of equal coefficients may be rejected.

The scatter plots and tests mentioned above characterize the data in the United Kingdom somewhat differently than in Sweden. Dispersion of observations is much more irregular in the case of the United Kingdom making estimation with OLS less plausible, even after correcting standard errors with the Newey-West procedure. The solution to the bias in the simple OLS estimator can be found by using the instrumental variable methods proposed by Anderson and Hsiao (1981, 1982) and Arellano and Bond (1991).

Table 3 Dummy variable approach for the United Kingdom

Period Variable	Pre-1997 OLS	Post-1997 OLS	Pre-1997 GMM	Post-1997 GMM
Interest rate	0,92***		0,93***	
($\rho_1+\rho_2$)	(0,1)		(0,11)	
Inflation	1,17**	-0,74	2,26**	-1,43
(β_π)	(0,57)	(0,67)	(1,14)	(2,08)
Output gap	-0,01	0,11	1,61	0,44
(γ_y)	(0,57)	(0,51)	(1,21)	(2,03)
Constant	2,78***	0,37	3,44*	0,46
(α)	(0,63)	(0,58)	(1,86)	(1,95)
usafed	0,04*		0,01	
	(0,02)		(0,02)	
No. Obs.	192	192	192	192

Notes: Standard errors in brackets, corrected with White heteroskedasticity. GMM with Kernel: Bartlett and instruments as specified in the text. Statistical significance at 1, 5, and 10% with ***, **, and * signs. usafed stands for the federal funds rate.

The Generalised Method of Moments (GMM) assumes the theoretical relation that the parameters should satisfy orthogonality conditions between some function of parameters and a set of instrumental variables. The GMM estimator selects parameter estimates so that the sample correlation between instruments and the function are as close to zero as possible (for more on GMM estimates, see Greene 2000: 476-491). To choose instruments, one can follow a general rule of choosing lagged values of independent variables. In this analysis, instruments chosen for the United Kingdom are interest rate lags (1,2,3,6), inflation rate lags (1,2,3,6,9,12), output gap lags (4,5), U.S. Federal Reserve System main interest rate lags (1,2,3,6) and three-month money growth lags (1,2,3). The use of U.S. interest rates is explained by the close international trade and financial relations between the two countries.

Estimations are based on the assumption that the inflation target is at the level of 2%. However, a replication of all estimations for the United Kingdom has been also done with the target for inflation at 2,5%. On its website,[5] the Bank of England explains that the inflation target was higher from June 1997 to December 2003, and was 2% after 10 December, 2003. Additionally, also corrected was the major inflation rate in the central bank's analysis, which was changed in 2003 from underlying inflation RPIX to CPI. The change in the inflation target has the greatest effect on equilibrium interest rates by making its value higher.

Before moving to panel analysis, one more test was performed. Based on the historical data and Taylor rule specification, it is possible to find predictions of a dependent variable, interest rate - i. This exercise helps to compare forecasts based on historical data with the actual decisions of central banks concerning the level of interest rates. In order to make such a comparison, forecasts were found (see Figure 3), first for the full period of analysis and later for the year of institutional change, as well as "around" the date (one year before and two years after). Forecasts have been made using the dynamic method (on forecasting see M.P. Clements and D.F. Hendry 1998, for example). A dynamic, as opposed to static, forecast calculates multi-step forecasts, starting from the first period in the forecast sample. Forecasted values for the lagged dependent variables are used in forming forecasts of the current value.

The largest discrepancies between predictions and data recorded can be noticed in the case of Sweden. In general, a higher degree of CBI should have helped keep the interest rate much higher, based on forecasts, than actually occurred. Shorter predictions suggest a rapid increase in the interest rate after the year 1999, with a decrease later, but not to the low levels recorded in past data. The full period forecast suggests that interest rates should have been kept higher after 2003. Forecasts for the United Kingdom are rather in accordance with actual time series, both with full period predictions and those starting around 1997.

The final analysis uses the panel data with three countries (Sweden, the United Kingdom and the United States) and equal time period 1993m01-2007m12. Considering the assumption of changing monetary policy due to a higher degree of independence, the most interesting results come from

[5] www.bankofengland.co.uk

Figure 4 Forecasts of interest rates in Sweden and the United Kingdom (upper and lower graphs respectively)

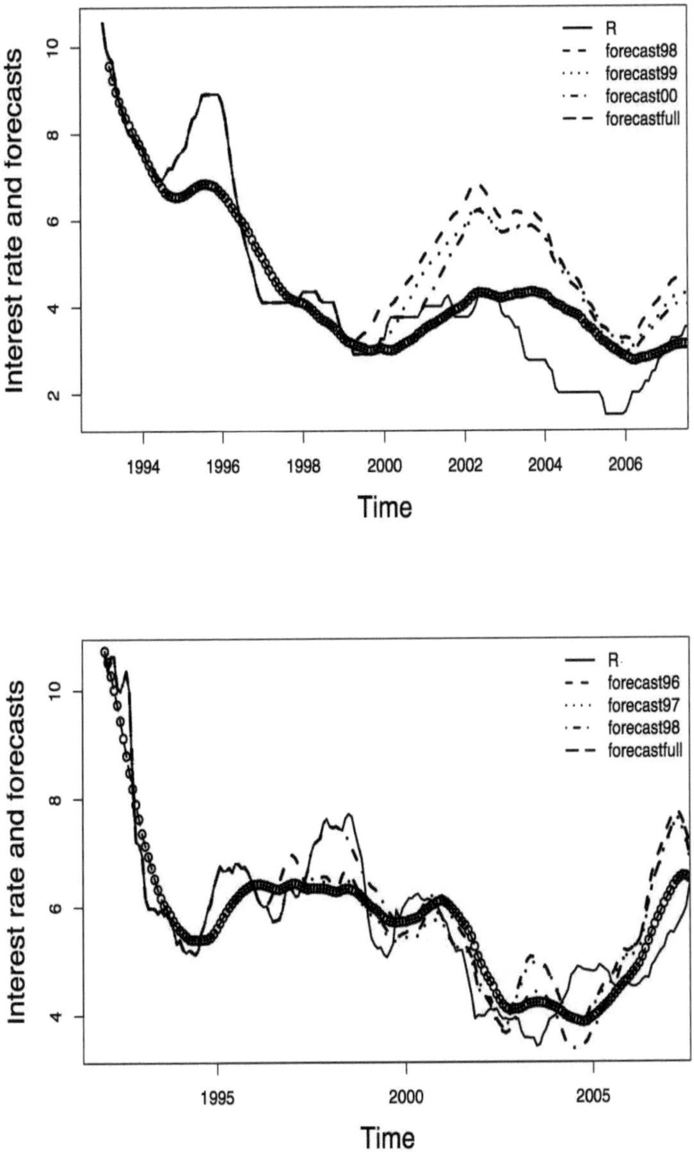

Table 4 Panel analysis with Sweden, the United Kingdom and the United States

Period Variable	Long period	Pre-change	Post-change
Interest rate			
$(\rho_1+\rho_2)$	(0,94)***		
(ρ_1)		0,76***	0.76***
Inflation rate	1,46***	1,82***	1,17***
Inflation rate*UK	0,72	-0,04	0,72**
Inflation rate*US	1,3*	-0,69***	1,56***
Output gap	0,63***	0,36***	-0,24**
Output gap*UK	-0,47**	-0,29***	0,20**
Output gap*US	-0,85*	-0,40***	0,19
Constant	4,38***	6,27***	-2,87***
Constant*UK	-2,51***	-4,82***	3,47***
Constant*US	-3,43***	-4,42***	2,73***

Notes: Panel (EGLS) with cross-section weights, White cross-section standard errors and covariance, Statistical significance at 1, 5, and 10% with ***, **, and * signs. Three cross sections included: panel with 534 observations. Weighted statistics for panel with country dummy: Adjusted R^2=0.99, S.E. of regression=0.24, D-W= 1.79. Weighted statistics for panel with country and time dummies: Adjusted R^2=0.98, S.E. of regression=0.22, D-W=1.39

output for the United States. Apart from differences found between countries, the Wald test with the null hypothesis that coefficients in pre- and post-change periods for the United States are the same has been rejected. This indicates that the presence of many macroeconomic factors around the world could have an effect on economies. One of those factors could be a higher degree of CBI, but not necessarily.

4. Conclusions

The aim of this paper was to connect increased central bank independence with the possible change in the type of monetary policy represented by chosen central banks. Unlike many previous studies on CBI, this one proposes an alternative method of analysis, namely estimating coefficients for the Taylor rule. It has been expected that a greater degree of CBI will have a visible effect on central banks' reactions to variability of inflation and output.

Data analysis for the case of Sweden allowed us to see a clear cut in the time series. Both the Chow and the unit-root tests, aiming to identify breakpoints in the data, showed a distinctive change around January 1999. Therefore, they confirmed not only the existence of two different regimes, but also that these regimes relate to legal status of the central bank. The key point in this analysis was to estimate coefficients of the Taylor rule. Results indicate that the adjustment of interest rate to changes in inflation was much stronger in the pre-independence period. Independently from the Taylor specification type (simple or modified), coefficients for inflation gap were much higher in the first period, even close to *2*. Although results for the output gap did not give such an obvious distinction between the two periods, the analysis of the equilibrium interest rate proved again the existence of two varying regimes. The rate, a constant term, being composed of nominal interest rate and inflation target, is much higher in the pre-independence period. This was confirmed with the simple Taylor rule specification estimated with the OLS and cointegration tests, as well as with the modified Taylor rules, as indicated. Wald tests supported the results that coefficients in two periods are different from each other.

The results of the analysis for the United Kingdom are not conclusive. Although the Chow test confirmed the hypothesis of the breakpoint in the data around the time of the new legislation for the Bank of England (1997), the unit root test did not support this hypothesis. The latter test suggested the year 2001 as a break indication, although the test had a low explanatory power. British economy is very dependent on international economic relations with the United States. We considered that fact in this analysis by including the U.S. federal funds rate in the equation. However, the Taylor estimations also failed to give an answer regarding whether the monetary regime really did change due to the increased independence of the Bank of England.

In this analysis it is difficult to exclude effects of other economic phenomena on interest and inflation rates, as well as on output. The dummy variable approach and inclusion of the United States, the country without any important change in the Fed legal status, was expected to correct for these unobservable variables. The panel results gave two kinds of information. First, there is a change in the policy for the United States that is caused by some varying economic phenomena. These could be connected with the general economic unease recorded worldwide over the year 2000, or the economic consequences of terrorist attacks in 2001 in the United States. The second type of information given by the panel is that the policy in all three countries differed from each other, and the size of changes was also dissimilar.

This paper enriches the discussion on whether "central bank independence matters," suggesting new methodology and presenting new results. The answer to the main question is again the same as in previous studies. Yes, independence of the central bank, the legal foundations of its existence in the market and relations with the public do matter. More precisely, they matter for some countries. In other cases, however, the general, domestic and international economic conditions of the country are the main prerequisites of a sound economic policy.

Acknowledgments

I would like to thank Matti Virén and Mika Widgrén for their invaluable mentor support. I also thank various participants at the European Public Choice Society Meeting in Athens (April 2009) and the International Conference on Macroeconomic Analysis and International Finance in Crete (May, 2009). In addition I benefited from the comments of two anonymous referees. The financial support of the Yrjö Jahnsson, OP-Pohjola, and Turun Kauppaseuran foundations is gratefully acknowledged. Responsibility for all errors and shortcomings remain mine alone.

References

Anderson, T.W. and Hsiao, C. (1981), Estimation of Dynamic Models with Error Components, *Journal of the American Statistical Association* 76.

Anderson, T.W. and Hsiao, C. (1982), Formulation and Estimation of Dynamic Models Using Panel Data, *Journal of Econometrics* 18.

Arellano, M. and Bond, S. (1991), Some Tests of Specification for Panel Data: Monte Carlo Evidence and an Application to Employment Equations, *Review of Economic Studies* 58.

Bade, R. and Parkin, M. (1988), *Central Bank Laws and Monetary Policy*, University of Western Ontario.

Barro R. and Gordon, D. (1983), Rules, Discretion and Reputation in a Model of Monetary Policy, *Journal of Monetary Economics* 12: 101-120.

Billmeier, A. (2004), *Ghostbusting: Which Output Gap Measure Really Matters?*, IMF Working Paper 146.

Brumm, H.J. (2000), Inflation and Central Bank Independence: Conventional Wisdom Redux, *Journal of Money, Credit, and Banking* 32(4): 807-819.

Campillo, M. and Miron, J. (1997), Why Does Inflation Differ across Countries?, in: C. Romer and D. Romer (eds.), *Reducing Inflation: Motivation and Strategy*, University of Chicago Press.

Chow, G.C. (1960), Tests of Equality between Sets of Coefficients in Two Linear Regressions, *Econometrica* 28(3): 591-605.

Clarida, R., Galí, J. and Gertler, M. (1998), Monetary Policy Rules in Practice: Some International Evidence, *European Economic Review* 42: 1033-1067.

Clarida, R., Galí, J. and Gertler, M. (1999), The Science of Monetary Policy: A New Keynesian Perspective, *Journal of Economic Literature* XXXVII: 1661-1707.

Clements, M.P. and Hendry, D.F. (1998), *Forecasting Economic Time Series*, Cambridge University Press.

Cukierman, A., Webb, S.B. and Neyapti, B. (1992), Measuring the Independence of Central Banks and its Effect on Policy Outcomes, *The World Bank Economic Review* 6(3): 353-398.

Dickey, D.A. and Fuller, W.A. (1979), Distribution of the Estimators for Autoregressive Time Series with a Unit Root, *Journal of the American Statistical Association* 74: 427-431.

Engle, R.F. and Granger, C.W.J. (1987), Cointegration and Error-Correction: Representation, Estimation, and Testing, *Econometrica* 55: 251-276.

Forder, J. (1999), Central Bank Independence: Reassessing the Measurements, *Journal of Economic Issues* XXXIII(1): 23-40.

Forder, J. (2005), Why is Central Bank Independence so Widely Approved, *Journal of Economic Issues* 39(4): 843-865.

Greene W.H. (2000), *Econometric Analysis*, Prentice-Hall, Inc.

Grilli V., Masciandaro, D. and Tabellini, G. (1991), Political and Monetary Institutions and Public Financial Policies in the Industrial Countries, *Economic Policy* 13: 341-392.

Gujarati, D.N. (1970), Use of Dummy Variables in Testing for Equality between Sets of Coefficients in Two Linear Regressions: A Note, *American Statistician* 24(1).

Gujarati, D.N. (2003), *Basic Econometrics*, McGraw-Hill, Inc.

Haan, J. de, Eijffinger, S.C.W. and Waller, S. (2005), The European Central Bank: Credibility, Transparency and Centralization, *CESifo Book Series.*

Hayo, B. and Hefeker, C. (2001), *Do We Really Need Central Bank Independence? A Critical Re-examination*, WWZ Discussion Paper, University of Basel.

Hetzel, R.L. (1998), Arthur Burns and Inflation, *Federal Reserve Bank of Richmond Economic* 84(1).

Judd, J.P. and Rudebusch, G.D. (1998), Taylor's Rule and the Fed, 1970-1997, *Federal Reserve Bank of San Francisco Economic Review* 3-16.

Kwiatkowski, D., Phillips, P.C.B., Schmidt, P. and Shin, Y. (1992), Testing the Null Hypothesis of Stationarity against the Alternative of a Unit Root, *Journal of Econometrics* 54: 159-178.

Kydland, F.E. and Prescott, E.C. (1977), Rules Rather than Discretion: The Inconsistency of Optimal Plans, *Journal of Political Economy* 85(3): 473-492.

Leeper, E.M. (1991), Equilibria under "Active" and "Passive" Monetary and Fiscal Policies, *Journal of Monetary Economics* 27: 129-147.

Mangano, G. (1998), Measuring Central Bank Independence: a Tale of Subjectivity and of its Consequences, *Oxford Economic Papers* 50: 468-492.

Mihailov, A. (2006), Operational Independence, Inflation Targeting, and UK Monetary Policy, *Journal of Post Keynesian Economics* 28(3): 395-42.

Nelson, E. (2000), *UK Monetary Policy 1972-97: A Guide Using Taylor Rules*, Bank of England Working Paper 120.

Newey, W.K. and West, K. (1987), A Simple Positive Semi-Definite Heteroscedasticity and Autocorrelation Consistent Covariance Matrix, *Econometrica* 55.

Orphanides, A. (2003), Historical Monetary Policy Analysis and the Taylor Rule, Board of Governors of the Federal Reserve System (U.S.), *Finance and Economics Discussion Series* 2003-36.

Phillips, P.C.B. and Hansen, B.E. (1990), Statistical Inference in Instrumental Variables Regression with I(1) Processes, *Review of Economic Studies* 57(1): 99-125.

Rogoff, K. (1985), The Optimal Degree of Commitment to an Intermediate Monetary Target, *Quarterly Journal of Economics* 100(4): 1169-1189.

Sauer, S. and Sturm, J.-E. (2007), Using Taylor Rules to Understand European Central Bank Monetary Policy, *German Economic Review* 8(3): 375-398.

Sturm, J.-E. and de Haan, J. (2001), *Inflation in Developing Countries: Does Central Bank Independence Matter?*, CCSO Working Papers 200101, University of Groningen, CCSO Centre for Economic Research.

Sveriges Report (1999), *Annual Report.*

Taylor, J. (1993), Discretion versus Policy Rules in Practice, *Carnegie-Rochester Conference Series on Public Policy* 39: 195-214.

Woodford, M. (2003), *Interest and Prices, Foundations of a Theory of Monetary Policy*, Princeton University Press.

Appendix

Table 5 Data descriptive

Variable	Obs	Mean	Std Dev.	Min	Max
Sweden					
Inflation rate	180	1,67	0,85	0,00	3,90
Interest rate	180	4,44	2,23	1,50	10,55
Production index	180	95,25	14,67	62,76	120,53
United Kingdom					
Inflation rate	192	2,71	0,70	1,50	5,70
Interest rate	192	5,76	1,47	3,42	10,65
Production index	192	98,73	4,20	86,70	104,60

Table 6 Data source

Variables	Source
Inflation rate	Statistics Sweden http://www.scb.se/ Office for National Statistic http://www.statistics.gov.uk/rpi Bureau of Labor Statistics www.bls.gov/cpi/
Interest rate	Riksbank www.riksbank.com Bank of England Federal Reserve System
Production index	Statistics Sweden Office for National Statistic http://www.statistics.gov.uk OECD

Homo Oeconomicus 27(4): 443–461 (2011)

www.accedoverlag.de

State Protection, Interest Groups and Government Spending in the Kingdom of Italy, 1876-1913

Nadia Fiorino
University of L'Aquila and CREI, Italy

Roberto Ricciuti
University of Verona, Italy and CESifo, Germany
(eMail: roberto.ricciuti@univr.it)

Abstract In the last two decades of the XIX century Italy became an industrial country. Historians maintain that this process was affected by the action of some interest groups that pursued both state protection from competition and specific public expenditure programs. Beginning with the economic literature of interest groups, this paper attempts to empirically investigate the role of the interest groups in public expenditure decisions in Italy from 1876 to 1913. We argue that a proper indicator of the role of interest groups is their output. The analysis suggests that government spending was sensitive to the preferences of heavy industry rather then those of textile and cereal cultivators. We therefore highlight the role of the political process in setting economic policy in the early stages of Italian development.

JEL Classifications H11, N43
Keywords special interest groups, public expenditure, Italian economic history

1. Introduction

In the last two decades of the XIX century, Italy experienced a change in its political system, and simultaneously became an industrial country. The law on tariff barriers to international trade, passed on July 14, 1887, represented a key event of this process, by protecting the grain, textile, sugar and steel industries. The Italian tariff was part of the generalized protectionism within Europe: Austria-Hungary in 1882, Germany in 1879 and France in 1881 followed similar policies. In the late XIX century only England, the Netherlands and Belgium carried on the free trade policy in Europe. The 1887 tariff originated from landed interests concerned about falling grain

ISBN 978-3-89265-075-1 ISSN 0943-0180

prices resulting from American and Russian competition in the context of rapidly declining transportation costs. As the landed interests did not carry sufficient lobbying power a *quid pro quo* was negotiated with both textile and heavy industry for mutual support in Parliament for the respective demand for protection.[1]

Economic historians have for a long time discussed the necessity of the protectionist trade policy choice in Europe and in Italy in the late XIX century. Most historians' contributions agree that only a protectionist trade policy would have allowed a solid industrialization to European late comers. With respect to the Italian case, Zamagni (1993) and Pescosolido (1998) followed this line of reasoning. Applying an infant industry argument, they maintained that without protection Italian industry would have been unable to survive foreign competition, and Italy would not have developed. Federico and O'Rourke (1999) found that the removal of trade barriers would have had only small welfare and income distribution effects.

Scholars have also emphasized that the protectionist choice in Italy was driven by the action of specific interest groups. Gerschenkron highlighted that public intervention, and more generally the activist state policy, was appropriate in the situation of the new Kingdom. Nevertheless, he argued that this policy was devoted to economically unproductive projects, like the promotion of the steel industry in Terni in 1884 and the subsidization of the shipbuilding and naval industry between 1885 and 1896 (Gerschenkron 1962). Fenoaltea (1978) condemned the choice of protecting the heavy industry because it strongly penalized the mechanical industry due to the higher costs of iron and steel. Federico and Tena (1998, 1999) have computed effective protection rates showing that some groups were strongly protected and others were not, without any coherence across sectors. They conclude that the lobbying activity of some interest groups was more effective than the activity of other groups in capturing politicians. The key element shared by these analyses is that some interest groups affected the mechanisms of capital formation, pursuing both protection from the competition and specific public spending programs (Bonelli 1975, 1978, Capone 1981).

A formal analysis of this hypothesis has yet to be carried out. So far the studies that have been developed do not go beyond descriptive statistics to motivate their arguments and do not provide any formal test.[2] Data limita-

---

[1] The law passed with 199 'yes' and 27 'no.' Toniolo (1990) described the 'horse trading' that took place among parliamentarians interested in helping specific firms in their constituencies.

[2] Brosio and Marchese (1986) built a model of demand in which the expenditure level is chosen by a median voter that belongs to an élite. They tested such a model for the period 1861 to 1914.

tions partly explain the absence of more rigorous inquiries on this issue.

This paper builds on this line of reasoning: according to the public choice theory of government, we empirically examine the role of the groups protected by the 1887 trade law exerted upon the expenditure decision-making process. We do not attempt to explain the economic and political determinants of the trade policy or relate revenues raised by tariffs with government spending. Rather, we use the protectionist trade policy of 1887 to identify the groups that emerged as *interest groups* and investigate the impact (*pressure*) of those groups on the size and the scope of the public sector from 1876 to 1913. We do so by applying the interest group theory as a formal positive economic analysis of government behavior as developed in the public choice literature. The starting point of the public choice view in analyzing the role of the interest groups in policy formation is the fundamental importance of the rational maximizing behavior of private actors, politicians and bureaucrats. Individual incentives, the prospect of personal gain and loss motivate public sector actors, just as they do those in the private sector. Thus, governmental policies follow from the decisions taken by self-interested individuals (politicians and bureaucrats) within the government organization. The central aspect of the public choice interest group theory concerns the *nexus* between politicians and voters (interest groups). Such a *nexus* can be stated more or less in conventional supply and demand terms (McCormick and Tollison 1981). On the one hand, interest groups maximize their utility functions by demanding certain policies (transfer, public goods, regulation). On the other hand, individual policy makers maximize the probability of winning elections and offer pieces of legislation. Thus, elected officials act as brokers amongst competing interest groups, pairing suppliers and demanders of regulation, legislatures are the place "to clear the market for wealth transfers" (Shughart and Tollison 1986). An important insight of interest group models is that the effectiveness of group lobbying activities is inversely related to its size, due to the heterogeneity of its memberships and goals (Olson 1965).

As a positive theory of government, the interest group theory has been applied and explains a large variety of historical and contemporary government activities (Ekelund and Tollison 1997), the government impact on income distribution (Congleton and Shugart 1990), economic growth (Olson 1982), and the activity of individual legislators (Bronars and Lott 1994). Yet, the main focus of the literature of interest groups has been the growth of government (Olson 1982, Mueller and Murrel 1986, Shugart and Tollison 1986). These models, by emphasizing the voting process within the legislature and the competition among different interest groups, predict a potential positive impact of interest groups seeking wealth transfers through the political process at the level of government activity, however measured (e.g. spending, regulation and so on).

The rest of the paper is organized as follows: Section 2 frames the historical and political background. The model is specified in Section 3 and tested in Section 4. The last section concludes.

2. Identifying interest groups: The historical background

In order to place our analysis in a historic perspective, this section provides an illustration of some historical events that motivate the empirical relationship we have identified and show the key role of the interest groups in shaping public policy.

In 1861 the Kingdom of Piedmont became the Kingdom of Italy. After that, most of the effort was finalized to enforce a homogeneous set of rules throughout the national territory and to build an economy able to compete with the more advanced European countries. In 1876 the Right (*Destra Storica*) was defeated and the Left (*Sinistra Storica*) came into power. These changes in government produced at last two distinctive processes. Firstly, the state became a financial institution that, by means of public debt and receipts, redistributed some of the resources generated in agriculture to other sectors of the economy (Aquarone 1981). Secondly, the political equilibrium based on the interests of landowners and traders came to an end. These processes were closely linked. On the one hand, the state had a prominent role in the accumulation of capital. The modernization of the economy started during the last ruling years of the Right. Inflows of foreign capital were favored by the abolition of the inconvertibility of the currency and by monetary stabilization. A large government expenditure program was set to give the opportunity for new industrial investments. In order to increase the stock of fixed social capital and to support the steel-mechanical industry, privileges to Italian firms for railway works were given through the so-called Baccarini Law in 1882 and, indirectly, through the nationalization of the railways by the establishment of the company *Ferrovie dello Stato* (National Railways Company) in 1905. This company gave procurements to the national industry by updating the rolling-stock. Furthermore, between 1885 and 1896, a program of subsidization of the shipbuilding and naval industry was promoted. Between 1885 and 1913 the national naval industry received an average of 22 million liras per year (Zamagni 1993). In 1884 a complete iron mill was created in Terni with public funds.

Overall government spending experienced a rapid growth throughout our sample. Simultaneously, changes in the composition of the government budget took place, in particular spending on public services, such as transport, communication and construction and, then later, spending on the provision of public goods, such as education, increased (Brosio and Marchese 1986, Aidt et al. 2006). On the other hand, this "new" role of the State, together with the agricultural crisis (due to the competition from overseas) and the failure of capitalistic development in agriculture changed both the economic and the political weight of the primary sector. Starting from the 1880s until World War I, the political system was characterized by the alliance between new entrepreneurial groups, mostly related to heavy industry and the traditional landowners of the South (Candeloro 1970, Capone 1981).

The effects on public policy of the consolidation of the alliance between traditional landowners and a more dynamic bourgeoisie appears more evident when we take into account two institutional issues that resulted in the electoral reform enacted in 1882. The reform extended the franchise for male voters, lowered the minimum voting age from 25 to 21 years and required, as the essential condition, capacity instead of socio-economic status. Meanwhile, status was considered to be an alternative to the accomplishment of the second year of primary school and was reduced from 40 to 19.80 liras. The gradual lifting of socio-economic restrictions on voting franchise strongly enlarged the constituency. In 1880 voters counted for 2.2% of the population of the Kingdom, while in 1882 they increased to 6.9% (Caracciolo 1977). The reform law also modified the electoral regulations. Beginning from 1882, the district size was broadened and the single-member districts replaced with a system of competing lists to favor competition between political-ideological groups.

The second important institutional factor derives from the social composition of the Left. The change in power from the Right to the Left was more sociological than ideological. In fact, the Left maintained a substantial continuity with previous policies. However, the Left was not homogeneous in bringing together landowners, the new financial aristocracy, speculators, urban professionals and new entrepreneurs (Farneti 1971). The electoral reform of 1882 was the result of the heterogeneous political composition of the *élites* and, at the same time, emphasized this heterogeneity by modifying both the constituency size and electoral districts.

3. The empirical model

Starting from the literature on interest groups, this section empirically estimates the influence of the interest groups on public expenditure programs between 1876 and 1913. The basic model used to describe the expenditure decision making process is the following:

$$EXP_t = \alpha_1 + \alpha_2 GDPpc_t + \alpha_3 CER_t + \alpha_4 TEX_t + \alpha_5 ISI_t + \alpha_6 OPEN_t + \alpha_7 POP_t + \alpha_8 VOT_t + \varepsilon_\tau$$

where ε_τ is a random error. The dependent variable of the model is the real total government expenditure (*EXP*). Our choice to use an aggregate measure of public spending, rather than particular expenditure areas, merits some discussion. Many empirical studies are concerned with narrow policy areas, as they evaluate the success or failure of an interest group in influencing policy in one particular area. However, non-voting activities such as making up the details of the laws, lobbying among representatives, formulating amendments and so on, are also crucial in determining legislative outcomes. In addition, the effect of lobbying is incremental and not only redistributive with respect to government spending: once some specific spending program has been captured by an interest group it is easier - for politicians - to add another in order to help another group, instead of shifting resources from one group to the other. Some sectors directly benefit from government spending via procurements. Amongst those considered here, iron and steel are the most important, since governments buy military equipment. However, government spending may indirectly benefit other sectors, for example, agriculture from public investments in irrigation, producers of equipment from capital transfers to build new factories, and so on. Based on these arguments, we prefer to use an aggregate policy outcome such as total government expenditure, rather than to analyze particular functions of public expenditure.

The main problem of empirical analyses in the field of interest groups is related to the identification of a proxy for the special group. In order to capture the pressure of the interest groups in shaping public policy, some models focus on their political activities, such as, the campaign contributions (Crain and Tollison 1977) and the lobbying activity in the legislative and executive branches of government (McCornik and Tollison 1981). As the data on interest group activities are sometimes not available, some contributions use the *structural characteristics* of the groups. Gardner (1987) employs the average size of the producers and the percentage of owner income. Mueller and Murrell (1986) estimate the strength of interest groups by the number of special interest organizations. When the interest group is not formally organized and membership data are unavailable, indirect *ex ante* proxies, such as the number of producers in an industry (Guttman 1978) or some measures of concentration, are applied. In this case, the results in support of the influence of the interest groups in public policy are not solid since the relationship between numbers and influence might be non-monotonic and may be dependent on the type of the interest group.

We use the law enacted in 1887 as an instrument to detect the special interest groups that acted as "pressure groups" on the public decision-making process. By means of duties and tariffs the entrepreneurs of textile, sugar, steel and grains were protected from international competition. All of them are considered in our analysis as the interest groups that affected government expenditure programs. One may wonder whether the political decisions which the 1887 law reflects were not the outcome of a coherent vision for supporting certain industries instead of others. Nevertheless, the relationship between public expenditure and the interest groups that benefited from the protectionist law seems historically correct and analytically sustainable. Some of the mechanisms implemented in 1887 (in particular, the willingness of the political system to compromise with interest groups) were kept in place for a long time (Bonelli 1978, Aquarone 1981).

Some models (e.g. Mueller and Murrel 1986) measure interest groups either by using the number of special interest organizations in a country or the number of members in each group. These kinds of proxies have the advantage of solving the free-riding problems that, as Olson's (1965) influential theoretical study highlighted, may arise from the increase in the group size. Because of the lack of data, it is impossible to replicate this procedure. Even so, the use of the number of workers is an unsatisfactory way to measure and compare the interest groups influence in our sample because the groups we identify present a quite different capital/labor ratio. For this reason, we cannot exclude *a priori* that a sector may have relatively few members due to a more intensive use of capital, but which may exert a large impact on the public decision-making process.

On the one hand, one may argue that an index of concentration would be a more appropriate measure. The degree of concentration, as well as the membership, allows the alleviation of the collective action problems (free-riding). However, the relationship between the independent variable and the proxies, like the membership or the degree of concentration, is not only driven by free-riding effects but also by effects which relate to the "political strength" of an interest group. In our sample, textile and grain production are fragmented in a wide number of medium and small sized enterprises; furthermore, in all of the industries we have analyzed importers co-exist with exporters, and then different goals exist within the same industry. Nevertheless, we do not know the internal organization of the group, for instance, whether the interests of some enterprise members of an industry are pivotal with respect to the interests of some other members of the same group, or if a larger group (with a larger free-riding problem) has more electoral resources. In other words, the relationship between number and influence is not a linear one, and perhaps not even a monotonic one. Based on the Olson argument, and considering the internal organization of the industries we have analyzed, an index of concentration might underesti-

Figure 1 Population and voter levels (1876-1913)

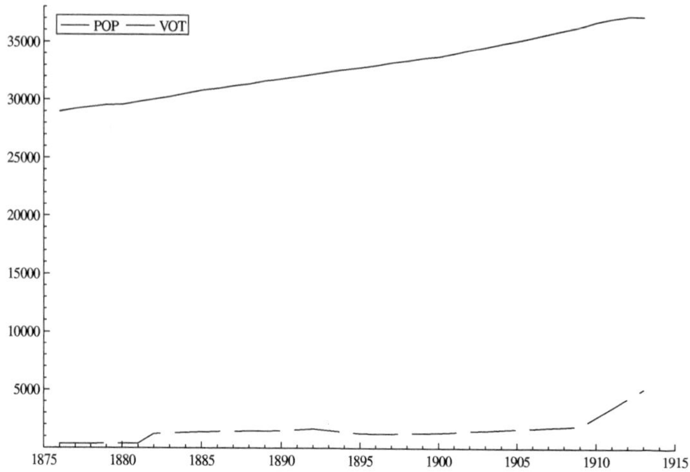

Figure 2 Real public expenditure 1876-1913 (million liras)

Figure 3 Deviation of real expenditure from trend (HP filtered)

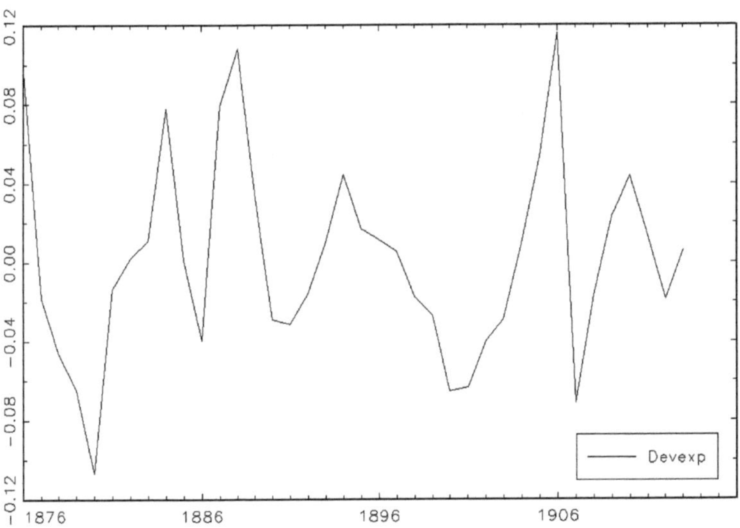

expenditure (mainly for personnel). In a number of works Giovanni Federico has reconstructed the statistical data for agriculture, showing that previous estimates from Istat (1957) overestimated grain production in the early 1870s and underestimated agricultural production from the 1880s until World War I. Federico (2000) reports the added value and gross sellable output data for benchmarks in 1891, 1911, 1938 and 1951, divided into the most important products.[8] In a subsequent paper (Federico 2003) he gives the gross sellable output for the whole agricultural production from 1861 to 1913. Our data, provided directly by Giovanni Federico, give the gross sellable output of cereals, which we take as a proxy for grain production. *TEX*, *ISI* and per capita GDP are taken from the new estimates of Italian industrial production given by Fenoaltea (2005). *OPEN* is taken from Fratianni and Spinelli (1991). All data are in 1911 prices.

---

[8] The gross sellable production is the value of all products minus their reinvestment in the agricultural sector. The added value is obtained from the gross sellable output by subtracting the cost of expenditures from other sectors of the economy. For the years 1891 and 1911 the expenditure to gross sellable output ratio was equal to 4.3% and 7.09%, respectively. Clearly, the choice of putting together different measures of production adds some noise in the estimations. However, we believe that this is not sizable, and removing expenditure based on the benchmark years from all years would have added even further noise, since we would have made assumptions on the distributions over time of expenditures that would not be soundly based.

4. Empirical results

4.1 *Tests for nonstationarity*

Before estimating the structural equation, the analysis of the stochastic properties of the series is applied in order to establish whether public expenditure and all explanatory variables used in the regression model share a long- or a short-run relationship. This information makes it possible to correctly specify the model by avoiding spurious regression problems. The stationarity has been verified by the Augmented Dickey-Fuller tests (ADF), and the autoregressive structure has been determined according to the Schwarz Information Criterion (SIC). The test specification includes a constant and a trend for all series. The results are presented in Table 1: nonstationarity can never be rejected.[9]

Table 1 Unit root tests

	ADF test statistics	Lags	Order of integration
CER	-3.8184	3	I(1)
DEVEXP	-2.3114	1	I(1)
EXP	-1.1513	1	I(1)
GDPpc	-0.1341	1	I(1)
ISI	-2.1285	1	I(1)
OPEN	-0.6960	1	I(1)
POP	-2.5931	2	I(1)
TEX	-2.1872	6	I(1)
VOT	-0.1595	1	I(1)

All specifications include trend and intercept. Critical values at the 1%, 5% and 10% for the ADF tests with trend and intercept are -3.96, -3.41, and -3.13, respectively.

4.2 *Regression results*

The assessment of the stochastic properties of the series allows us to express equation (1) by first differencing all the variables in order to prevent spurious regression. Therefore, the estimated regressions are short-term relations. From an econometric point of view, the specification test cannot reject the validity of the instruments, and the variables are jointly different from zero at the usual significance levels.

[9] The variable *GDPpc* is I(1) since the ADF test rejects the null of nonstationarity on the first-differenced series (the test statistic is -4.1192, with 1 lag according to the SIC).

Table 2 2SLS results for *EXP*

	(1)	(2)	(3)	(4)
Constant	0.447* (0.259)	0.448* (0.256)	0.474* (0.262)	0.468 (0.261)
dGDPpc	0.003* (0.002)	0.003* (0.002)	0.003* (0.002)	0.003* (0.002)
dCER	6.717e-6* (3.607e-6)	6.722e-6* (3.555e-6)	7.232e-6** (3.645e-6)	-7.194e-6* (3.609e-6)
dTEX	-0.001 (0.001)	-0.001 (0.001)		
dISI	0.092** (0.037)	0.097** (0.037)	0.116** (0.064)	-0.095* (0.046)
dOPEN	0.006 (0.009)	0.006 (0.009)	0.005 (0.009)	
dPOP	0.0004* (0.0002)	0.0004** (0.0002)	0.0004** (0.0002)	0.0004* (0.0002)
dVOT	-0.002 (0.004)			
N	34	34	34	34
Specification test	2.376	2.327	1.927	2.185
Testing $\beta = 0$	10.471*	9.902*	8.592*	8.206*

The specification test is distributed under the null of the validity of the instruments as a χ^2 with degrees of freedom equal to the number of instruments minus one. The test $\beta = 0$ is distributed as a χ^2 with degrees of freedom equal to the number of variables minus one. Heteroskedasticity consistent standard errors are in parentheses. The operator *d* indicates first differences. ***, ** and * indicate significance at the 1%, 5% and 10% levels, respectively.

We comment on the results of both tables together because they share strong similarities. The variable *CER* is statistically different from zero in Table 2, but from an economic point of view its effect is almost null, and it is not significantly different from zero in Table 3. The class of grain cultivators mainly represented elderly landowners. They were not interested in the capitalistic development of agriculture; rather they operated in order to keep their property rights and to crystallize social and productive relationships.[10] Therefore, it is reasonable to maintain that they controlled more on the receipts side of the budget, rather than on expenditure. Indeed,

[10] Most likely, the interest of the grain entrepreneurs in the infrastructures, such as ports for sea-transportation, would grow stronger during World War I.

Table 3 2SLS results for *DEVEXP*

	(1)	(2)	(3)	(4)
Constant	0.085** (0.034)	0.081** (0.031)	0.078*** (0.023)	0.064*** (0.017)
dGDPpc	0.346 (0.903)	0.305 (0.855)	0.267** (0.092)	0.249** (0.099)
dCER	-0.077 (0.187)	-0.079 (0.192)		
dTEX	-0.052 (0.374)			
dISI	0.244* (0.129)	0.237** (0.114)	0.241** (0.116)	0.087*** (0.014)
dOPEN	-0.010 (0.008)	-0.010 (0.008)		
dPOP	0.891** (0.434)	0.916** (0.378)	0.808** (0.297)	0.889*** (0.262)
dVOT	0.059 (0.047)	0.064 (0.062)		
N	34	34	34	34
Specification test	2.1230	2.1782	2.1605	2.2532
Testing $\beta = 0$	10.882*	10.182*	9.962**	10.005**

The specification test is distributed under the null of the validity of the instruments as a χ^2 with degrees of freedom equal to the number of instruments minus one. The test $\beta = 0$ is distributed as a χ^2 with degrees of freedom equal to the number of variables minus one. Heteroskedasticity consistent standard errors are in parentheses. The operator *d* indicates first differences. ***, ** and * indicate significance at the 1%, 5% and 10% levels, respectively.

between 1885 and 1910 the estate tax decreased from 125 to 84 million liras (Castronovo 1975: 143). Nevertheless, the requests of the traditional landowners were focused on the tariff of wheat, that scholars (Toniolo 1978, among others) consider the *pactum sceleris*, i.e. the agreement between the protected industrial and agricultural sectors to *buy* their privileges.[11]

The coefficient of *ISI* is significantly positive in both specifications. Empirical evidence suggests the idea, maintained by historians, that the State helped the iron and steel industry through procurement both in the

[11] Maffeo Pantaleoni (1901) in a speech at the Chamber of Deputies highlighted that the tariff on wheat: 1) solely rewarded the landowners (about 50,000 units) and harmed both the sharecroppers and the tenants waiting for relocation; 2) guaranteed to the landowners a return (150 million liras) higher than costs represented by the estate tax (107 million liras).

military and in the railway sectors (in particular after nationalization in 1905). In addition, government grants supported the naval industry. Despite the fact that such an industry was founded with the direct support of the state this result emphasizes that it was a private business. It was able to put pressure on the government to guarantee a satisfying utilization of the productive capacity, overcoming the small size of the national market. The establishment of the *Società degli Altoforni, Acciaierie e Fonderie di Terni* in 1884 is the most evident sign of the role of the interest groups in the political framework, and of logrolling within the legislature (Bonelli 1975: 15). The company, whilst remaining private, was the result of both the private capital led by V. S. Breda, who was also elected to the Senate, and state capital: the government advanced 12 million liras to the company, buying some components of military ships. Furthermore, the interest group of metal-makers also benefited from monetary and credit policy: Terni's iron mills avoided bankruptcy by receiving loans funded by the Bank of Italy (Bonelli 1975, Cerioni 2001).

The variable *TEX* is insignificant in both Tables. The different behavior of the textile and steel entrepreneurs already emerged from the *Inchiesta Industriale*, a document framed during the last years of the government of the Left (1870-1874) and considered by historians to be the most important source of information to reconstruct the origin of the protectionist choice realized in 1878 and 1887.[12] The *Atti dell'Inchiesta Industriale* emphasized that textile and steel entrepreneurs demanded aid from the state, especially in the form of protectionist measures. However, while the textile entrepreneurs did not put such a request into a strategy oriented to a qualitative reinforcement of their firms, the steel entrepreneurs asked for public investments also in education in order to obtain a skilled labor force.

Population is positive and significantly different from zero. This result shows that an increase in population has the same effect on residual government expenditure. The variable for the extension of the franchise is insignificant, probably because the number of effective voters remained small. Indeed, during this period governments faced the so-called banditry (*brigantaggio*) in Southern Italy and the *fasci siciliani*, a separatist political movement in Sicily, which represented a way to express social discontent without going through the poorly representative institutional and political system. Openness is not significantly different from zero. Indeed, tariffs had only a short-run effect in reducing imports, and both imports and exports increased over time. Finally, per capita GDP is mostly significant.

---

[12] See on this point Baglioni (1974) and Marongiu (1995: 311-312).

5. Conclusions

The trade tariffs imposed in 1878 and confirmed in 1887 are usually indicated as milestones of Italian policy in the 19th century. It is reasonable to maintain that these political decisions were not the outcome of a careful and systematic attempt to set favorable conditions for the birth and the development of particular industries. However, historiography emphasizes that these *episodes* were the result of positive answers to the requests of powerful interest groups. Such requests strengthened the alliance between political and entrepreneurial groups.

Interest groups can seek several goals: protection from international competition and public expenditure programs, but also tax breaks and long-term contracts with government agencies. Starting from these considerations we have tested the influence that the groups protected in 1887 exerted on the expenditure decision-making process over 1876-1913. The main result points to the role of the iron and steel industries as the most powerful interest group.[13]

This is in line with a traditional view dating back from the liberal school of the early 20th century. Luigi Einaudi (and in the same line the "L'Unità" edited by Gaetano Salvemini) in a number of articles attacked those he sarcastically called the 'drillers'. *Strictu sensu*, they were drilling in Northern Italy looking for oil, but in a more general way Einaudi referred to all entrepreneurs whose investment choices were distorted by government subsidies and tariffs. In particular, he showed that the excessive production costs of the iron and steel industry and its behavior as a trust were detrimental for the machine industry, the unreliability of the balance sheets of the companies, and quantified the total costs of the protection and subsidies of the iron and steel industry in 260 million liras in 1910.[14] In the view of the free-trade scholars the protectionist tariffs were a signal that policy makers were responsive to the requests of some interest groups (Cardini 1981, Tedesco 2002). Furthermore, Pantaleoni, de Viti de Marco and Mazzola used the "Giornale degli Economisti" to emphasize the relevance

---

[13] A referee argued that since the main components of total expenditure are interests on debt and military expenditure, which mostly consists of personnel expenses, there is no reason to expect that they are caused by iron and steel production. We think that having as dependent variable the deviation of government spending from its trend mostly removes these components (especially the part that is brought from one year to the following as salaries and interests on outstanding debt), therefore strengthening to our claim. Furthermore, government spending had a very limited redistributive role and total government spending was basically the sum of specific interventions in a number of fields, including those affected by interest groups.

[14] See, among others, Einaudi (1911a and 1911b; 1912) and Einaudi and Riboni (1912).

of the "heavy" industry interests for an understanding of political behavior. The Agriculture Minister Bruno Chimirri was one of the most criticized by Mazzola for his defense of vested interests. Cardini (1981: 109) reported a statement in which Chimirri described the intimate link between government spending and industries:

> There is nothing sadder for the economy than the smokestacks of the bankrupted factories in Savona, the heavy mallets of Terni for which we hear at every blow taxpayers groaning, the factories in Pozzuoli producing machines paid by Italian (our translation).

Probably none of these free-market economists could have said it better.

Acknowledgements

We thank Stefano Fenoaltea, Emma Galli, Fabio Padovano, Gaetano Sabatini, two anonymous referees and the editor Manfred Holler for useful comments, Giovanni Federico for sharing his data and for comments, and Sukhvinder Kaur and Ian Chadwich for editing. The usual *caveat* applies.

References

Aidt, T.S., Dutta, J. and Loukoianova, E. (2006), Democracy Comes to Europe: Franchise Extension and Fiscal Outcomes 1830-1938, *European Economic Review* 50: 249-283.

Aquarone, A. (1981), *L'Italia Giolittiana (1896-1915)*, Bologna: Il Mulino.

Baglioni, G. (1974), *L'Ideologia della Borghesia Industriale dell'Italia Liberale*, Torino: Einaudi.

Bonelli, F. (1978), *Il Capitalismo Italiano: Linee Generali di Interpretazione, Annali di Storia d'Italia*, Torino: Einaudi.

Bonelli, F. (1975), *Lo Sviluppo di una Grande Impresa in Italia: La Terni dal 1884 al 1962*, Torino: Einaudi.

Bronars S.G. and Lott, J.R. (1997), Do Campaign Donations Alter How Politicians Vote?, *Journal of Law and Economics* 40: 317-350.

Brosio, G. and Marchese, C. (1986), *Il Potere di Spendere: Economia e Storia della Spesa Pubblica dall'Unificazione ad Oggi*, Bologna: Il Mulino.

Candeloro, G. (1970), *Storia dell'Italia Modern*, Milano: Feltrinelli.

Capone, A. (1981), Destra e Sinistra da Cavour a Crispi, *Storia d'Italia*, Vol. XX, Torino: UTET.

Caracciolo, A. (1977), *Stato e Società Civile: Problemi dell'Unificazione Italiana*, Torino: Einaudi.

Cardini, A. (1981), *Stato Liberale e Protezionismo in Italia (1890-1900)*, Bologna: Il Mulino.

Castronovo, V. (1975), *La Storia Economica*, Torino: Einaudi.

Cerioni, I. (2001), *La Banca d'Italia e il Consorzio Siderurgico: Fonti per la Storia della Siderurgia in Età Giolittiana nelle Carte dell'Archivio della Banca d'Italia*, Quaderni dell'Ufficio Ricerche Storiche della Banca d'Italia, 2.

Crain, W.M. and Tollison, R.D. (1977), The Influence of Representation on Public Policy, *Journal of Legal Studies* 6: 355-362.

Congleton, R. and Shugart II, W.F. (1990), The Growth of Social Security: Electoral Push or Electoral Pull?, *Economic Inquiry* 28: 109-132.

Einaudi, L. (1911a), I Trivellatori di Stato, *La Riforma Sociale* 22, 1-14.

Einaudi, L. (1911b), Nuovi Favori ai Siderurgici?, *La Riforma Sociale* 22: 97-112.

Einaudi, L. (1912), I Fasti Italiani Degli Aspiranti Trivellatori della Tripolitania, *La Riforma Sociale*, 23, 161-193.

Einaudi, L. and Riboni, P. (1912), Polemizzando con i Siderurgici, *La Riforma Sociale* 23, 850-888.

Ekelund, R.B. and Tollison, R.D. (1997), *Politicized Economies: Monarchy, Monopoly and Mercantilism*, College Station: Texas A&M University Press.

Farneti, P. (1971), *Sistema Politico e Società Civile: Saggi di Teoria e Ricerca Politica*, Torino: Giappichelli.

Federico, G. and Tena, A. (1998), Was Italy a Protectionist Country?, *European Review of Economic History* 2, 73-97.

Federico, G. and Tena, A. (1999), Did Trade Policy Foster Italian Industrialization?: Evidence from Effective Protection Rates 1870-1930, *Research in Economic History* 19, 111-130.

Federico, G. and O'Rourke, K. (1999), Much Ado about Nothing?: The Italian Trade Policy in the 19th Century, in: J. Williamson and S. Pamuk (eds.), *The Mediterranean Response to Globalisation before 1950*, London: Routledge.

Federico, G. (2000), Una Stima del Valore Aggiunto in Agricoltura, in: G.M. Rey (ed.), *I Conti Economici dell'Italia, 3.2 Il Valore Aggiunto per il 1891, 1938 e 1951*, Bari: Laterza, 3-112.

Federico, G. (2003), Le Nuove Stime della Produzione Agricola Italiana, 1860-1910: Primi Risultati ed Implicazioni, *Rivista di Storia Economica* 19, 359-381.

Federico, G. (2008), *Always on the Brink: Piedmont and Italy*, mimeo.

Fenoaltea, S. (1978), Riflessioni sull'Esperienza Industriale Italiana dal Risorgimento alla Prima Guerra Mondiale, in: G. Toniolo (ed.), *L'Economia Italiana 1861-1940*, Bari: Laterza.

Fonoaltea, S. (2001), The Growth of Italy's Cotton Industry, 1861-1913: A Statistical Reconstruction, *Rivista di Storia Economica* 17: 139-171.

Fenoaltea, S. (2003), Product Heterogeneity Trade and Protection: The Cotton Industry in Post-Unification Italy, in: A.M. Falchero, A. Giuntini, G. Nigro and L. Segreto (eds.), *La Storia e l'Economia. Miscellanea di Studi in Onore di Giorgio Mori*, Varese, Edizioni Lativa.

Fenoaltea, S. (2005), Notes on the Rate of Industrial Growth in Italy, 1861-1913, *Journal of Economic History* 63: 695-735.

Fratianni, M. and Spinelli, F. (1991), *Storia Monetaria d'Italia*, Milano: Mondadori.

Gardner, B.L. (1987), Causes of U.S. Farm Commodity Programs, *Journal of Political Economy* 95: 290-310.

Gerschenkron, A. (1962), *Economic Backwardness in Historical Perspective*,

Cambridge MA: Harvard University Press.

Ghisalberti, C. (1986), *Storia Costituzionale d'Italia 1848-1948*, Bari: Laterza.

Guttman, J.M. (1978), Interest Groups and the Demand for Agricultural Research, *Journal of Political Economy* 86: 467-484.

ISTAT (1957), *Annali di Statistica: Le Rilevazioni Statistiche in Italia dal 1861 al 1956*, Serie VIII, Vol. 8-9, Roma.

ISTAT (1958), *Sommario di Statistiche Storiche Italiane 1861-1955*, Roma.

Kamath, S.J. (1989), Concealed Takings: Capture and Rent-seeking in the Indian Sugar Industry, *Public Choice* 62: 119-138.

Marongiu, G. (1995), *Storia del Fisco in Italia: La Politica Fiscale della Destra Storica (1861-1876)*, Torino: Einaudi.

Meltzer, A.H. and Richard, S.F. (1981), A Rational Theory of the Size of Government, *Journal of Political Economy* 89: 914-927.

Mueller, D.C. and Murrel, P. (1986), Interest Groups and the Size of Government, *Public Choice* 48: 125-145.

Olson, M. (1965), *The Logic of Collective Action: Public Goods and the Theory of Groups*, Cambridge, MA: Harvard University Press.

Olson, M. (1982), *The Rise and Decline of Nations: Economic Growth, Stagflation and Social Rigidities*, New Haven CT, Yale University Press.

Pantaleoni, M. (1901), Discorso Pronunciato alla Camera dei Deputati, 20 marzo 1901, *Atti parlamentari*, Camera dei Deputati, Discussioni, XXI legislatura, I sessione.

Pescosolido, G. (1998), *Unità Nazionale e Sviluppo Economico*, Bari: Laterza.

Ragioneria Generale dello Stato (1969), *Il bilancio dello Stato italiano dal 1862 al 1967*, Roma: Istituto Poligrafico dello Stato.

Rodrik, D. (1998), Why Do More Open Economies Have Bigger Governments?, *Journal of Political Economy* 106: 997-1032.

Shughart, W.F. and Tollison, R.D. (1986), The Political Economy of Legislation and the Growth of Government, *Research in Law and Economics* 9: 111-127.

Tedesco, L. (2002), *L'Alternativa Liberista in Italia: Crisi di Fine Secolo, Antiprotezionismo e Finanza Democratica nei Liberali Radicali (1898-1904)*, Soveria Mannelli: Rubbettino.

Toniolo, G. (1977), Effective Protection and Industrial Growth: The Case of Italian Engineering, *Journal of European Economic History* 6: 659-673.

Toniolo, G. (1978), Alcune Tendenze dello Sviluppo Economico Italiano 1861-1940, in: G. Toniolo (ed.), *L'Economia Italiana 1861-1940*, Bari: Laterza.

Toniolo, G. (1990), *An Economic History of Liberal Italy, 1850-1918*, London: Routledge.

Zamagni, V. (1993), *The Economic History of Italy 1860-1990*, Oxford: Clarendon Press.

Homo Oeconomicus 27(4): 463–479 (2011)

www.accedoverlag.de

Fair Voting Rules in Committees, Strict Proportional Power and Optimal Quota

František Turnovec
Charles University in Prague, Institute of Economic Studies, Prague, Czech Republic
(eMail: turnovec@fsv.cuni.cz)

Abstract In simple weighted committees with a finite number of members, fixed weights and changing quota, there exist a finite number of different quota intervals of stable power with the same sets of winning coalitions for all quotas from each of them. If in a committee the sets of winning coalitions for different quotas are the same, then the power indices based on pivots, swings, or minimal winning coalitions are also the same for those quotas. If the fair distribution of voting weights is defined, then the fair distribution of voting power means to find a quota that minimizes the distance between relative voting weights and relative voting power (optimal quota). The problem of the optimal quota has an exact solution via the finite number of quotas from different intervals of stable power.

JEL Classifications C71, D72, H77
Keywords simple weighted committee, fairness, optimal quota, strict proportional power, voting and power indices

1. Introduction

Let us consider a committee with n members. Each member has some voting weight (number of votes, shares etc.) and a voting rule is defined by a minimal number of weights required for passing a proposal. Given a voting rule, voting weights provide committee members with voting power. Voting power means an ability to influence the outcome of voting. Voting power indices are used to quantify the voting power.

The concept of fairness is being discussed related to the distribution of voting power among different actors of voting. This problem was clearly formulated by Nurmi (1982): "If one aims at designing collective decision-making bodies which are democratic in the sense of reflecting the popular support in terms of the voting power, we need indices of the latter which enable us to calculate for any given distribution of support and for any

ISBN 978-3-89265-075-1 ISSN 0943-0180

decision rule the distribution of seats that is 'just'. Alternatively, we may want to design decision rules that - given the distribution of seats and support - lead to a distribution of voting power which is identical with the distribution of support" (Nurmi 1982: 204).

Voting power is not directly observable: as a proxy for it voting weights are used. Therefore, fairness is usually defined in terms of voting weights (e.g. voting weights are proportional to the results of an election). Assuming that a principle of fair distribution of voting weights is selected, we are addressing the question of how to achieve equality of voting power (at least approximately) to voting weights. The concepts of strict proportional power and the randomized decision rule introduced by Holler (1982a, 1985, 1987), of optimal quota of Słomczyński and Życzkowski (2007), and of intervals of stable power (Turnovec 2008b) are used to find, given voting weights, a voting rule minimizing the distance between actors' voting weights and their voting power.

Concept of fairness is frequently associated with so-called square root rule, attributed to British statistician Lionel Penrose (1946). The square root rule is closely related to indirect voting power measured by the Penrose-Banzhaf power index.[1] Different aspects of the square root rule have been analysed in Felsenthal and Machover (1998, 2004), Laruelle and Widgrén (1998), Baldwin and Widgrén (2004), Turnovec (2009). The square root rule of "fairness" in the EU Council of Ministers voting was discussed and evaluated in Felsenthal and Machover (2007), Słomczyński and Życzkowski (2006, 2007), Hosli (2008), Leech and Aziz (2008), Turnovec (2008a) and others. Nurmi (1997a) used it to evaluate the representation of voters' groups in the European Parliament.

In the second section basic definitions are introduced and the applied power indices methodology is shortly resumed. The third section introduces the concept of quota intervals of stable power and optimal quota. While the framework of the analysis of fairness is usually restricted to the Penrose-Banzhaf concept of power, we are treating it in a more general setting and our

[1] The square root rule is based on the following propositions: Let us assume n units with population $p_1, p_2, \ldots, p_n$, and the system of representation by a super-unit committee with voting weights $w_1, w_2, \ldots, w_n$ of units' representations. It can be rigorously proved that for sufficiently large p_i the absolute Penrose-Banzhaf power of individual citizen of unit i in unit's referendum is proportional to the square root of p_i. If the relative Penrose-Banzhaf voting power of unit i representation is proportional to its voting weight, then indirect voting power of each individual citizen of unit i is proportional to the product of voting weight w_i and square root of population p_i. Based on the conjecture (not rigorously proved) that for n large enough the relative voting power is proportional to the voting weights, the square root rule concludes that the voting weights of units representations in the super-unit committee proportional to square roots of units' population lead to the same indirect voting power of each citizen independently of the population unit she is affiliated with.

results are relevant for any power index based on pivots or swings and for any concept of fairness.

2. Committees and voting power

A simple weighted committee is a pair $[N,\mathbf{w}]$, where N will be a finite set of n committee members $i=1,2,...,n$, and $\mathbf{w}=(w_1,w_2,...,w_n)$ will be a non-negative vector of the committee members' voting weights (e.g. votes or shares). By 2^N we denote the power set of N (set of all subsets of N). By voting coalition we mean an element $S\in 2^N$, the subset of committee members voting uniformly (YES or NO), and

$$w(S)=\sum_{i\in S} w_i$$

denotes the voting weight of coalition S. The voting rule is defined by quota q satisfying $0<q\leq w(N)$, where q represents the minimal total weight necessary to approve the proposal. Triple $[N,q,\mathbf{w}]$ we call a *simple quota weighted committee*. The (voting) coalition S in committee $[N,q,\mathbf{w}]$ is called a winning one if $w(S)\geq q$ and a losing one in the opposite case. The winning coalition S is called critical if there exists at least one member $k\in S$ such that $w(S\backslash k)<q$ (we say that k is critical in S). The winning coalition S is called minimal if any of its members is critical in S.

A priori voting power analysis seeks an answer to the following question: Given a simple quota weighted committee $[N,q,\mathbf{w}]$, what is an influence of its members over the outcome of voting? The absolute voting power of a member i is defined as a probability $\Pi_i[N,q,\mathbf{w}]$ that i will be decisive in the sense that such a situation appears in which she would be able to decide the outcome of voting by her vote (Nurmi 1997b and Turnovec 1997), and a relative voting power as

$$\pi_i[N,q,w]=\frac{\Pi_i[N,q,w]}{\sum_{k\in N}\Pi_k[N,q,w]}$$

Three basic concepts of decisiveness are used: swing position, pivotal position and membership in a minimal winning coalition (MWC position). The *swing position* is an ability of an individual voter to change the outcome of voting by a unilateral switch from YES to NO (if member j is critical with respect to a coalition S, we say that he has a swing in S). The *pivotal position is* such a position of an individual voter in a permutation of voters expressing a ranking of attitudes of members to the voted issue (from the most preferable to the least preferable) and the corresponding order of forming of the winning coalition, in which her vote YES means a YES outcome of voting and her vote NO means a NO outcome of voting (we say that j is pivotal in the permutation considered). The MWC position is an ability of an individual voter to contribute to a minimal winning coalition (i.e. membership in the minimal winning coalition).

Let us denote by $W(N,q,\mathbf{w})$ the set of all winning coalitions and by $W_i(N,q,\mathbf{w})$ the set of all winning coalitions with i as a member, $C(N,q,\mathbf{w})$ as the set of all critical winning coalitions, and by $C_i(N,q,\mathbf{w})$ the set of all critical winning coalitions i has the swing in, by $P(N,q,\mathbf{w})$ the set of all permutations of N and $P_i(N,q,\mathbf{w})$, the set of all permutations i is pivotal in. Moreover, $M(N,q,\mathbf{w})$ represents the set of all minimal winning coalitions, and $M_i(N,q,\mathbf{w})$ is the set of all minimal winning coalitions with i. By $\text{card}(S)$ we denote the cardinality of S, therefore $\text{card}(\emptyset)=0$.

Assuming many voting acts and all coalitions equally likely, it makes sense to evaluate the a priori voting power of each member of the committee by the probability to have a swing, measured by the absolute Penrose-Banzhaf (PB) power index (Penrose 1946, Banzhaf 1965):

$$\Pi_i^{PB}(N,q,w)=\frac{\text{card}(C_i)}{2^{n\text{-}1}}$$

Here, $\text{card}(C_i)$ is the number of all winning coalitions the member i has the swing in and 2^{n-1} is the number of all possible coalitions with i. To compare the relative power of different committee members, the relative form of the PB power index is used:

$$\pi_i^{PB}(N,q,w)=\frac{\text{card}(C_i)}{\sum\limits_{k\in N}\text{card}(C_k)}$$

While the absolute PB is based on a well-established probability model (see e.g. Owen 1972), its normalization (relative PB index) destroys this probabilistic interpretation, the relative PB index simply answers the question of what is the voter i's share in all possible swings.

Assuming many voting acts and all possible preference orderings equally likely, it makes sense to evaluate an a priori voting power of each committee member by the probability of being in pivotal situation, measured by the Shapley-Shubik (SS) power index (Shapley and Shubik 1954):

$$\Pi_i^{SS}(N,q,w) = \frac{\text{card}(P_i)}{n!}$$

Here, $\text{card}(P_i)$ is the number of all permutations in which the committee member i is pivotal, and $n!$ is the number of all possible permutations of committee members. Since $\sum_{i \in N} \text{card}(P_i) = n!$ it holds that

$$\pi_i^{SS}(N,q,\mathbf{w}) = \frac{\text{card}(P_i)}{\sum_{k \in N} \text{card}(P_k)} = \frac{\text{card}(P_i)}{n!}$$

i.e. the absolute and relative form of the SS-power index is the same.[2]

Assuming many voting acts and all possible coalitions equally likely, it makes sense to evaluate the voting power of each committee member by the probability of membership in a minimal winning coalition, measured by the absolute Holler-Packel (HP) power index:

$$\Pi_i^{HP}(N,q,\mathbf{w}) = \frac{\text{card}(M_i)}{2^n}$$

Here, $\text{card}(M_i)$ is the number of all minimal winning coalitions with i, and 2^n is the number of all possible coalitions.[3] Originally the HP index was defined and is usually being presented in its relative form (Holler 1982b, Holler and Packel 1983)

---

[2] Supporters of the Penrose-Banzhaf power concept sometimes reject the Shapley-Shubik index as a measure of voting power. Their objections to the Shapley-Shubik power concept are based on the classification of power measures on so-called I-power (voter's potential influence over the outcome of voting) and P power (expected relative share in a fixed prize available to the winning group of committee members, based on cooperative game theory) introduced by Felsenthal et al. (1998). The Shapley-Shubik power index was declared to represent P-power and as such is unusable for measuring influence in voting. We tried to show in Turnovec (2007) and Turnovec et al. (2008) that objections against the Shapley-Shubik power index, based on its interpretation as a P-power concept, are not sufficiently justified. Both Shapley-Shubik and Penrose-Banzhaf measure could be successfully derived as cooperative game values, and at the same time both of them can be interpreted as probabilities of being in some decisive position (pivot, swing) without using cooperative game theory at all.

[3] The definition of an absolute HP power index is provided by the author (a similar definition of absolute PB power can be found in Brueckner (2001), the only difference is that we relate the number of MWC positions of member i to the total number of coalitions, not to the number of coalitions of which i is a member).

$$\Pi_i^{HP}(N,q,\mathbf{w}) = \frac{\text{card}(M_i)}{\sum_{k \in N} \text{card}(M_k)}$$

The above definition of the absolute HP index allows a clear probabilistic interpretation. Multiplying and dividing it by the $\text{card}(M)$, we obtain

$$\frac{\text{card}(M_i)}{\text{card}(M)} \frac{\text{card}(M)}{2^n}$$

In this breakdown the first term gives the probability of being a member of a minimal winning coalition, provided the MWC is formed, and the second term the probability of forming a minimal winning coalition assuming that all voting coalitions are equally likely. The relative HP index has the same problem with a probabilistic interpretation as the relative PB index.[4]

In the literature there are still two other concepts of power indices: the Johnston (J) power index based on swings, and the Deegan-Packel (DP) power index, based on membership in minimal winning coalitions.

The Johnston power index (Johnston 1978) measures the power of a member of a committee as a normalized weighted average of the number of her swings, using as weights the reciprocals of the total number of swings in each critical winning coalition. (The swing members of the same winning coalition have the same power, which is equal to $1/[\#$ of swing members].)

The Deegan-Packel power index (Deegan and Packel 1978) measures the power of a member of a committee as a normalized weighted average of the number of minimal critical winning coalitions he is a member of, using as weights the reciprocals of the size of each MWC

It is difficult to provide some intuitively acceptable probabilistic interpretation for relative J and DP power indices. They provide a normative scheme of the division of rents in the committee rather than a measure of an a priori power (and in the sense of Felsenthal and Machover (1998) classification they can be considered as measures of P-power).

It can be easily seen that for any $\alpha > 0$ and any power index based on swings, pivots or MWC positions it holds that $\Pi_i[N,\alpha q,\alpha \mathbf{w}] = \Pi_i[N,q,\mathbf{w}]$. Therefore, without the loss of generality, we shall assume throughout the text that

---

[4] For a discussion about the possible probabilistic interpretation of the relative PB and HP, see Widgrén (2001).

$$\sum_{i \in N} w_i = 1 \quad \text{and} \quad 0 < q \leq 1$$

using only relative voting weights and quotas in the analysis.

3. Quota interval of stable power, fairness and optimal quota

Let us formally define some concepts that we shall use in this paper.

Definition 1 A simple weighted committee $[N, \mathbf{w}]$ has a property of *strict proportional power* with respect to a power index $\boldsymbol{\pi}$, if there exists a voting rule q^* such that $\boldsymbol{\pi}[N, q^*, \mathbf{w}] = \mathbf{w}$, i.e. the relative voting power of committee members is equal to their relative voting weights.

In general, there is no reason to expect that such a voting rule exists. Holler and Berg (1986) extended the concept of a strict proportional power in the model with randomized voting rule.

Definition 2 Let $[N, \mathbf{w}]$ be a simple weighted committee, $\mathbf{q} = (q_1, q_2, ..., q_m)$ be a vector of different quotas, $\boldsymbol{\pi}^k$ be a relative power index for quota q_k, and $\boldsymbol{\lambda} = (\lambda_1, \lambda_2, ..., \lambda_m)$ be a probability distribution over elements of $\mathbf{q}$. The *randomized voting rule* $(\mathbf{q}, \boldsymbol{\lambda})$ selects within different voting acts by random mechanism quotas from $\mathbf{q}$ by the probability distribution $\boldsymbol{\lambda}$. Then $[N, \mathbf{w}]$ has a property of *strict proportional expected power* with respect to a relative power index $\boldsymbol{\pi}$, if there exists a randomized voting rule $(\mathbf{q}^*, \boldsymbol{\lambda}^*)$ such that the vector of the mathematical expectations of power is equal to the vector of voting weights:

$$\boldsymbol{\pi}(N, (\mathbf{q}, \boldsymbol{\lambda}), \mathbf{w}) = \sum_{k=1}^{m} \lambda_k \boldsymbol{\pi}^k (N, q_k, \mathbf{w}) = \mathbf{w}$$

The concept of randomized voting rule and strict proportional expected power was introduced by Holler (1982, 1985), and studied by Berg and Holler (1986).

Definition 3 Let $\mathbf{w} = (w_1, w_2, ..., w_n)$ be a fair distribution of voting weights (with whatever principle is used to justify it) in a simple weighted committee $[N, \mathbf{w}]$, $\boldsymbol{\pi}$ is a relative power index, ($\boldsymbol{\pi}[N, q, \mathbf{w}]$ is a vector valued function of q), and d is a distance function, then the voting rule q_1 is said to be *at least as fair* as voting rule q_2 with respect to the selected $\boldsymbol{\pi}$ if $d(\mathbf{w}, \boldsymbol{\pi}(N, q_1, \mathbf{w})) \leq d(\mathbf{w}, \boldsymbol{\pi}(N, q_2, \mathbf{w}))$.

Intuitively, given $\mathbf{w}$, the voting rule q_1 is preferred to voting rule q_2 if q_1 generates a distribution of power closer to the distribution of weights than q_2.

Definition 4 The voting rule q^* that minimizes a distance d between $\pi[N,q,\mathbf{w}]$ and $\mathbf{w}$ is called an optimal voting rule (*optimal quota)* with respect to the selected power index π.

Let $[N,q,\mathbf{w}]$ be a simple weighted quota committee and C_{is} be the set of critical winning coalitions of the size s in which i has a swing, then

$$\text{card}(P_i) = \sum_{s \in N} \text{card}(C_{is})(s-1)!(n-s)!$$

is the number of permutations with the pivotal position of i in $[N,q,\mathbf{w}]$. The number of pivotal positions corresponds to the number and structure of swings. If in two different committees sets of swing coalitions are identical, then the sets of pivotal positions are also the same.

Proposition 1 Let $[N,q_1,\mathbf{w}]$ and $[N,q_2,\mathbf{w}]$, $q_1 \neq q_2$, be two simple quota-weighted committees such that $W[N,q_1,\mathbf{w}] = W[N,q_2,\mathbf{w}]$, then

$$C_i(N,q_1,\mathbf{w}) = C_i(N,q_2,\mathbf{w})$$

$$P_i(N,q_1,\mathbf{w}) = P_i(N,q_2,\mathbf{w})$$

$$M_i(N,q_1,\mathbf{w}) = M_i(N,q_2,\mathbf{w})$$

for all $i \in N$.

From Proposition 1 it follows that in two different committees with the same set of members, the same weights and the same sets of winning coalitions, the PB-power indices, SS-power indices and HP-power indices are the same in both committees, independently of quotas. Moreover, since the J-index is based on the concept of swing and the DP power index is based on membership in minimal winning coalitions, the J and DP indices are also the same.

Proposition 2 Let $[N,q,\mathbf{w}]$ be a simple quota weighted committee with a quota q,

$$\mu^+(q) = \min_{S \in W[N,q,w]} (w(S) - q) \quad \text{and}$$

$$\mu^-(q) = \min_{S \in 2^N \setminus W(N,q,w)} (q - w(S))$$

Then for any particular quota q we have $W[N,q,\mathbf{w}] = W[N,\boldsymbol{\gamma},\mathbf{w}]$ for all $\gamma \in (q - \mu^-(q),\ q + \mu^+(q)]$.

Proof
a) Let $S \in W[N,q,\mathbf{w}]$, then from the definition of $\mu^+(q)$

$$w(S) - q \geq \mu^+(q) \geq 0 \Rightarrow w(S) - q - \mu^+(q) \geq 0 \Rightarrow S \in W(N,q+\mu^+,w)$$

hence S is winning for quota $q+\mu^+(q)$. If S is winning for $q+\mu^+(q)$, then it is winning for any quota $\gamma \leq q+\mu^+(q)$.

b) Let $S \in 2^N \setminus W[N,q,\mathbf{w}]$, then from the definition of $\mu^-(q)$

$$q - w(S) \geq \mu^-(q) \geq 0 \Rightarrow q - \mu^-(q) - w(s) \geq 0 \Rightarrow S \in 2^N \setminus W(N,q-\mu^-(q),w)$$

hence S is losing for quota $q - \mu^-(q)$. If S is losing for $q - \mu^-(q)$, then it is losing for any quota $\gamma \geq q - \mu^-(q)$.

From (a) and (b) it follows that for any $\gamma \in (q - \mu^-(q),\ q+\mu^+(q)]$

$$S \in W(N,q,\mathbf{w})\} \Rightarrow S \in W(N,\gamma,\mathbf{w})\}$$

$$S \in \{2^N \setminus W(N,\gamma,\mathbf{w})\} \Rightarrow S \in \{2^N \setminus W(N,q,\mathbf{w})\}$$

which implies that $W(N,q,\mathbf{w}) \Rightarrow W(N,\gamma,\mathbf{w})$.

From Propositions 1 and 2 it follows that swing, pivot and MWC-based power indices are the same for all quotas $\gamma \in (q - \mu^-(q),\ q + \mu^+(q)]$. Therefore the interval of quotas $(q - \mu^-(q),\ q + \mu^+(q)]$ we call an *interval of stable power* for quota q. Quota $\gamma^* \in (q - \mu^-(q),\ q + \mu^+(q)]$ is called the marginal quota for q if $\mu^+(\gamma^*) = 0$.

Now we define a partition of the power set 2^N into equal weight classes $\Omega_0, \Omega_1, ..., \Omega_r$ (such that the weight of different coalitions from the same class is the same and the weights of different coalitions from different classes are different). For the completeness set $w(\varnothing) = 0$. Consider the weight-increasing ordering of equal weight classes $\Omega^{(0)}, \Omega^{(1)}, ..., \Omega^{(r)}$ such that for any $t < k$ and $S \in \Omega^{(t)}$, $R \in \Omega^{(k)}$ it holds that $w(S) < w(R)$. Denote $q_t = w(S)$ for any $S \in \Omega^{(t)}$, $t = 1, 2, ..., r$.

Proposition 3 Let $\Omega^{(0)},\Omega^{(1)},...,\Omega^{(r)}$ be the weight-increasing ordering of the equal weight partition of 2^N. Set $q_t = w(S)$ for any $S \in \Omega^{(t)}$, $t = 1,2,...,r$. Then there is a finite number $r \leq 2^n - 1$ of marginal quotas q_t and corresponding intervals of stable power $(q_{t-1}, q_t]$ such that $W[N, q_t, \mathbf{w}] \subset W[N, q_{t-1}, \mathbf{w}]$.

Proof follows from the fact that card $(2^N) = 2^n$ and an increasing series of k real numbers $a_1,...,a_k$ subdivides interval $(a_1, a_k]$ into $k-1$ segments. An analysis of voting power as a function of the quota (given voting weights) can be substituted by an analysis of voting power in a finite number of marginal quotas.

Proposition 4 Let $(N,q,w]$ be a simple quota weighted committee and $(q_{t-1}, q_t]$ is the interval of stable power for quota q. Then for any $\gamma = 1 - q_t + \varepsilon$, where $\varepsilon \in (0, q_t - q_{t-1}]$ and for all $i \in N$

$$\mathrm{card}(C_i(N,q,\mathbf{w})) = \mathrm{card}(C_i(N,\gamma,\mathbf{w}))$$

$$\mathrm{card}(P_i(N,q,\mathbf{w})) = \mathrm{card}(P_i(N,\gamma,\mathbf{w}))$$

Proof Let S be a winning coalition, k has the swing in S and $(q_{t-1}, q_t]$ is an interval of stable power for q. Then it is easy to show that $N \setminus S \cup k$ is a winning coalition, k has a swing in $N \setminus S \cup k$ and $(1-q_t, 1-q_{t-1}]$ is an interval of stable power for any quota $\gamma = 1 - q_t + \varepsilon \, (0 < \varepsilon \leq q_t - q_{t-1})$. Let R be a winning coalition, j has a swing in R, and $(1-q_t, 1-q_{t-1}]$ is an interval of stable power for quota $\gamma = 1 - q_t + \varepsilon \, (0 < \varepsilon \leq q_t - q_{t-1})$. Then $N \setminus R \cup j$ is a winning coalition, j has a swing in $N \setminus R \cup j$ and $(q_{t-1}, q_t]$ is an interval of stable power for any quota $q = q_{t-1} + \tau$ where $0 < \tau \leq q_t - q_{t-1}$.

While in $[N,q,\mathbf{w}]$ the quota q means the total weight necessary to pass a proposal (and therefore we can call it a *winning quota*), the *blocking quota* means the total weight necessary to block a proposal. If q is a winning quota and $(q_{t-1}, q_t]$ is a quota interval of stable power for q, then any voting quota $1 - q_{t-1} + \varepsilon$ (where $0 < \varepsilon \leq q_t - q_{t-1}$) is a blocking quota. From Proposition 4 it follows that the blocking power of the committee members, measured by swing and pivot-based power indices, is equal to their voting power. It is easy to show that voting power and blocking power might not be the same for power indices based on membership in minimal winning coalitions (i.e. HP and DP power indices). Let r be the number of marginal quotas, then from Proposition 4 it follows that for power indices based on swings and pivots the number of majority power indices does not exceed int $(r/2)+1$.

Proposition 5 Let $q_1, q_2, ..., q_m$ be the set of all majority marginal quotas in a simple weighted committee $[N, \mathbf{w}]$, and $\boldsymbol{\pi}^k$ be a vector of Shapley-Shubik relative power indices corresponding to a marginal quota q_k, then there exists a vector $(\lambda_1, \lambda_2, ..., \lambda_r)$ such that:

$$\sum_{k=1}^{m} \lambda_k = 1, \ \lambda_k \geq 0, \ \sum_{k=1}^{m} \lambda_k \boldsymbol{\pi}^k = \mathbf{w}$$

The proof follows from Berg and Holler (1986). They provide the following property of simple weighted committees: Let $[N, Q, \mathbf{w}]$ be a finite family of simple quota weighted committees with the same weights $\mathbf{w}$ and a finite set of different relative quotas $Q = \{q_1, q_2, ..., q_m\}$. Let $\lambda(Q)$ be a probability distribution over Q where φ_k is a probability with which a random mechanism selects the quota q_k and $\pi_{ik}(N, q_k, \mathbf{w})$ be SS relative power index in the committee $[N, q_k, \mathbf{w}]$ with a quota $q_k \in Q$, then

$$\overline{\pi}_i(N, Q, \mathbf{w}) = \sum_{k: q_k \in Q} \pi_{ik}(N, q_k, \mathbf{w}) \lambda_k$$

is an expected SS relative power of the member i in the randomized committee $[N, \boldsymbol{\lambda}(Q), \mathbf{w}]$. For any vector of weights there exist a finite set Q of quotas q_k such that $0.5 < q_k \leq 1$, and a probability distribution $\boldsymbol{\lambda}$ such that

$$\overline{\pi}_i(N, Q, \mathbf{w}) = \sum_{k: q_k \in Q} \pi_{ik}(N, q_k, \mathbf{w}) \lambda_k = w_i$$

The randomized voting rule $\boldsymbol{\lambda}(Q)$ leads to strict proportional expected SS power. Clearly, if there exists an exact quota q^* such that $\pi_i[N, q^*, \mathbf{w}] = w_i$, we can find it among finite number of marginal majority quotas.

In general, the number of majority power indices can be greater than the number of committee members, and the system

$$\sum_{k=1}^{r} \lambda_k = 1, \ \lambda_k \geq 0, \ \sum_{k=1}^{r} \lambda_k \boldsymbol{\pi}^k = \mathbf{w}$$

might not have the unique solution. To solve the system we can use the optimization problem:

$$\text{minimize} \sum_{i=1}^{n} abs\left(\sum_{k=1}^{r} \pi_i^k \lambda_k - w_i\right)$$

$$\text{subject to} \sum_{k=1}^{r} \lambda_k = 1, \ \lambda_k \geq 0$$

that can be transformed into an equivalent linear programming problem (Gale, 1960):

$$\text{minimize} \sum_{i=1}^{n} y_i$$

$$\text{subject to} \sum_{k=1}^{r} \pi_i^k \lambda_k - y_i \leq w_i \qquad \text{for } i=1,\ldots,n$$

$$\sum_{k=1}^{r} \pi_i^k \lambda_k + y_i \leq w_i \qquad \text{for } i=1,\ldots,n$$

$$\sum_{k=1}^{r} \lambda_k = 1$$

$$\lambda_k, y_i \geq 0 \qquad \text{for } k=1,\ldots,r, \ i=1,\ldots,n$$

This problem is easy to solve by standard linear programming simplex methods. Although we can apply a randomized voting rule to any relative power index, based on pivots and swings, the problem is with the interpretation of what we get. The relative PB index has no probabilistic interpretation, so the randomized voting rule calculated for it by Proposition 5 does not provide the mathematical expectation of the number of swings, leading to a relative PB power equal to weights.

One can hardly expect that randomized voting rules leading to the strict proportional expectation of power would be adopted by actors in real voting systems. However, the design of a "fair" voting system can be based on an approximation provided by the quota generating the minimal distance between vectors of power indices and weights, which is called an *optimal quota*.

The optimal quota was introduced by Słomczyński and Życzkowski (2006, 2007) as a quota minimizing the sum of square residuals between the power indices and the voting weights by $q \in (0.5, 1]$

$$\sigma^2(q) = \sum_{i \in N} (\pi_i[N,q,\mathbf{w}]) - w_i)^2$$

Słomczyński and Życzkowski introduced the optimal quota concept within the framework of the so-called Penrose voting system as a principle of fairness in the EU Council of Ministers voting. Here power is measured by the Penrose-Banzhaf power index. The system consists of two rules (Słomczyński and Życzkowski 2007: 393):

a) The voting weight attributed to each member of the voting body of size n is proportional to the square root of the population he or she represents;

b) The decision of the voting body is taken if the sum of the weights of members supporting it is not less than the optimal quota.

Looking for a quota providing a priori voting power "as close as possible" to the normalized voting weights, Słomczyński and Życzkowski (2007) are minimizing the sum of square residuals between the power indices and voting power for $q \in (0.5, 1]$. Based on a simulation they propose heuristic approximations of the solution for the PB index:

$$\underline{q} = \frac{1}{2}\left(1 + \frac{1}{\sqrt{n}}\right) \le q \le \frac{1}{2}\left(1 + \sum_{i \in N} w_i^2\right) = \overline{q}$$

Clearly $\underline{q} = \overline{q}$ if and only if all the weights are equal, but in this case any majority quota is optimal.

Definition 5 By the index of the fairness of a voting rule q in $[N,q,\mathbf{w}]$ we call:

$$\varphi(N,q,\mathbf{w}) = 1 - \sqrt{\frac{1}{2}\sum_i (\pi_i[N,q,\mathbf{w}] - w_i)^2}$$

It is easy to see that

$$0 \le \sqrt{\frac{1}{2}\sum_i (\pi_i[N,q,\mathbf{w}] - w_i)^2} \le 1$$

(zero in the case of the equality of weights and power, e.g. $w_1 = 1/2,\ w_2 = 1/2,\ \pi_1 = 1/2,\ \pi_2 = 1/2$, and 1 in the case of an extreme inequality of weights and power, e.g. $w_1=1,\ w_2=0,\ \pi_1=0,\ \pi_2=1$), hence $0 \le \varphi(N,q,w) \le 1$. We say that a voting rule q_1 is "at least as fair" as a voting rule q_2 if $\varphi(N,q_1,\mathbf{w}) \ge \varphi(N,q_2,\mathbf{w})$.[5]

Looking for a "fair" voting rule we can maximize φ , which is the same as to minimize $\sigma^2(q)$. Using marginal quotas and intervals of stable power we do not need any simulation.

Proposition 6 Let $[N,q,\mathbf{w}]$ be a simple quota-weighted committee and $\pi_i(N,q_t,w)$ be relative power indices for marginal quotas q_t , and q_{t^*} be the majority marginal quota minimizing

$$\sum_{i\in N} (\pi_i[N,q_j,\mathbf{w}]-w_i)^2$$

($j=1,2,\dots,r$, r is the number of intervals of stable power such that q_j are marginal majority quotas), then the exact solution of Słomczyński and Życzkowski's optimal quota (SZ optimal quota) problem for a particular power index used is any $\gamma\in(q_{t^*-1},q_{t^*})$ from the quota interval of stable power for q_{t^*} .

The proof follows from the finite number of quota intervals of stable power (Proposition 4). The quota q_{t^*} provides the best approximation of strict proportional power that is related neither to a particular power measure nor to a specific principle of fairness.

4. Concluding remarks

In simple quota weighted committees with a fixed number of members and voting weights there exists a finite number r of different quota intervals of stable power ($r \le 2^n - 1$) generating a finite number of power indices vectors. For power indices with a voting power equal to blocking power the number of different power indices vectors corresponding to majority quotas is equal at most to int $(r/2)+1$.

If the fair distribution of voting weights is defined, then the fair distribution of voting power is achieved by the quota that maximizes the index

[5] The index of fairness follows the same logic as measures of deviation from proportionality used in political science to evaluate the difference between results of an election and the composition of an elected body - e.g. Loosemore and Hanby (1971) is based on the absolute values of the deviation metric, or Gallagher (1991) using a square roots metric.

of fairness (minimizes the distance between relative voting weights and relative voting power). The index of fairness is not a monotonic function of the quota.

The problem of optimal quota has an exact solution via the finite number of majority marginal quotas. Słomczyński and Życzkowski introduced an optimal quota concept within the framework of the so called Penrose voting system as a principle of fairness in the EU Council of Ministers voting and related it exclusively to the Penrose-Banzhaf power index and the square root rule. However, the fairness in voting systems and approximation of strict proportional power is not exclusively related to the Penrose square-root rule and the Penrose-Banzhaf definition of power, as it is usually done in discussions about EU voting rules. In this paper it is treated in a more general setting as a property of any simple quota weighted committee and any well-defined power measure. Fairness and its approximation by optimal quota are not specific properties of the Penrose-Banzhaf power index and square root rule.

Acknowledgements

This research was supported by the Czech Government Research Target Program, project No. MSM0021620841 and by the Grant Agency of the Czech Republic, project No. 402/09/1066 "Political economy of voting behavior, rational voters' theory and models of strategic voting" and by the Max Planck Institute of Economics in Jena. The author would like to thank Manfred J. Holler, Andreas Nohn and an anonymous referee for valuable comments to an earlier version of the paper.

References

Baldwin, R. and Widgrén, M. (2004), Winners and Losers under Various Dual Majority Rules in the EU's Council of Ministers, in: M. Wiberg (ed.), *Reasoned Choices*, Turku: The Finnish Political Science Association.

Banzhaf, J.F. (1965), Weighted Voting Doesn't Work: A Mathematical Analysis, *Rutgers Law Review* 19: 317-343.

Berg, S. and Holler, M.J. (1986), Randomized Decision Rules in Voting Games: A Model for Strict Proportional Power, *Quality and Quantity* 20: 419-429.

Brueckner, M. (2001), Expected Probabilistic Characterization of Power Indices, in: M.J. Holler. and G. Owen (eds.), *Power Indices and Coalition Formation*, Boston-Dordrecht-London: Kluwer.

Deegan, J. and Packel, E.W. (1978), A New Index of Power for Simple n-Person Games, *International Journal of Game Theory* 7: 113-123.

Felsenthal, D.S. and Machover, M. (2007), *Analysis of QM Rule Adopted by the Council of the European Union, Brussels, 23 June 2007,* Research report online, LSE, London [http://eprints.lse.ac.uk/archive0000431].

Felsenthal, D.S. and Machover, M. (2004), *Analysis of QM Rule Adopted by the EU Inter-Governmental Conference, Brussels, 18 June 2004,* Research report online, LSE, London [http://eprints.lse.ac.uk/2531].

Felsenthal, D.S. and Machover, M. (1998), *The Measurement of Voting Power, Theory and Practice,* Cheltenham: Edward Elgar.

Felsenthal, D.S., Machover, M. and Zwicker, W. (1998), The Bicameral Postulates and Indices of A Priori Voting Power, *Theory and Decision* 44: 83-116.

Gale, D. (1960), *The Theory of Linear Economic Models,* New York: McGraw-Hill.

Gallagher, M. (1991), Proportionality, Disproportionality and Electoral Systems, *Electoral Studies* 10: 33-51.

Holler, M.J. (1987), Paradox Proof Decision Rules in Weighted Voting, in: M.J. Holler (ed.), *The Logic of Multiparty Systems,* Dordrecht: Martin Nijhoff Publishers.

Holler, M.J. (1985), Strict Proportional Power in Voting Bodies, *Theory and Decision* 19: 249-258.

Holler, M.J. (1982a), An Introduction to the Analysis of Power, Voting, and Voting Power, in: M.J. Holler (ed.), *Power, Voting and Voting Power,* Würzburg, Wien: Physica Verlag.

Holler, M.J. (1982b), Forming Coalitions and Measuring Voting Power, *Political Studies* 30: 262-271.

Holler, M.J. and Packel, E. (1983), Power, Luck and the Right Index, *Zeitschrift für Nationalökonomie (Journal of Economics)* 43: 21-29.

Hosli, M.O. (2008), Council Decision Rules and European Union Constitutional Design, *AUCO Czech Economic Review* 2(1): 76-96.

Johnston, R.J. (1978), On the Measurement of Power: Some Reaction to Laver, *Environment and Planning* A10: 907-914.

Laruelle, A. and Widgrén, M. (1998), Is the Allocation of Voting Power among EU States Fair?, *Public Choice* 94: 317-339.

Leech, D. and Aziz, H. (2008), *The Double Majority Voting Rule of the EU Reform Treaty as a Democratic Ideal for an Enlarging Union: an Appraisal Using Voting Power Analysis,* presented at the 2008 EPCS meeting in Jena.

Loosemore, J. and Hanby, V.J. (1971), The Theoretical Limits of Maximum Some Analytical Expression for Electoral Systems, *British Journal of Political Science* 1: 467-477.

Nurmi, H. (1982), The Problem of the Right Distribution of Voting Power, in: M.J. Holler (ed.), *Power, Voting and Voting Power,* Würzburg, Wien: Physica Verlag.

Nurmi, H. (1997a), The Representation of Voter Groups in the European Parliament: A Penrose-Banzhaf Index Analysis, *Electoral Studies* 16: 317-322.

Nurmi, H. (1997b), On Power Indices and Minimal Winning Coalitions, *Control and Cybernetics* 26(4): 609-611.

Owen, G. (1972), Multilinear Extensions of Games, *Management Science* 18: 64-79.

Penrose, L.S. (1946), The Elementary Statistics of Majority Voting, *Journal of the Royal Statistical Society* 109: 53-57.

Shapley, L.S. and Shubik, M. (1954), A Method for Evaluation the Distribution of Power in a Committee System, *American Political Science Review* 48: 787-792.

Słomczyński, W. and Życzkowski, K. (2007), From a Toy Model to Double Square Root System, *Homo Oeconomicus* 24(3-4): 381-400.

Słomczyński, W. and Życzkowski, K. (2006), Penrose Voting System and Optimal Quota, *Acta Physica Polonica* B37(11): 3133-3143.

Turnovec, F. (2009), Fairness and Squareness: Fair Decision Making Rules in the EU Council, *Badania Operacyjne i Decyzje* 4: 109-124.

Turnovec, F. (2008a), National, Political and Institutional Influence in European Union Decision Making, *AUCO Czech Economic Review* 2(2): 154-173.

Turnovec F. (2008b), Efficiency of Fairness in Voting Systems, *Homo Oeconomicus* 25(3-4): 335-348.

Turnovec, F. (2007), New Measure of Voting Power, *AUCO Czech Economic Review* 1(1): 4-14.

Turnovec, F. (1997), Power, Power Indices and Intuition, *Control and Cybernetics* 26(4): 613-615.

Turnovec, F., Mercik J.W. and Mazurkiewicz, M. (2008), Power Indices Methodology: Decisiveness, Pivots and Swings, in: M. Braham and F. Steffen (eds.), *Power, Freedom and Voting: Essays in Honor of Manfred J. Holler*, Berlin, Heidelberg: Springer Verlag.

Widgrén, M. (2001), On the Probabilistic Relationship Between the Public Good Index and the Normalized Banzhaf Index, in: M.J. Holler and G. Owen (eds.), *Power Indices and Coalition Formation*, Boston-Dordrecht-London: Kluwer.

Homo Oeconomicus 27(4): 481–491 (2011)

www.accedoverlag.de

Human Nature or Cultural Constructs: A Phenomenological Account of Justice and Efficiency Conflict

Tõnu Viik
Tallinn University, Estonia
(eMail: tonu.viik@ehi.ee)

Abstract The paper proceeds from the paradoxical results of the ultimatum game theory experiments suggesting that contrary to the expectations of the free market theory people often do not behave as economic agents attempting to maximize their self-interests. Rather, their choices are influenced by moral ideals, and what makes the situation more complicated - their behavioral patterns are reported to vary from culture to culture. As a solution to this problem it is suggested by many that we need to revise the psychological assumptions of the Rational Actor that is commonly used in the microeconomic theories. This paper gives a phenomenological sketch of this revision. It is argued that in order to explain the choices people make in the ultimatum game experiments we cannot describe their situation as choosing between a particular amount of monetary gain and a moral value, but as acting according to what is most meaningful for an actor in economic, but also in ethical, religious, and ideological sense at a given moment. The article presents a phenomenological account of such meaning-formation and attempts to explain how these meaning-formation processes are dependent on culture.

1. Introduction

Manfred J. Holler and Martin Leroch (2010) come back to the conflict between justice and efficiency, regarded as principles of human behavior. Justice is a moral ideal that humans strive to in various everyday life situations. People attempt to make just decisions, they evaluate the actions of others on its basis, and sometimes they ignore its call, but usually this is not a desirable or a pleasant thing to do. In other situations the same people behave as economic agents who attempt to maximize their self-interests. And this is how they are expected behave in market relationships, or at least this is regarded as a way of conduct naturally characteristic to human

ISBN 978-3-89265-075-1 ISSN 0943-0180

beings according to the proponents of free market theory. Now, since ethical and economical agents are the same people acting in one and the same world there must be situations when the ethical ideal of justice and the economical ideal of maximizing self-profit overlap and the ideals conflict.

This conflict is brought to the fore in the ultimatum game experiments, where, as it turns out, the respondents do not behave as monetarily self-interested agents all the way down. Rather, when confronted with a monetary deal, which seems to be a purely economical market situation, they act as moral agents and reject offers that they would benefit from, but which strike them as unfair. From the point of view of economical theory we can just wonder why would a self-interested agent whose goal should be to maximize economic gain act in such an irrational and non-purposive manner. And yet, as Holler and Leroch (2010: 312) report, thousands of respondents around the globe rejected the offer of less than $20 out of $100, and a substantial share was not willing to accept less than $50. The mean offer in industrial societies is between 40 and 50% of the sum total, which allows us to interpret the proposal as a rational self- interested choice of the proponent, provided that we take into account the proposers' expectations about the fairness concerns of the respondents. But that does still not explain where these expectations, and most notably the seemingly irrational choice of the respondents, come from.

The issue becomes more complicated when Holler and Leroch turn to anthropological data and include the results of empirical research by Joseph Henrich (2000) about the ultimatum game results among the Machiguenga people from the Peruvian Amazon area, as well as Frank Marlow's (2004) results about the Hadza tribe in Tanzania. Henrich reports that, on the average, Machiguenga proposers offered only 26% of the sum total, and that only 1 out of 31 proponents refused their share. Among the Hadza tribe the mean offer was 33% and rejection rate 24%. Given these results it is difficult to avoid the conclusion that culture – in the anthropological sense of the word – has something to do with how people behave as economic agents. Paradoxically the people from capitalist societies seem to care less about money and more about fairness than people from non-capitalist cultures. But once we do away with human nature and adhere to the cultural relativism position assuming that human behavior and values are dependent on culture, it is difficult to maintain, as Holler and Leroch point out (2010: 313), the Kantian notion of a universal concept of justice that is valid for all human beings. But it is not just the universalist versions of ethical theories that are at stake here. The economical theory has a double problem: not just does the *homo oeconomicum* behave at times ethically instead of maximizing his self-interest, but this ethical "inclination" seems to be a culture-specific feature of his conduct. As Henrich (2000: 14) puts it, "If cultural differences do greatly influence economic behavior, then the implicit assumption that all humans share the same economic decisionmaking processes, the same sense of fairness, and/or the same taste for punishment must be brought into question."

Thus if the microeconomic theory that is able to predict human behavior in market relations wants to maintain its integrity, it has to revise its assumptions about the nature of acting subjects. In other words, the economic theory needs to modify its paradigmatic views on human nature, and to provide some kind of account of the cultural influences on the behavior of humans. Holler and Leroch are doing this by supplementing Adam Smith's philosophical psychology behind the economical theory in the "Wealth of the Nations" with his views on human nature from "The Theory of Moral Sentiments." It does not mean that they want to do away with the self-interested behavior, for it certainly has its place in everyday life and it can be widely observed in market relationships. The issue lies rather in complementing the psychology of acting human agent in such a way that it would explain why in these very market relationships humans do not behave with the sole purpose of maximizing their profits and how is this "deviation" from the expected pattern dependent on culture.

2. Cultural impact of the behavior of the rational actor

Holler and Leroch derive their answer from Adam Smith's account of human empathetic faculty for sympathy, which is developed (already by Smith) beyond face to face situations, and which actually provides a mechanism of cultural regulation of human behavior. Smith calls it the imagined "impartial spectator" that a subject himself applies to his conduct. And as Holler and Leroch (2010: 316) conclude, "the impartial spectator perspective, which derives from sympathy, thus becomes operational to evaluate, to control and to restructure our behavior." What is more, they point out that the impartial spectator perspective presupposes "some common platform of experience" that needs not to be the same for all mankind (Kant), but that defines the range of subjects whose cultural regulator would bear similar features. Because Smith's impartial spectator is derived from the actual feelings of empathy, it comes in degrees, being stronger and more defined about persons whom we have closer connections to, and less defined when it concerns persons that the subject has never met. From here it is possible to derive a view that explains why people would have a more uniform "impartial spectator" with the members of the same class, society or country. Holler and Leroch use Ken Binmore's theory of evolutionary ethics to build out this connection. Hence, they conclude, it is possible to develop a culturally informed account on the basis of Smith's texts in which there is no inconsistency between the self-interested and culturally influenced moral behavior.

In what follows I would like to contribute to this argument, but I'll do so by giving an alternative explanation about bringing self-interest and moral sentiments to the same plane. This alternative derives from phenomenology, and here I am following the lead of Edward Rubin (1998, 2001). He argues that phenomenology does provide a more realistic psychological model of human motivation than the one used in microeconomics. As Holler and Leroch, he thinks that the economical account of human motivation needs not to be washed away, but complemented by a more overarching theory of human behavior which can be achieved by revising the psychological account that is used in economics. But first, do we really need to assume that economics is based on a kind of psychology? Yes, Rubin (1998: 1705) argues, "any model that states the way human beings behave under specified circumstances is necessarily a theory of the way the human mind functions, and thus belongs in the category of psychology." The particular brand of psychology that microeconomics is based on, Rubin claims, is called rational actor theory, the weaker version of which states that an actor generally attempts to maximize his ability to achieve his goals, and the stronger version specifies that the goal is always to be seen as his *material* self-interests (Rubin 1998: 1705f).

The rational actor theory consists of three premises according to Rubin. The first is methodological individualism which asserts that human beings are autonomous active forces of the social world, and which contrasts to the theories of general will and any other anthropomorphized collective entities that might have a will of their own or take actions independently of particular human beings. The second premise of the rational actor psychology is the belief in instrumental rationality: the claim that social actors try to achieve their goals in the most effective manner, which in turn presupposes that people's preferences can be rank ordered. This assumption runs the risk to overlook such impediments to optimal action as the cognitive limitations of the individual, the structural limitations of an organization, or the lack of information, but it might still work if just assume that the actors *attempt* to make the best to achieve their goals. The third is utility maximization, which, if we define the goals to be achieved very broadly, then it should account for such mutually exclusive behavioral patterns as the one of a workaholic and the one of a couch potato, in which case the theory loses precision and predictability, or, if we define goals as being material or monetary only, then the theory obviously gains in precision, but is unable to deal with such cases that are discussed here (Rubin 1998: 713ff).

Given not just the anthropological evidence about the "irrational" concern with fairness in the ultimatum game experiments, but also other "deviations" that include endowment effects, regret, and excessive optimism, as well as the widely observed phenomena of altruism, self-sacrifice, ideological commitment, and cooperation, we are forced to conclude, Rubin argues, that the rational actor theory is simply inadequate as a view of human psychology, even though it works in a limited range of situations. Hence we are in need of a theory that would be able to account both for these limitations, and why it works within them. Phenomenology, Rubin (1998: 1707) claims,

> accounts for all the explanations that rational action and rational choice theory offer for human behavior, and also accounts for the limitations of those theories. It defines the boundaries between the areas where people will behave rationally, in either sense of the term, and the areas where they will not, and it offers an explanation for human behavior in those areas where rational choice does not apply.

How is phenomenology going to do this? – By means of analyzing meaning-formation in the "natural attitude." Natural attitude can be defined as our mode of being engaged in everyday life when we experience the world, things within it, events that take place, other people and ourselves as entities that have a certain meaning and objective existence. The phenomenological reflection of the natural attitude has revealed that how things appear cannot be explained by a psychological view of a passive human mind which is subjected to the inflowing sensory data and who is sorting this data into clusters of similar and dissimilar qualities. Rather, our perception of things is an active process of interpreting the inflowing data by means of several types of meaning-bestowing operations, starting from categorization and ending with identifying things and events according to highly complex meaning-formations, such as mathematical concepts or moral ideals. Thus the experiencing subject in the natural attitude is all but a passive receptor of what is outside in the objective world. Depending on the meaning-bestowing activities in his consciousness things and events are construed in his mind as good or bad, important or unimportant, friendly or hostile, pleasant or repulsive, just or efficient, etc.

This feature makes the phenomenological theory a kin to the rational actor theory, for they both proceed from the assumption of methodological individualism which rejects a view that humans are subjected to the collective cultural forces, and therefore do not make individual choices in their own minds. However, phenomenology provides an account of the emergence of motifs in the consciousness of an individual. Motifs, in turn, derive from meanings that a subject applies to certain objects, events and situations. To return to our example of the choice between self-gain and concern for fairness in the ultimatum game, before one is choosing one or the other, both options need to be comprehended by him, which means that they are made meaningful for him. Only after that the situation can be described as a choice.[1]

3. Phenomenological account of meaning formation

Now the question is, how are such meanings created in the mind of an individual. As we said above, the subject is to be seen as an active agent of meaning-formation. Edmund Husserl (1995: §17-22) describes the processes of meaning-formation as different types of syntheses of the contents of consciousness, as most notably in the case of empirical perception when we experience different appearances of something from different perspectives at different points of time to be the appearances of one and the same thing. Consciousness accomplishes this effect of sameness by uniting various sensory data that come from the different acts of perception of different aspects of an object around the very temporal and spatial substantiality of it. The substantiality of the object is therefore not empirically perceived, but applied to empirical data. As a consequence the subject always experiences things as having a certain substantial integrity that transcends beyond what is empirically given by means of sense-data.

In Husserl's terms, synthetic activities of consciousness constitute intentional objects - the objects that I am aware of; or what is the same, the objects as they are experienced. Now, the most important component of the process of constitution is the application of meaning to something that appears as having a substantial integrity. Whenever I experience something, I experience it ***as*** something, i.e. any object of experience is identified (and in fact as a result of this its substantionality is formed) by means of its meaning. As Husserl (2001: 113-122) would claim in the "Logical Investigations," an intentional object is constituted by means of its "grasping sense," or what is the same, its "matter."

This epistemology allows us understand why different people (or different groups of people) interpret one and the same situation differently and act differently on the basis of this interpretation. Put simply, this is because they apply different meanings to it, or what is the same, they experience the situation either *as* this or *as* that depending not on the empirical data, but on their subjective meaning-bestowing activity. As said above, to make a choice in the ultimatum game presupposes that the deal is meaningful for

[1] While I do agree with Rubin's thesis about the usefulness of phenomenology on this level of generality, I will provide a different account of how exactly we have to deal with this problem from the phenomenological point of view.

the respondent. However, the deal is not meaningful for him from the beginning on, but it *becomes* meaningful for him as he comes to terms with the situation; as he comprehends what he can win or lose in terms of money, what these options mean to him, etc. That is, the subject needs to process the deal offered to him and he does so by applying meanings to it. The outcome can be economical or theoretical, but also moral, ideological, religious, etc.

Now, from the phenomenological point of view, it is these particular meanings that are created by the subject in the course of interpreting the deal - that motivate him to make one or the other choice, and not the particular sum of money itself versus universal or culture-dependent moral ideals. For obviously, what is on one side of his scales depends on how important a given sum is for the respondent, how desperate or how indifferent one is towards the possible gain. Thus on one side of the scales is not the sum as such with its objective monetary value, but its meaning for the subject at a given time. Students from industrial societies may well reject \$20 as an unfair share out of \$100: this could be partly explained by the fact that an extra \$20 does not make a substantial difference in their day. Clearly the situation would be evaluated differently by somebody who will have something to eat or not, depending on this choice. Or how would a relatively well-off student from industrial societies react if the choice is even more unfair, but the offered sum is one million out of a hundred? Will he still reject it? He could do so, but at this time the deal must have a very different meaning for him. Thus we need to base our psychology on subjectively experienced meanings of the deal, rather than on the objectively measured value of money.

4. Cultural impact from the phenomenological point of view

On the other side of the scales the meaning of the deal is dependent on the collectively held idealities, such as cultural, religious, ideological or ethical ideals. How do these ideals influence the choice of the respondent and proposer, and how do they participate in forming the meaning of the deal for them? This is the question of how does culture influence our experiences; and more precisely; what is the agent of culture within our mind that performs the function similar to Smith's impartial spectator. We know that our individual choices tend to be stereotypical, and consequently our individual meaning-formation processes bear collective similarities.

To answer this question by means of Husserl's phenomenological theory we need to turn to his conception of life-world (*Lebenswelt*) which is defined as the world of "valid realities" (*geltende Wirklichkeiten*) that we are engaged with in our natural attitude. Among the valid realities are material things that we are dealing with, landscapes and material circumstances, but life-world also includes ideal things that we know to be true, existing or valuable, such as the contents of religious beliefs, common sense knowledge, scientific theories, famous artworks, etc. (Husserl 1970: 357, 1989: 250-255). Thus the life-world is not the world of physical objectivities around us, but the world as it is experienced by human beings. For example the historical life-world of Ancient Greeks, Husserl (1970: 272) argues, "… is not the objective world in our sense but rather their 'world-representation,' i.e. their own subjective validity with all the actualities which are valid for them within it, including, for example, gods, demons, etc."

What is the nature of the "ideal things" that belong to the life-world? Who are the subjects to whom they count as "valid realities?" And how is their validity constituted? According to Husserl (1970: 356-357) the ideal things possess s specific "ideal objectivity" which means that they are perceived by a certain range of subjects *as existing*. These idealities might be difficult to discover from the external point of view. Thus, for example, Euclid's theorem is experienced as existing and as having a truth value by mathematicians when they advance their theories and talk to each other about it, but a non-mathematician (a person who knows nothing about mathematics) may not be able to understand what it is, or whether such a thing exists at all, by observing the actions of mathematicians. He might detect that there is a certain regulative principle that structures their talk and actions, but he might fail to understand why it determines their action in the way it does. The same can be said about other ideal objects, such as God, nation, homeland, communism, or democracy, and the communities of subjects who experience these idealities as objectively valid.

According to Husserl the very objectivity of the constituents of the life-world is constituted intersubjectively. This applies even to the objectivity of material objects. If it were the case that I know myself to be only one in the world who sees an object - a man with a hat smoking in the corner in almost any room I go - and everyone else denies his existence ("What man?", "In which corner?"), then the very objectivity of this man will become doubtful for me even if I really do visually perceive him. Usually only these objects are real for me that I see others subjects experiencing as real. Needless to say, this is even more obviously so with ideal objects. All ideal forms are valid for me because I experience them to be valid for people around me, and there is often no other way to prove their reality. In this sense the objectivity of ideal objects consists in nothing but their intersubjectively constituted validity.

As a result, Husserl (1970: 163) argues, a certain "intersubjective harmony occurs, [establishing what is] 'normal'" for a community of subjects. Based on Husserl's manuscripts Anthony Steinbock (1995: 8) has construed a branch of phenomenology ("generative phenomenology") that deals with the intersubjective constitution of home and alien life-world as "normatively significant territories" for a particular community of egos. Dan Zahavi (2001: 100) has also pointed out that one type of intersubjective constitution of reality operates at the level of the creation of normality, as "I am in the midst of a world that has already been provided with sense by others, and my formation of judgments, my self-apprehension, my evaluations, and my interpretation of the world are guided by a linguistically articulated pre-understanding. Thus I understand the world - and through it, myself - by virtue of a handed down linguistic conventionality." As a result my individual experience is always already "communalized," as Husserl (1970: 161ff) puts it.

Thus similarly to Smith's impartial spectator, the cultural regulator of human behavior is seen here as an internalized feature of consciousness that comes to existence as a result of interaction with others, and by means of which a certain "common platform of experience" is created in each community of subjects. The communalization of experience occurs as the subject applies the idealities that are collectively hold as valid in a particular community to the particular cases. Thus the respondent may regard a particular deal offered to him as fair or unfair (but also as religiously or ideologically intriguing, tempting, bothering, etc.) by means of the "ideal things" that are regarded as existing in a given society. These collective idealities define the way in which the respondent, as well as the proponent, experience the offer. They define not just its contents but its emotional significance, they categorize possible choices as an economical, moral, or religious decision, etc.

5. Concluding remarks

Now, if the meaning of a particular event (the deal offered to a respondent) is derived by applying the meanings that are derived from the collectively hold idealities, we arrive at the phenomenological account of culturally influenced, and yet individually performed, meaning formation. If on one side of the scales is the perspective of the monetary gain - with everything that this means for the subject, then on the other side of the scales are "ideal things." But the action is not triggered, as the justice and efficiency puzzle might suggest, by either side which then supposedly weighs over the other side, but the subject creates a unified meaning from the point of which it is most meaningful to do what he does. This unified meaning certainly includes weighing the alternative prospects, but it is a meaning-formation of its own that includes a multitude of evaluations of various possibilities, of situation of the subject himself, other subjects, his life in general, his social surroundings, etc. Thus similarly to the second premise of microeconomic psychology (instrumental rationality) the phenomenological account of meaning-formation suggests that people rank order their preferences, but they do so not by measuring or counting the benefits between gaining self-interest and a particular moral virtue, but they choose what is most meaningful for the subject as he or she makes sense of the deal in all possible perspectives that occur to him.

Thus, as Rubin (2001: 333) concludes, the phenomenological account is in agreement with the rational actor theory about methodological individualism and about the behavioral premise of instrumental rationality. But the choice is not motivated by self-interest, but by the desire for meaning:

> At the level of their life experience, they make decisions so that their life will be meaningful to them. Sometimes, what is most meaningful is to maximize the material well-being of themselves and their children. In other situations, what is most meaningful is to serve God, to serve one's country, to become famous, to experience adventure, to prove one's masculinity or femininity, to help others, or to inflict pain on amphibians (Rubin 2001: 333f).

As we see, the phenomenological account does not dismiss the motive for a monetary gain, but places it on a common plane of meaning. Money matters because it *means* something for a subject, and consequently its objective value has only an indirect impact. What is more, money is experienced with future projections about what this sum will do for a subject, and that makes the value of the deal to be dependent on a variety of other things. But what is most important from the point of view of methodology is that subjectively experienced meaning provides a common denominator for self-gain possibilities versus the other options for choice. This is why it is actually not money on one side of the scales and moral virtues on the other, but these two and many other alternative meanings are all ordered on the scale of what is or seems to be most meaningful for the subject at the given point of time.

People certainly do seek money, but this is not because at times they are placed in anonymous market relations, but because money contributes to the way they want to view their life. There is no such distinct area in the life-world as free market (even though certain aspects of the life-world can well by characterized by it), as there are no such situations when all the other ideal objects besides money are "switched off." At any given moment there are large varieties of alternative idealities that could be used for making sense of a particular situation, even if some of them are more habitual to us than others. This makes it always possible for a human being to come up with alternative meanings and to make an unexpected choice. This explains why "even pathologically self-centered people will often exchange material resources for power or fame, while normal people will exchange material resources for aesthetic or lifestyle benefits that are more meaningful for them" (Rubin 2001: 334f). These exchanges simply make sense to them, and the sense is what matters.

References

Henrich, J. (2000), Does Culture Matter in Economic Behavior? Ultimatum Game Bargaining among the Machiguenga of the Peruvian Amazon, *American Economic Review* 90(4): 973-979.

Holler, M.J. and Leroch M. (2010), Efficiency and Justice Revisited, *European Journal of Political Economy* 26(3): 311-319.

Husserl, E. (1995), *Cartesian Meditations: An Introduction to Phenomenology*, Dordrecht: Kluwer Academic Publishers.

Husserl, E. (1989), Ideas Pertaining to a Pure Phenomenology and to a Phenomenological Philosophy, Studies in the Phenomenology of Constituion, Dordrecht: Kluwer Academic Publishers.

Husserl, E. (2001), *Logical Investigations*, London: Routledge.

Husserl, E. (1970), The Crisis of European Sciences and Transcendental Phenomenology, An Introduction to Phenomenological Philosophy, Evanston, Illinois: Northwestern University Press.

Marlowe, F.W. (2004), Dictators and Ultimatums in an Egalitarian Society of Hunter-gatherers: The Hadza of Tanzania, in: J.P. Henrich (ed.), *Foundations of Human Sociality: Economic Experiments and Ethnographic Evidence from Fifteen Small-scale Societies*, Oxford: Oxford University Press.

Rubin, E.L. (2001), Public Choice, Phenomenology, and the Meaning of the Modern State: Keep the Bathwater, but Throw out that Baby, *Cornell Law Review* 87: 309-361.

Rubin, E.L. (1998), Putting Rational Actors in their Place: Economics and Phenomenology, *Vanderbilt Law Review* 51: 1705-1727.

Steinbock, A.J. (1995), *Home and Beyond: Generative Phenomenology after Husserl*, Evanston, Illionois: Northwerstern University Press.

Zahavi, D. (2001), *Husserl & Transcendental Intersubjectivity*, Athens, Ohio: Ohio University Press.

Homo Oeconomicus 27(4): 493–495 (2011)

www.accedoverlag.de

The Letter to the Queen: CReBB, the Sequel[1]

Ray Rees
CES, University of Munich, Germany
(eMail: Ray.Rees@lrz.uni-muenchen.de)

In her visit to the London School of Economics in November 2008, HM the Queen asked her now-famous question: why had no-one foreseen the banking crisis that was now devastating the Western economies? In response, the British Academy swiftly convened a conference with leading representatives of business and the City of London, financial regulators, academic economists and civil servants to find an answer. This answer was contained in a letter written to her Majesty by Professor Tim Besley and his colleague Professor Peter Hennessy, which I'm sure many of you have read. The result of this was the formation of the Commission to Re-educate Bad Bankers (CReBB), whose activities are the subject of this note.

The Commission decided to set up a School of Banker Re-education and gave the well-known behavioral psychologist Professor T Sharpe of Porterhouse College, Cambridge, the job of designing the re-education program. Since the government now owns large parts of most of the major British banks, it was able to require the senior bankers to attend the short courses held at the School, which Professor Sharpe designed.

On entering the program, the first thing the bankers received was a good haircut. Then, they were ushered into a darkened cinema-like room with comfortable seats and a large screen. The bankers were asked to put on a headset which, unknown to them, contained a set of sensors. A sequence of words was then flashed on the screen: *bonus; stock options; mortgage-backed securities; credit default swaps*; and so on. If the sensors registered a warm glow of pleasure or approval from the banker, the seat was programmed to deliver to him a small but perceptible electric shock. This is of course a very standard behavioral training device.

[1] See Manfred J. Holler (ed.), Letter to the Queen (Homo Oeconomicus 27(3)), Munich: Accedo, 2010, for further material and discussion.

ISBN 978-3-89265-075-1 ISSN 0943-0180

Unfortunately, the supervisors found, after a few repetitions of this treatment, that there was in fact an *increase* in the warm glow the bankers experienced at the sight of these words, even after the shocks had been administered. This made them suspect that bankers were not at all like the standard subjects in psychological tests. Professor Sharpe's request to be allowed to increase the voltage of the shock considerably was turned down at the highest level, and so he had to rethink his strategy.

His next idea was the Bad Bankers' Maze. Each banker, alone, equipped with a briefcase labeled *risky assets* and a rolled-up umbrella, had to enter a maze of corridors. He was then led by a series of subliminal signals to a small room with a door marked *exit.* Just to the left of the door was a recess set into the wall, and on a shelf in this recess was a large pile of bundles of one-hundred pound notes. A small sign above the notes said: *capital reserves.* If, as they all did, a banker took some of these reserves and stuffed them into his risky assets briefcase, a loud noise would sound, red lights would flash, and a small stick, labeled *regulator*, would come down and rap the banker lightly on the back of his hand. The door would then open onto the start of the maze and the banker would have to go through the maze again

Unfortunately this did not work either. The bankers responded by running back through the maze as fast as they could go to the shelf with the money, and then stuffing more of the capital reserves into the risky asset briefcases. They would then take the regulator's rap on the knuckles with a smile, and set off back through the door to go around the circuit again. Some of them even used their rolled-up umbrellas to lever the bundles of notes into their briefcases more quickly, and so they received a second rap on the knuckles for "excessive leverage." They did this until only about 5% of the original pile of money was left. The supervisors labeled this the "take the money and run" strategy. Once again, Professor Sharpe's request to have the Regulator deliver a sharper rap on the knuckles was rejected. Clearly major rethinking was necessary.

The members of the CReBB were very unhappy at this lack of progress under Professor Sharpe and asked Professors Besley and Hennessy to explain to him the main point they had made in their letter to the Queen. This was that the chief underlying cause of the crisis had been that each part of the banking system concentrated only on the risks it itself took in its investment banking activities, but no-one had taken account of the way in which all these risks interacted to undermine the stability of the system as a whole, the systemic risk. Once he had understood this, Professor Sharpe hurried off to design the definitive re-educational instrument.

This he called the Banker's Dilemma Game. A large wooden platform was constructed over a big plastic tank containing very cold water, to a depth of about five-and-a-half feet. On the platform were 10 computer screens, placed in what looked like voting booths, so that no screen was visible to anyone but the banker who sat in front of it. On each screen were two small circles. Next to the first circle was the message:

> I give you 2% return with no systemic risk.

Next to the second circle was the message:

> I give you 25% return with huge systemic risk.

Each banker had to touch one of the circles on the screen. If 5 or more bankers chose the 25% return, the platform floor would open up and gently but firmly all ten bankers would be propelled into the cold water.

Professor Sharpe assured the Commission that no banker would come to any physical harm. All they had to do was to wade through the water, helping themselves along by flailing their arms in a kind of swimming motion, until they reached the side of the tank, where they would be helped out by attendants who would wrap them in soft towels and give them a warming drink. A little to his surprise, he was given permission to go ahead with this game.

Unfortunately, on its first trial, things went badly wrong. Eight bankers chose the 25% return and according to plan all the bankers were tipped into the water. But Professor Sharpe had overlooked the fact that some of the bankers were rather large and overweight and not able to propel themselves to the side of the tank. They were, so to speak, too big to flail. It took some time to rescue them and some of them contracted bad chills and had to be released from the course.

For the moment the School's activities have been suspended, Professor Sharpe has been fired and CReBB is deeply divided on the next steps to take. So if you have any suggestions you could send them to Professors Besley and Hennessy, or perhaps to Her Majesty the Queen, who I'm sure will warmly welcome them.

Homo Oeconomicus 27(4): 497–499 (2011)

www.accedoverlag.de

EURAS* Yearbook of Standardization, Volume 6

The EURAS conference in Lithuania this year was very much a success story. The attendance was good, the quality of the papers high, not least in the poster session, and Kaunas itself remarkable. There were representatives from as far afield as Japan, China and Australia and of course across Europe. More and more we are welcoming participation from Eastern Europe with representatives from Latvia, Lithuania, Russia, Serbia and Slovakia. My understanding is that Kaunas has fared badly in the global recession. Europe too faces considerable problems, not least in dealing with the sovereign debt crisis, an aftershock of the credit crisis itself. Power has shifted eastwards, political power, economic power and perhaps cultural power too. The way forward for Europe lies in strengthening its economic base and in this it must pay particular attention to manufacturing as well as the service sectors. Innovation is critical. In facilitating innovation, standards have a role to play, with perhaps the classic example being provided by GSM.[1]

Yet the governance structures of the EU lag behind, perhaps, in appreciating this and in giving standards and standardization the emphasis which they warrant. We should not overstate the case. Standards are but one piece of the jigsaw, but they are an important piece. Several Asian countries, notably Korea, have put standards at the heart of their innovation strategy and, for example, place considerable emphasis on educating the next generation of managers, administrators and technicians in standards. EURAS has noted this and is in the process of launching a White Paper arguing the need for more emphasis on standards in our university courses and institutes of education. This in itself is a landmark step for EURAS and we await with interest the consequences.

Standardization itself is a varied discipline with contributions to the literature being made from across both the social sciences and the sciences. It is also a discipline which combines contributions from those in practice

* The European Academy for Standardization.

[1] Global System for Mobile Communications.

ISBN 3-89265-075-1 ISSN 0943-0180

and academia. This is fully reflected in this edition of the Yearbook. The paper by Michael Spring is a reflective one looking at the evolution of standards research over a forty year period. It suggests that we have learned that there are different types of standards and the processes by which they emerge are different and evolving. Spring also suggests that an open multi-disciplinary discussion heavily seeded with experienced practitioners to identify a set of practice based questions is a suitable means of minimizing discipline based biases that sometime shade research. The paper by Peter Walsh provides a perspective from practice in looking at the principle of consensus in arriving at a standard. The paper outlines the criteria used to define consensus by international (ISO/IEC), regional (CEN/CENELEC) and one national standards body (Standards Australia) when approving new standards projects and final acceptance for publication. He also explores the concept of one vote, one value when such a formula based approach is taken.

The third paper in this issue is by Hans Teichmann. He argues that a comprehensive and standardized technical-scientific terminology, is essential for efficient communication in vital sectors like economy, science and technology. Thus, even when composed by native speakers, standards written in world languages may not be universally useful in all countries where these languages are spoken. Examples are given when standards have actually been "translated" from ISO English into American English for use in the United States and from Spanish for a South American audience. These examples also emphasise the importance of terminological precision per se. Poonam Mehra is from academe and her paper is a technical analysis of conflict among antitrust authorities in different countries. The paper is largely theoretical and develops a two-country, three-firm model. She shows that if countries maximize their national welfare there is a possibility of conflict that blocks welfare-enhancing mergers. It is also shown that convergence to a reference standard based on global welfare or consumer surplus resolves conflicts, but may not always lead to an efficient outcome. Efficiency can however be ensured through transfer payments coupled with the total welfare standard. Finally the paper concludes that there is scope for institutions like the WTO to assume the role of supranational authority to ensure conflict-free, efficient outcomes. The final paper by Jasper Paasch discusses a standardized, terminological approach for describing real property rights and public regulations. Real property rights are e.g. the right to perform some activities on another's real property such as rights of way or to take water from a well. Public regulations are officially imposed burdens like planning regulations, etc. Real property rights and regulations are an important part of the legal domain and function as instruments of conflict resolution regulating the use of real property. The outcome of the approach is a classification of rights and regulations in order to further cross-border transfer of real property information.

These are a wide range of issues, analysed from a wide range of perspectives and illustrate, with fascinating insights, the heterogeneous nature of the discipline. We welcome future contributions in this tradition and indeed others such as ones with a more empirical emphasis. We are excited at the possibilities. This is a propitious time to analyse standards and standardization. They are both important issues and issues in flux. On the empirical side, data which was previously in short supply is becoming increasingly available, for example both on firms and consumers use of standards. In international terms the Asian countries are becoming increasingly involved with standards. How will this change the global standards architecture? How will it change the process of achieving consensus? In the EU, CEN, CENELEC and ETSI play important roles in governance and yet they are all but invisible to most people. Is this an example of good governance? Platform technologies are becoming increasingly important and present a challenge to both intellectual property rights and the standards bodies. How will they adapt in the face of this challenge? As mentioned earlier, the world faces a crisis, indeed not one crisis, but several. Apart from the continuing credit crisis, there are the environmental, energy, raw material and food crises. Standards will have their part to play as the world attempts to meet these challenges, but equally they will change both standards and standardization. We look forward in future years to seeing how this all evolves and to both documenting these changes and facilitating them via the papers that will appear in future volumes.

Manfred J. Holler (University of Hamburg and PCRC, University of Turku)

John Hudson (University of Bath)

Managing Editors of EYS (EURAS Yearbook of Standardization)

Homo Oeconomicus 27(4): 501–517 (2011)

www.accedoverlag.de

What Have We Learned about Standards and Standardization?

Michael B. Spring
School of Information Sciences, University of Pittsburgh, USA
(eMail: spring@pitt.edu)

Abstract Over the last 40 years, standards have been a subject of interest to academic researchers from a number of disciplines. Early research on standardization focused on economic models and predictions. More recently, research has emphasized business models and perspectives where standards have become a tool that helps to shape markets. During the middle years, a multidisciplinary approach was taken to looking at standards and standardization as a phenomenon in its own right. This paper reviews the history of standards research in an effort to identify what has emerged from the work. The paper suggests that we have learned that there are different types of standards and the processes by which they emerge are different and evolving. The author suggests that one focal point for future research might be an effort to validate the findings from earlier research. Finally, the author suggests some ways to move forward. In particular, an open multidisciplinary discussion heavily seeded with experienced practitioners to identify a set of practice based questions is proposed as a means of minimizing discipline based biases that sometime shade research.

Keywords standards, research, models, theory, standardization

1. Introduction

Recently, Purao, Bagby and Umapathy (2008) explored two important issues in standardization: anticipatory standards and the roles of participants in the standards development process. The paper makes carefully considered observations on the process. Having some familiarity with the topics, I glanced at the references to see what literature had been cited. While some older references existed related to research methods, most of the standards research cited was recent. The only "old" standards reference was to a first book on standards by Carl Cargill. Cargill (1989) is almost universally cited as the beginning of critical thinking about standards and

ISBN 978-3-89265-075-1 ISSN 0943-0180

standardization. However, as Cargill himself points out, he owes much to earlier literature, notably Hill (1972) and Cerni (1984).

I was curious that two pieces of work, with which I had been involved, were not referenced. (This is not a criticism of the authors in any way. In general, the premise of what follows is that we, as a discipline of inquiry, lack a good mechanism for keeping track of the diverse and generally uncoordinated literature related to standards and standardization.) I could be wrong, but I think the paper, which I wrote with a graduate student – Bonino and Spring (1991) – was the first one to use the term "anticipatory standardization." That being said, I think the impetus for the paper was a discussion with Carl Cargill who I have no problem crediting with the concept, although I think my good friend often credits me. The other paper that came to mind was related to work done in 1992 and published two years later (Spring et. al 1994). It addressed roles in the standardization process across different Standards Developing Organizations (SDOs). While I think the paper was useful in its time, it is by no means an important predecessor to the quality work done by Purao, Bagby and Umapathy, but it is clearly closely related work. Their work, in a different era of standardization, and using a different framework is quality work and important to understanding what actions we might take today. At the same time, I am frequently left with the gnawing suspicion that many of us who come to this fascinating area of study, come thinking that little or no related work has been done before. (Or at best, being aware only of the work done in our particular field.)

The premise of what follows is that our collective memory is spotty. I believe we might better position our future work by taking a longer term view of what we do and don't know about standards and standardization. Hopefully, this particular look embodies some insights and is not simply the mutterings of an old curmudgeon. Before turning to the main point of this article let me provide a little background.

2. Background

In the mid 1980's, in the course of research on collaborative authoring, I began to look at standards for documents. At that time, I was working with the Xerox Corporation on a system called Compuprep, which was designed to do "unstructured text conversion." More explicitly, we were exploring the design of virtual machines that would convert procedurally copy marked text to structurally copy marked text. We designed a system that used a set of rules to read a file in which text was intermingled with commands such as "center and bold the following text at the top of a page" and conclude that that text should be marked as "Title" – we converted procedural (do this) copy marks to structural (this is) copy marks (Spring 1989).

I needed to know more about the emerging standards for structural copy marking – Digital's "Office Document Architecture (ODA)" and IBM's "Standard Generalized Markup Language (SGML)." Colleagues didn't seem to know much about the standards and they were not to be found in the University Library, so I began a quest to learn more. With that simple task, I began an adventure that would span more than two decades. The adventure began with the acquisition of standards for review and proceeded to the development of a graduate course at the University of Pittsburgh on Information Technology Standards and Standardization and continued on to participation in strategic planning for the standardization process through X3[1] as well as membership on governmental oversight boards related to standards.

Along the way, we began to do research on standards and proposed the development of a center for the study of standards using any and all means at our disposal. We sought corporate support, government agency support, and NSF funding – with little success. In many ways, my active involvement came to a conclusion with the development of a collaborative authoring system, called CASCADE,[2] which was designed to improve the standardization process. Specifically, our goal was to cut costs for IT standards by 50% and reduce the time required to develop standards by 50%. When we began the development of CASCADE in 1994, by our estimate, we might reduce the average total cost of developing an IT standard by $5 million (USD) and reduce the development time from 10 years to 5 years. Funding for CASCADE was completed in 1998. While the system was briefly adopted by some SDO's, my failure to commercialize the system ultimately led to its down fall – although the hegemony of Word and the emergence of the WWW probably would have killed it anyway.

In this article, I reflect on some of the lessons learned in that decade of active work on standards and standardization. I do so after a further decade of casual observation of the research on standards and standardization. I

---

[1] X3 is the U.S. standards committee for computer and information processing standards. This effort was sanctioned by ANSI and supported by the Computer and Business Equipment Manufacturers Association (CBEMA). X3 is now known as InterNational Committee for Information Technology Standards (INCITS), and CBEMA has been replaced by the Information Technology Industry Council (ITI), a trade association representing the leading U.S. providers of information technology products and services.

[2] CASCADE stands for "Computer Augmented Support for Collaborative Authoring and Document Editing." Research on the basic concepts and processes and development of a prototype distributed system was funded by the National Institute of Standards and Technology Information Technology Laboratory from 1994-1998.

am excited about the work being done in Europe, China and the US. While my particular research agenda has moved in other directions, I continue to read about the developments in standards research. Occasionally, like many old academics, I sometimes feel like we are "breaking new ground again." This article reflects on what I think we have learned.

3. The older literature on standardization

The space allocated for this article does not allow a complete review of the literature on standardization. At the same time, it should be noted that there are publications that have rather good reviews of the older literature. Others are far more qualified to provide a definitive review and organization of the significant recent and critically important work of Henk J. de Vries, Nicholas Economides, Tineke M. Egyedi, Manfred J. Holler, Kai Jakobs, Ken Krechmer, and Andrew Updegrove, among others. (Please note that these are in alphabetical order and off the top of my head. There are many others.) The point is that we would all benefit from such a meta review. It would help to establish a preliminary reading list for our graduate students. It might also serve to help define the structure of what everyone has and has not been doing. A comprehensive review of the literature might begin with Computer Standards and Interfaces, StandardView, the International Journal of IT Standards & Standardization Research, the EURAS Yearbook of Standardization, and the Standards Edge as beginning points with careful attention to the other conferences and journals that frequently serve as hosts to standards related research, such as RAND Journal of Economics and Economics of Innovation and New Technology.

In terms of the older literature, a serious scholar of standards might track down copies of two particular early works: Marjorie Hill's 1972 "The World of EDP Standards" and Dorothy Cerni's 1984 "Standards in Process: Foundations and Profiles of ISDN and OSI Studies." In the late 80's, there were numerous contributions that were made by colleagues in economics, and the economic analysis of standards continues to this day. Surely, Paul David, Joe Farrell, Garth Saloner, Shane Greenstein, Nicholas Economides, and William Lehr all need to be looked at carefully. (At the very least, the economists provided some of the best titles and some of the cleanest analogies in the early literature. The title of my 1994 paper "*Improving the standards process: working with bulldogs and turtles*" was in part a tribute to Farrell and Saloner's 1987 paper *"Competition, Compatibility, and Standards: The Economics of Horses, Penguins, and Lemmings."*)

Both of Carl Cargill's books should be analyzed (1989, 1996), as should both of Martin Libicki's (1995, 2000). In terms of building a complete bibliography of the work in the field, Martin Weiss's 1988 dissertation at

Carnegie Mellon University, which many consider to be the first empirical study of the standards process, contains a good review of the literature to that point in time. (The dissertation title was "Compatibility Standards and Product Development Strategies: A Retrospective of Data Modem Developments".) I also like to believe that the special edition of JASIS that I edited in 1992 on Information Technology Standards summarized the best of what was being discussed through the 1980's. Significant scholarly contributions came from the U.S. Congress thanks to the consummate research skills of D. Linda Garcia. She was responsible for a number of reports from the Office of Technology Assessment, including "Critical Connections: Communication for the Future," "Global Standards: Building Blocks for the Future," and "Electronic Enterprises: Looking to the Future." My article on Information Technology Standards (Spring 1991) in the Annual Review of Information Science and Technology was an early effort to survey the literature and organize it. There are other pieces that can be collected from the references cited in these works, but this would provide a good start.

4. What have we learned?

It would seem that we have learned a couple of things over the last few decades. Little of it seems to have been ascertained via experimental methods that have been carefully validated, but that may be too high a standard at this point in time. I choose four things that have been the subject of research and reflection by a number of people. I have listed them in order of decreasing confidence related to what we know.

4.1 Not all standards are the same

There are many different kinds of standards. While this will be obvious to most readers, it is not clear to me that we yet use such information to inform and delimit our research. Few papers begin with: "This study looked at reference standards developed by early stage consortia for global application." Similarly, few conclusions begin with delimitations and suggest possible extension of the findings based on the subject of the research. The fact that standards are of different identifiable classes is an important beginning in the process of defining this field.

Beyond obvious differences such as the area of standardization, or descriptive attributes of the documents – length, longevity, complexity, etc., standards have been classified along a number of dimensions. Standards may reflect accepted practice in the marketplace, or they may endeavor to shape a market that doesn't yet exist. Standards may break new ground, or incrementally extend existing standards. Standards of each of these types will vary in many ways, e.g. the time required to develop them, the size of the committee that will be involved, the process used to develop them. If our research on standards is to benefit from aggregation of findings, it will be important that we qualify our findings in some way that allows meaningful comparisons.

A number of researchers have suggested standards typologies. While none of them are perfect, we can use those that have been developed as the basis of a shared typology of standards. Crawford (1986) suggests that standards can be classified by their scope - organizational, industry-wide, national, multinational (or regional), and international or global. It should be noted that multinational efforts, are a recent phenomenon, and were not a part of Crawford's original classification. The efforts of the European Community are a commonly used example of a multinational or regional effort that includes less than the full international community. Thus, standards may be grouped into at least five categories.

- Company
- Industry or Enterprise
- National
- Regional
- Global

Paul David (1987) suggested a simple yet elegant classification scheme that allows us to look at standards more closely. His suggestion was simple. Consider all standards to be one of six classes, varying on two dimensions - function and type.

	Technical	Behavioral
Measurement	Meter	professional licensing
Minimum attribute	steam pressure	Job qualifications
Compatibility	RS-232	Contracts

Farrell and Saloner (1985) suggest that technical compatibility standards, which include most information and telecommunications standards, may further be classified as:

- physical compatibility
- communications compatibility
- compatibility by convention

Cargill(1989: 26-35) suggested a typology of consensus standards across three dimensions which I will call importance, focus and type. The first is a measure of to whom the standard is important, and how it is important. The second is a rough classification of the standard as an implementation or a conceptualization. Finally, the standard may specify the particulars of the solution, or simply the interface (inputs and the outputs). Cargill calls the former a product solution and the latter a process solution.

Over the years, I have used these and other metrics in thinking about my work. What seems to ring true after twenty years are three dimensions that are both concrete enough to be applied accurately, and conceptually rich enough to help clarify research questions. They are:

- *Scope:* Organization, industry, enterprise, nation, region, world
- *Class:* Reference/model; base/syntax, implementation, derivative
- *Origin:* Voluntary Consensus, consortium, public specification, government regulation, product

While I would be satisfied with any shared classification that served to clarify what we might say about standards, this one has allowed me to think productively about both the products and processes. Consider the class of standard. POSIX or OSI serve as reference models for many other standards. The complexity of a reference model is such that they take longer to develop and have little direct return on investment, but they are incredibly important to guiding or controlling the development of base standards (Spring and Weiss 1994). Another interesting phenomenon relates to the origin of the standard. Increasingly, with fast tracking, standards are moving from one origin classification to another. A public specification becomes an international consensus standard. Finally, standards on the edges are interesting. I would suggest that the standards of both the W3C and the IETF are becoming more like the standards developed by the traditional SDOs as the scope of their impact increases.

4.2 *The standards development process is evolving*

If we ask how a standard is developed, the immediate answer is "it depends." It depends on at least three things. First, it depends on whether it is consciously developed or emerges in the marketplace. Second, for each of the broad categories, there are distinct subcategories. For example, under voluntary consensus standards, we will distinguish between formal Standards Developing Organizations (SDOs) and consortia. Third, if we look back over time, it is clear that the process is evolving. For example, "fast-tracking" is a relatively new phenomenon which seeks to incorporate externally developed specifications into formal processes. Despite the rules set out on paper by the SDOs, my sense is that standards development is sometimes as much serendipity and/or chaos as plan. The history of standardization is ripe with stories and anecdotes. The history of early standardization is a study in and of itself.[3] There are many stories about standards that are worth thinking about. Consider just three as examples that tell us something about the changing nature of the process: steam boiler safety, the Manufacturing Automation Protocol (MAP), and VHS.

The American Society of Mechanical Engineers was founded in 1880 and is responsible for more than 600 standards, ranging from screw threads to safety standards. As the use of steam power increased in the U.S., so did the number of boiler explosions, sometimes more than 1000/year. The larger accidents raised significant public concern. "By 1910 the rate jumped to 1,300 to 1,400 a year… A Boiler Code Committee was formed in 1911 that led to the Boiler Code being published in 1914-15."[4] Some early and significant standards were driven by public pressure and the ethical concerns of the engineering profession. Standardization was a solution demanded by public concern and professional responsibility. There are many such stories worth telling. The standardization of building codes and fire equipment under the auspices of the National Fire Protection Association and National Bureau of Standards is another significant one.[5] This period of professionally dominated standardization, it seems to me, was a

---

[3] Standard time is something few of us think about. It is difficult to imagine every city operating on a unique locally determined time. Yet, until the 1800's that was exactly the case. Standardized time begins with the railroads. One can imagine the problems associated with scheduling stops for a train when every major city in which the train stopped had a different locally determined time. The British were the first to adopt standard time – London Greenwich Mean Time (GMT). The Great Western Railway did so in 1840. By 1850, most railways had adopted standard time despite the fact that the legal system still maintained local time. In 1880, the legal system finally adopted standard time. The situation was similar in the U.S. U.S. railways adopted standard time at noon on November 18, 1883 despite the continued use of local time for all other purposes. Over the years, people began to make more use of standard time. The legal process of adopting standard time culminated with the Standard Time Act of 1918, enacted on March 19, 1918. Congress adopted standard time zones based on those set up by the railroads.

[4] http://www.asme.org/Communities/History/ASMEHistory/Brief_History.cfm

[5] I was surprised when I first visited the National Institute of Standards and Technology to find that one of the Laboratories, right next to Physics and Chemistry was the Building and Fire Research Laboratory. While somewhat oversimplified, as much as Congress was concerned with standards for weights and measures, it was concerned with the losses of life and property related to fires and in particular as a result of the 1904 Baltimore fire. The devastation of that fire was worsened by the lack of standard fire hose connections at the time of the fire. The newly established National Bureau of Standards took up the challenge along with the National Fire Protection Association and others. The impact of that concern is still reflected today in the structure of the labs.

sort of golden age of standardization. Technical committees of engineers and scientists developed singular standards in formal processes that addressed constrained issues of importance to society.

Fast forward to the 1980's as things grew more complex, particularly in the computer and telecommunications arena. This was an era of multitudes of incompatible standards and complex organizational choices. This is the era of system standardization! Perhaps it is best characterized by the effort to develop International Standardized Profiles. These have now largely passed into oblivion thanks to the hegemony of Microsoft and Intel, but this was the era in which GM, Ford, Boeing and others were creating profiles of standards. For manufacturing it was the Manufacturing Automation Profile (MAP). For the office it was the Technical Office Profile (TOP). For government it was the Government Open Systems Interconnection Profile (GOSIP). There was the European Standards and Promotion Group (SPAG). And on and on it went. This was the era of systems of standards. A time when there were dozens of computer manufacturers, multiple operating systems, hundreds of incompatible data formats – remember writing code to covert EBCDIC to ASCII! Remember when word processing formats including 100 different forms? Remember when TCP/IP and Ethernet were only two of 100 network protocols? This was the era of standardization of systems of standards for interoperability. It was the era in which end users became heavily invested in the process demanding standards that worked together.

This same era saw the emergence of what I will call business standards. A prime example of this is the war between VHS and Betamax. These standards were created by business to create a market. Most readers understand that while the Betamax standard provided a signal of superior quality, the VHS standard allowed for more recording time at a lower level of quality and was selected by vendors, and consumers, for marketing purposes. More recently we have seen the battle between Blu-Ray and HD-DVD standards. While this era of standardization involves engineers in the same way the "golden era" did, there is a much stronger presence of business advocacy in the standardization process. Now the committees also include standards managers and other organizational members who are less concerned with purely technical aspects of the standard.

These three processes of standardization continue to coexist today. The existence of technical, systems, and business oriented processes are not mutually exclusive. There are related phenomena as well. Consortia are often associated with business standards. Perhaps the most memorable example was reflected in the Unix wars where competitive approaches were put forward by Unix International and the Open Software Foundation.

The other notable evolution of the standards process relates to rapid prototyping. Perhaps the best example of this is the emergence of sophisticated mail handling systems. In the 1980, the ITU proposed X.400 and X.500 as mail and directory standards of some sophistication. While these extensive standards came out of a carefully reasoned committee process, the IETF proposed and deployed alternative standards on an as needed basis. This led to several standards including POP1, POP2, POP3, IMAP, IMAP2, IMAP4, MIME, etc. In an article I published with Stephen Oksala (Unisys, SCTE, ANSI, JTC1 TAG) and Tony Rutkowski (Internet Society), we discussed various approaches to standardization (Oksala, Rutkowski, Spring, and O'Donnell 1996). While Oksala and I tend to favor singular standardization, such as might be characterized by X.400, Rutkowski advocated a form of rapid prototyping or competitive standardization such as might be envisioned by the various IETF email standards.

So, we do know that the processes used to develop standards are different and have changed over time. We can probably even make some statements about the nature of those changes, identifying some of the trends, and if we are very good, predict future changes. I will suggest three meta trends that I believe have and will continue to govern the evolution of the standardization process, based on what I have outlined above.

1. Any standardization process that impacts a significant audience will be subject to increased formalization to minimize liabilities related to standardization.

2. The individuals involved in the standardization process will grow to include increased representation from the business side of organizations as standards impact market share and from the commerce and trade branches of government as standards impact international trade.

3. As standards processes slow down the production of standards, especially in areas of rapid technological change, new standardization processes will emerge that will bypass existing processes to speed the production of standards, at least until the new processes slow down as a result of trends 1 and 2. (In the 1990, consortia appeared able to develop standards faster than the traditional SDOs. In the last ten years, as consortia like the W3C have grown and become slower, fast tracked public specifications emerged.)

4.3 Standards can be used to restrict free trade

With the growth of free trade agreements, tariffs began to disappear as barriers to free trade. Whether there was any conscious effort to use standards proactively to restrict free trade will be a matter of ongoing debate. It is clear that standards can have an impact on free trade, and with the elimination of tariffs as a barrier, standards emerge as an important mechanism. The debate over the ISO 9000 standards and the certification of quality manufacturing processes related to the European Free Trade Agreement was an early salvo in this discussion. Of primary concern to many U.S. organizations was the external review and certification of quality assurance in the manufacturing process. In 2004, questions were raised about the impact of standards and licensing related to Wi-Fi encryption standards that were slated to control the devices that could be sold in China. (The encryption technology was only licensed to Chinese companies requiring U.S. and European companies that wanted to enter the market to have to partner with the Chinese companies.) While pressure brought an acceptable resolution to the issue, it was yet another example of how standards might be used to restrict free trade.

4.4 It is hard to determine who is responsible for "good" standards

Our daily experience is impacted significantly by standards, but few recognize the extent of that impact. We wake to an alarm set to standardized time, and moan at the arrival of daylight savings time. The flow of water in showers and the quality of the water we drink are the result of standards. The contents of breakfast cereals and the processing of the milk we use are safeguarded by standards. The frequencies on which television signals are transmitted and the connections that allow our phones to function are controlled by standards. The accuracy with which we can navigate using GPS is limited by the ability to measure time. The fuel we put in our cars and the oil we use to lubricate them is controlled by standards. All of these standards impact us before we begin a day of work. Yet most people are unaware of these standards.

Who is responsible for the development of 'good' standards? Is it the businesses that produce the products? Is it the governments that protect the public? Is it the professional societies that develop the technologies? The answer of course is that all of these groups play an important role. Perhaps the more interesting question is who is responsible for making sure that the process of standardization is carried out in a timely and cost effective manner? Because good standards tend to be invisible to both the public and the policy makers, this question is difficult to answer. We as academic researchers have as yet been unsuccessful in raising this issue in such a way that the involved parties can clearly see the impact of poor standards or flawed standardization processes. So long as standards emerge before there is public outrage, the process goes on carried forth by its own momentum.

5. What we need to determine

I believe there is sufficient literature and scholarship to defend the points I have made in the previous section. Yet there is more. When I started to work with the standards community, it bothered me that the senior practitioners "knew" a lot about standards. I have no doubt that these ladies and gentlemen were not only supremely confident, but correct, about what they knew. The fact of the matter is that while they knew things with certainty, it was not based on empirical research so much as tacit knowledge. I kept thinking "prove it," not because I doubted them, but because my academic tradition is based on replicable empirical research. Now, more than 20 years later, I find myself in a similar position. I don't know that I can defend or prove the things I have come to believe, but I do have confidence that they are true. Just as I set out as a dispassionate academic observer to form hypotheses about what my friends told me was true and study them empirically, so now I would suggest that there are several things I am convinced are true based on the tacit knowledge gained over the years. Over the coming years, we need to ascertain if that tacit knowledge lives up to empirical assessment. The funds to conduct research are still meager so we need to carefully choose what we want to study. I believe we can make a strong case that we "know" five or more things that might become a focal point for validation through focused studies. These include:

1. The difficulty of developing a standard is a function of many factors, but the two most significant factors are the size of the community impacted by the standard, the degree to which entrenched approaches exist and differ.

2. Participants in the standardization process fill different roles functionally (i.e. writers, editors, reviewers, voters, etc.) and intentionally (i.e. contributing technical ideas, free riding to gather intelligence, protecting company positions, etc.).

3. The return on investment in standardization differs by class of standard and as a result reference standards will be undersupplied in a standards environment driven by market pressures. As a corollary, potentially competitive base standards will be oversupplied in environments in which reference standards do not exist.

4. The state of the maturity of a technology impacts standardization in several ways:

- the volume of standardization is highest at the early stages of the development of a technology
- anticipatory standardization occurs most frequently when technological theory is moving toward first generation products and

- competitive standardization occurs more frequently when technological alternatives are not significantly different

5. In an ideal world, we develop a singular set of standards based on an overall conceptual plan. I would suggest that the Open System Interconnection Reference Model and the OSI standards represent such an ideal. However, this approach takes time and can front load standardization cost. This makes it appear cheaper to develop ad hoc or competitive standards. However, in the long run, I believe ad hoc or competitive standards are frequently more expensive. If one considers the long term costs to organizations and consumers of developing and implementing the IETF array of mail standards including the costs of changing from one to the other, I believe the cost ended up being much greater than would have been the cost of a phased deployment of X.400 and X.500.

For all of these hypotheses, we should be able to gather data or do focused simulations that help us to provide useable answers to questions of significant import to our companies, our nations, and the emerging global society.

6. Conclusions

In 1989, we convened a group of interested individuals from industry, government, and academia to discuss a modest proposal for the study of standards and standardization. The center was to have three primary goals:

- to provide a focal point for multidisciplinary research on information technology standardization.
- to develop programs and materials to assist professionals who are or may be involved in the standards process.
- to provide a clearinghouse for information about standards and the standards process.

The research goal was broken down into two major objectives:

- Observe and analyze the standardization process in order to determine: (a) costs and procedures for cost containment, (b) costs and returns, and (c) critical paths and delay points avoidable in the process.
- Develop and assess models for standards and standardization that focus on particular aspects such as (a) characterization of the process, similarities and differences, across Standards Developing Organizations (SDO), (b) the

classification of application and interchange standards, (c) a reference model for non-interconnect information technology standards, (d) characterization of inter and intra standard interactions, and (e) the life cycle of standards from the point of view of a sponsoring, implementing, and using organization.

We did our best to carry out that research despite the lack of funding to do so. We also tried to keep track of what others were doing. The major point of this paper is that we have been lax in trying to catalog and keep track of the growing body of literature on what is known about standards and standardization. It may be a good time to create a comprehensive annotated bibliography of the work that has been done in the area. It would be nice to find a framework within which we might also identify gaps in the literature. Related to the literature review, I think that a timeline of the major events in standardization would be provocative. There might be any number of such timelines – e.g. the rise of consortia, the emergence of fast-tracking, the growth of IT standards, etc. Many years back, as an exercise in PostScript programming, I developed a plot of the growth of various classes and numbers of IETF standards over time. I can imagine any number of such timelines that might help us to understand aspects of what is going on that would merit further investigations.

Some of the best research on standards comes from the fields of economics and business, and this would seem appropriate given what we know about standards as business and economic instruments. The results of this research yield what one might expect – economic or business models of standards. Generally speaking these say little about the micro process of standardization. When sociological, anthropological, or engineering analyses are conducted, they again yield what might be expected – confirmation or contradiction of theories from the relevant field. Recently, Hendler et. al. (2008) suggested that the impact and importance of the World Wide Web merited consideration of a new field of study "Web Science." This suggestion has been received in different ways, but a compelling case has been made for consideration. When I arrived in my current department in 1986, it was named "The Interdisciplinary Department of Information Science." About a decade later, we dropped the word "Interdisciplinary." Standards are not of such importance that they merit their own science. At the same time, it is clear that no one discipline has the scope to study all of the facets of standardization. More importantly, I do think that we know that highly focused discipline based research, while interesting, is less than optimal in describing and predicting things about standards or standardization processes.

What is needed is an open multidisciplinary discussion heavily seeded with experienced practitioners to identify a set of practice based questions.

The five points made in section 5 might be among the starting points for such a discussion. Based on the issues identified we can do a better job of identifying the questions that need to be answered and the talents and expertise that need to be brought to bear to answer them. At very least, an ideal research team will need engineers, business researchers, economists, information scientists, sociologists, and public policy researchers. Starting with such a group, we will have a better chance of defining the questions that require the expertise of a single discipline and those that can only be answered using a multi-disciplinary approach.

References

Aden, M. and Harris, M. (1993), A Practitioner's Guide to Standards and the Government, *StandardView* 1(2): 25-34.

Arthur, W.B. (1983), *Competing Technologies and Lock-in by Historical Small Events: The Dynamics of Allocation under Increasing Returns*, Tech. Rep. 43, Center for Economic Policy Research, Stanford Univ., Palo Alto, CA.

Berg, S.V. (1988), Duopoly Compatibility Standards with Partial Cooperation and Standards Leadership, *Information Economics and Policy* 3: 35-53.

Berg, S.V. (1989), Technical Standards as Public Goods: Demand Incentives for Cooperative Behavior, *Public Finance Quarterly* 17(1): 29-54.

Berg, S.V. (1990), Technical Standards and Technological Change in the Telecommunications Industry, in: A.L. Link and V.K. Smith (eds.), *Advances in Applied Microeconomics*, JAI Press.

Berg, S.V. (1989), The Production of Compatibility: Technical Standards as Collective Goods, *Kyklos* 42(3): 361-83.

Besen, S. and Johnson, L. (1986), *Compatibility Standards, Competition, and Innovation in the Broadcasting Industry*, RAND Corporation.

Bonino, M. and Spring, M.B. (1991), Standards as Change Agents in the Information Technology Market, *Computer Standards and Interfaces* 12(2): 97-107.

Buckley, F.J. (1987), An Overview of the IEEE Computer Society Standards Process, *Computer Standards and Interfaces* 6(2): 267-274.

Cargill, C.F. (1989), Information Technology Standardization: Theory, Process, and Organizations, *Digital Press*, ISBN 1-5558-022-X.

Cargill, C.F. (1989), *Open Systems Standardization: A Business Approach*, Prentice Hall, ISBN 0132683199.

Cerni, D.M. (1984), Standards in Process: Foundations and Profiles of ISDN and OSI Studies, *NTIA Report* 84-170.

Crawford, W. (1986), *Technical Standards: An Introduction for Librarians*, Knowledge Industry Publications, White Plains, N.Y.

David, P.A. (1987), Some New Standards for the Economics of Standardization in the Information Age, in: P. Dasgupta and P. Stoneman (eds.), *Economic Policy and Technological Performance*, Cambridge: Cambridge University Press.

Homo Oeconomicus 27(4): 519–526 (2011)

www.accedoverlag.de

Arriving at a Consensus when Developing and Publishing Standards: An Australian Perspective

Peter Walsh
Managing Director of Conformance and Standards Services, Vice-President of European Academy for Standardization, and Associate of Centre for European Studies, Australian National University, Sydney, Australia
(eMail: peter.walsh@casserv.com)

Abstract Although decision making during the development of standards generally relies on the principle of *consensus*, there is often differences of opinion and interpretation of what this means especially if numerical acceptance criteria are used. This paper outlines the criteria used to define *consensus* by international (ISO/IEC), regional (CEN/CENELEC) and one national standards body (Standards Australia) when approving new standards projects and final acceptance for publication and explores the concept of *one vote, one value* when such a formula approach is taken.

1. Fundamental principles for developing standards

Generally the development of Standards by international, regional, national or consortia organizations, involve the following three fundamental principles:

(a) *Transparency*, both at the project initiation stage and by issue of a draft for comment

(b) *Involvement* of a balance of interested parties for international and regional standards development this is achieved at the national level

(c) *Consensus* decision making

Of these principles, the least understood is *consensus* that underpins decision making at varying times during the process of developing standards, be they international, regional, national or consortia. There are a number of trigger points where decisions need to be made, when developing stan-

ISBN 978-3-89265-075-1 ISSN 0943-0180

dards: as to whether and when to proceed to the next major phase of development, and options within content and coverage. This paper concentrates on the achievement of *consensus* in the first of these trigger points, and especially the rules and methodology used by Standards Australia, the Australian National Standards Body and the Australian member of the International Organization for Standardization (ISO) and the International Electrotechnical Commission (IEC).

Many definitions and meanings of consensus are contained in the policies and procedures of international regional and national standards bodies. In particular ISO/IEC Guide 2, *Standardization and related activities - General vocabulary*, defines *consensus* as follows:

> General agreement, characterized by the absence of sustained opposition to substantial issues by any important part of the concerned interests and by a process that involves seeking to take into account the views of all parties concerned and to reconcile any conflicting arguments.

However, while some dictionary definitions infer "*unanimity*," when quoting the ISO/IEC definition Standards Australia's Standardization Guide SG-001, *Preparing Standards*, adds "*Consensus need not imply unanimity.*" A better definition of *consensus* in respect of standards development is the following from the Business Dictionary:

> Middle *ground* in decision making between total assent and total disagreement. Consensus depends on *participants* having *shared values* and *goals*, and on having broad *agreement* on specific *issues* and overall direction. Consensus implies that everyone *accepts* and *supports* the *decision*, and understands the reasons for making it.

2. *Consensus* in national and international standards development

In national standards development organizations, generally the concept of involving "*all parties concerned*" or "*all relevant interests*" as provided for in Standards Australia's Standardization Guide SG-002, *Structure and Operation of Standardization Committees*, is applied when arriving at *consensus*. SG-002 further defines those to be involved in standards development to be "*individuals who are nominated by organisations that represent the views of large groups of interested and affected parties with a common interest.*"

In international and regional standards development organizations, generally the United Nations General Assembly principle of "*one country, one vote*" is applied when arriving at *consensus*, often to the chagrin of the US when faced in ISO and IEC with block voting by multiple European

Countries. There is an assumption in regional and international standards development organizations that national positions that are brought forward have been agreed to by a *consensus* of *"all relevant interests"* on a national basis.

3. Arriving at *consensus*

Most decisions made during the development of standards do not use a formula approach. Usually the Committee Officers (Chairperson and Secretary/Project Manager) of the standards development committee recognise that discussion indicates that a *consensus* is emerging and this view is summarised. Occasionally where it is not clear that a single common view is emerging, a *"straw poll"* or *"show of hands"* vote may be taken; in such cases, a decision to proceed would generally require a substantial positive vote but not unanimity. In general the principles proposed in the Business Directory definition (see above) can be taken as a guideline.

While less formal decision making during the standards development process can be reasonably controlled where development work is undertaken in face-to-face meetings, a different paradigm applies when standards development is undertaken electronically. While the Committee Officers can sometimes recognise that a *consensus* is emerging by monitoring the exchange of electronic messages, it is probably prudent to inject some form of voting during development. It is only when participants are forced to vote that a good indication of acceptance emerges.

4. Consensus by formal voting

4.1 International Organisation for Standardization (ISO) and the International Electrotechnical Commission (IEC)

ISO/IEC Directives Part 1, *Procedures for the technical work*, when ascertaining if a new technical committee or subcommittee should be formed to undertake a new standards development project (new work item), requires

(a) a "2/3 majority of the national bodies voting" to be in favour, and

(b) at least 5 national bodies to express an interest in participating in the work.

Where the new work item comes within the terms of reference of an existing technical committee or subcommittee that have a number of national bodies that have previously agreed to participate in the work, the ISO/IEC Directives requires

(a') agreement by simple majority of the participating members (i.e. P-members) of the technical committee or subcommittee voting, and

(b') at least 5 national bodies to express an interest in participating in the work.

The formal stages for approval during the ISO and IEC standards development process are at the enquiry draft (transparency) stage and the Draft International Standards (DIS) stage where approval to proceed requires

(a") a 2/3 majority of the votes cast by the P-members to in favour, and

(b") not more than 1/4 of the total number of votes cast are negative.

However, the ISO/IEC Directives do make provision for the Chairperson of the technical committee to propose, even where the voting rules have been complied with, that the DIS be further considered where there is objection to publication by major countries that have a major trade involvement in the subject covered by the standard. Thus, major countries may have a veto in practical terms and the *"one vote, one country"* concept is not really *"one vote, one value."* Moreover, the ISO/IEC Directives also include less onerous approval requirements for lower consensus documents such as Technical Specifications, Publicly Available Specifications and Technical Reports.

4.2 European Commission for Standardization (CEN) and the European Commission for Electrotechnical Standardization (CENELEC)

The CEN/CENELEC Common Rules for Standardization Work provide for most decisions during the standards development stage and for the approval of lower-consensus normative documents, such as technical specifications, guides, handbooks and the like, to be taken at meetings. However the publication of a European Standard, known as an EN for CEN or as a Harmonization Document (HD) for CENELEC, requires *acceptance by 71% of the weighted votes cast (abstentions not being counted)* with CEN or CENELEC members having the voting weights as listed in Figure 1. When CEN and CENELEC are developing European Standards in response to a mandate from the European Union, the 71% vote must also be achieved without the inclusion of the non-EU CEN and CENELEC members (i.e. Croatia, Iceland, Norway and Switzerland).

Figure 1 Voting weights in CEN/CENELEC

Weighting	CEN/CENELEC Members
29	FRANCE, Germany, Italy, United Kingdom
27	Poland, Spain
14	Romania
13	Netherlands
12	Belgium, Czech Republic, Greece, Hungary, Portugal
10	Austria, Bulgaria, Sweden, Switzerland
7	Croatia, Denmark, Finland, Ireland, Lithuania, Norway, Slovakia
4	Cyprus, Estonia, Latvia, Luxemburg, Slovenia
3	Iceland, Malta

4.3 National Standards Bodies (NSBs), especially Australia

National Standards Bodies generally make decisions during the standards development process by negotiation and consensus. Some such as the British Standards Institute (BSI), as outlined in BS 0, *A standard for standards*, resolves disagreements at the final approval stage by negotiation with ongoing objections being escalated to a higher level committee. Others, such as Standards Australia, use a formal voting procedure at the *"approval for publication"* stage.

Standards Australia SG-001, as well as replicating the ISO/IEC definition of *consensus*, includes the following voting rules for the approval by technical committees of Australian Standards they develop, noting that members of such committees are voting as representatives of nominating bodies:[1]

> While a unanimous affirmative vote is the desirable outcome, this is not always possible. Where there are unresolved negative votes, the Accreditation Board for Standards Development Organisations (ABSDO) has specified when consensus can be deemed to have been achieved. Currently the consensus rules are:
>
> - a minimum of 67% of those eligible to vote have voted affirmatively; and
> - a minimum of 80% of votes received are affirmative; and

[1] "If a committee member casts a negative vote, the committee is obliged to give thorough consideration to the reasons for the negative vote and to attempt to find a resolution that is acceptable to the committee as a whole. Committee members are voting on behalf of their Nominating Organisation and not acting as individuals or a representative of their employer" (Standards Australia SG-001).

- no major interest involved with the subject of the Standard has collectively maintained a negative vote. Consensus need not imply unanimity.

ABSDO is administered by a board elected by the membership of Standards Australia but does not report to the Board of Directors of Standards Australia. It accredits Standards Australia and other Australia Standards Development Organisations to develop Australian Standards.

This Standards Australia definition of *consensus* has been crafted to maintain the integrity of the final standard while enabling abstention from voting by those committee members who may not have an interest in the subject of a specific standard as this can be the case where committees cover multiple standards on a variety of (related) subjects. However it does require some judgement by the Committee Officers and the Standards Australia Executive as to

- whether or not a sufficient cross section of relevant interests have voted affirmatively, and
- if there are negative votes, what represents a (collective) major interest.

Following voting the Committee Officers arrange for any negative votes to be considered at a committee meeting or in a smaller group involving, at least, the Committee Officers and the negative voters. Where all steps are exhausted at this committee stage and a major (collective) interest maintains negative vote(s), the issue can be escalated to a higher level committee, which is a similar process as that used by BSI, as described in BS 0.

Under the Standards Australia voting rules the following selection of scenarios can occur with a committee of 20 stakeholder representatives that are eligible to vote provided there is an overarching assessment by the Committee Officers and Standards Australia that there is a sufficient cross section of stakeholders voting affirmatively:

(1) 12 affirmative votes, 0 negative votes, 8 abstentions. Although less than 67% affirmatively, as there are no negative votes, this can be accepted.

(2) 12 affirmative votes, 2 negative votes, 6 abstentions. As the votes fail to meet the minimum of 67% affirmative vote required, i.e. 14 votes, this is rejected.

(3) 14 affirmative votes, 3 negative votes (not representing a major collective interest). As the affirmative votes meet the minimum of 80% of those eligible to vote who actually voted, this is accepted.

(4) 14 affirmative votes, 4 negative votes (not representing a major collective interest). As the affirmative votes fail the minimum of 80% of those eligible to vote who actually voted, this is rejected.

5. Concluding observations

To a large extent, the development of standards avoids the use of voting as a means of arriving at *consensus* of the parties involved. Where voting is used, there is often capacity for the management team involved in the conduct of the relevant standards development committee to take advantage of some flexibility in interpreting the voting rules. This leads to the observation that *"one vote, one value,"* a term invented when considering representation in parliaments in Australia, is not entirely correct in the standards development arena. In this respect it is interesting to note that the European standards bodies CEN and CENELEC have, to a large extent, avoided this issue by using weighted voting whereas the international standards bodies ISO and IEC are restricted by the UN concept of *"one vote, one country."*

Acknowledgements

The Author wishes to recognise the comment provide on a draft of this paper by Colin Blair (Chief Executive Officer, Standards Australia), Anne McNaughton (College Of Law, Australian National University and Associate, Centre for European Studies, ANU), Manfred J. Holler (Institute of SocioEconomics, University of Hamburg, and Public Choice Research Centre, Turku), and John Hudson (Department of Economics & International Development, University of Bath).

References

British Standards Institute, London, UK (BS 0, *A standard for standards*) – www.bsi-global.com

BusinessDictionary.com – www.businessdictionary.com

European Commission for Standardization and the European Commission for Electrotechnical Standardization, Brussels, Belgium (CEN/CENELEC, *Common* Rules for Standardization Work) – www.cen.au and www.cenelec.eu

International Organization for Standardization and the International Electrotechnical Commission, Geneva, Switzerland (ISO/IEC Directives Part 1, Procedures for the technical work) – www.iso.org and www.iec.ch.

Standards Australia, Sydney, Australia (Standardization Guide SG-001, *Preparing Standards* SG-002, *Structure and Operation of Standardization Committees*) – www.standards.org.au.

Homo Oeconomicus 27(4): 527–543 (2011)

www.accedoverlag.de

International Standardization of Technical and Scientific Terminology

Hans Teichmann
Avenue du Temple 13C, Lausanne, Switzerland
(eMail: teichmann.hans@bluewin.ch)

Abstract The development of international terminology is an important and demanding task: without a comprehensive and standardized technical-scientific terminology, efficient communication in vital sectors like economy, science and technology would not be possible. Following a general review of basic issues in technical terminology development, relevant lexicographical aspects are considered. As a result, conclusions on the impact and specific challenges of the international standardization of technical-scientific terminology can be formulated. These findings may serve as a starting point for the assessment and comparison of competing methodologies.

Keywords international terminology development, lexicography, technical-scientific terminology

1. Introduction

So much has life in the 20th century been intertwined with the development and application of technology that any mention of the term "technical dictionary" will raise in the minds of most people associations of modern, sophisticated engineering and industrial processes. Science-based industries introduce completely new processes, developed in the laboratory or experimental farm or plant, and they are introduced in their totality often via a foreign language. So a new "special" language, which is expected to be multi-disciplinary and transnational, has to be formulated.

This study aims at the *fundamental aspects* of the international standardization of technical-scientific terminology. It is intended to open the door to the assessment and comparison of the alternative methodologies that are used in global terminology development (for instance by ISO, International Organization for Standardization; ITU, International Telecommunication

ISBN 978-3-89265-075-1 ISSN 0943-0180

Union; and IEC, the International Electrotechnical Commission). With respect to *terminology,* this study takes into particular consideration the following contributions: Wüster (1931, 1991), Galinski and Budin (1993), Galinski and Hjulstad (1998), Rey (1979), and Wright (2004). The following contributions on *special-subject languages* were taken into consideration: Sager et al. (1980), von Hahn (1983), Kocourek (1982), and Pinchuck (1977).

Knowledge is developing in our time faster and changing more fundamentally than is *language*. The formation of new terms is impeded primarily by the very limited number of term elements available in any language for naming new concepts. The number of these concepts, on the other hand, increases more or less at the same pace as knowledge grows, i.e. at a very rapid pace. Therefore, the quantitative development of *concepts* tends to diverge considerably from that of terms (Galinski and Budin 1993).

Translating into other languages is an uncontested necessity. The translation of *technical texts* requires considerable specific knowledge, i.e. not only knowledge about linguistic rules and structures, but also knowledge about the relevant technical-scientific topic (Maillot 1981). Knowledge about just one of these two aspects does not suffice to produce a correct translation. There is also a need for *terminology management.* Its main contribution can be seen in its crucial role in the process of acquiring, storing and applying both the linguistic and the subject-specific knowledge required for the production of target texts.

This study will consider the following fundamental aspects: *Need for developing* technical-scientific terminology; *Basic issues* arising in technical-scientific terminology work; and finally related *Lexicographical aspects.* - Like in other fields, there are limitations also to well-intended interventions, and the linguists' contributions have not always been appreciated. As Delbridge (1983) reports, the well-known American terminologist *Noah Webster* asserted that "the principal corruptions of our language, within the last five hundred years, are the work not of the vulgar, but of authors and writers *pretending to purify and refine* the language."

2. Need for developing technical/scientific terminology

2.1 General remarks

Is the international standardization of technical-scientific terminology a task of fundamental importance, rather than a pastime for introverted word collectors? The complexity of this question stems from the fact that terminology development concerns a rather diverse range of aspects as well as various stakeholders. First of all, *the development* of such a terminology is not easy. It is common knowledge that different languages lexicalise semantic space differently, the extent of overlapping or difference depending, among other things, on the *cultural differences* between these languages. At the one end of the continuum there are the rare cases of one-to-one correspondence, and at the other end there are items in one language that have no equivalent at all in the other language. If no lexical equivalent in a language exists, when talking or writing about the meaning they convey, one will have to resort to circumlocution, definition, etc. (Tomaszczyk 1983). It is definitely wrong *to simply translate* a term into a language where no equivalent seems to exist. Drame (2010) stressed the need for developing and implementing a *coherent terminology policy* in any large organization because otherwise the costs of possible incidents may be considerable.

The role of technical-scientific terminology may sometimes be underestimated. In fact, essential activities in the multinational environment of regional standards setting organizations can be described as "multilingual, collective technical writing" and "multilingual, cross-cultural communication" (Teichmann 2010a): *linguistic aspects* are undoubtedly important. However, the following publications investigated an array of issues concerning *regional* standardization *without any mentioning of terminology-related problems,* witness the following publications: (a) "Electrotechnical Standardization in Europe – A Tool for the Common Market" by Winckler (1994): This booklet deals with the European Committee for Electrotechnical Standardization (CENELEC). (b) "Wie funktioniert die Normung?" by Niedziella (2007). This booklet was published by the German VDE (Verband der Elektrotechnik Elektronik Informationstechnik) and considers national as well international standardization. (c) "Standardization: Fundamentals, Impact, and Business Strategy," a book published by APEC, the Asia Pacific Economic Cooperation (APEC 2010).

2.2 Aim of terminology development

The need for terminology development in a *given language* varies in function of its status and of economic facts. Even *within a given language*, any terminology presents problems of *internal coherency* (Schnieder 2010 and IEC 2008). The reason is that in different sectors of the fundamental sciences, from mathematics to philosophy, the *different groups* will tend to use *different concepts.*

When it comes to *language for special purposes*, such as languages used in the spheres of education, economics, science and technology, *standardized terminologies* have to be in place in order to facilitate successful conceptualisation, knowledge transfer and acquisition (Alberts 2006, IEC 2008, Drame 2010, and Teichmann 2010a).

On the *national level*, the aim of language development (respectively of language modernisation) is the provision of standardized terminology in varied domains in order to ensure (a) an accurate information transfer, (b) information acquisition, and (c) creative thinking in the first language, (d) to promote technical, scientific and economical communication ensuring better education and training results, and (e) to equip learners, students and workers for utilisation of knowledge.

2.3 *Classes of terminology users*

In the context of developing terminologies and conceptual systems, the different interests of *varied classes* of users have to be taken into account (Rahmstorf 1993). These classes are in principle the following:

(a) *General users, students, etc.* use terminological information presented within a book or another source for studying a particular domain. Such definitions communicate term knowledge, semantic knowledge and conceptual knowledge.

(b) *Translators* use definitions as a help for understanding terms and texts, and for translating technical terms and texts. In fact, *even specialized translators* cannot always be experts for the domain the texts are dealing with. Definitions stored in terminological data bases can support translators which are not so familiar with the subject of their text.

(c) *Scientists, engineers* use, develop and communicate theoretical positions and results of the analysis of a subject. Scientific definitions have to be prepared by experts of the domain. The primary scientific achievement of a good definition is the *new conceptual construction.* The *term* is a secondary invention, but it does have some impact on the successful communication of the new concept.

(d) *Standard experts* working in terminological standardization analyze, control and improve the usage of terms. Finding and recommending suitable new terms for new concepts (observations, ideas, views, constructions, products, etc.) by publishing recommended terms for concepts is an important technical function.

(e) *Technical experts* participating in the technical work of national, regional or global standards setting organizations (Teichmann 2010b).

(f) *Information scientists, indexers, retrieval experts* and other specialists for knowledge organization use terminological definitions for technical purposes such as documentation, ordering, and communicating information. Terms can be used as descriptors for indexing and retrieving documents and for indicating hierarchical positions in a clarification system.

(g) *Epistemologists, psychologists* and other researchers study definitions for meta-scientific analysis. Various logical and cognitive problems of definitions are discussed here such as their adequateness, and the formal structure. Other questions are related to the limits of definitions.

(h) *Knowledge engineers* may use definitions for developing knowledge bases for expert systems.

(j) Finally, *Linguists and terminologists* have studied definitions in word semantics. They can use terminological definitions collected in dictionaries and terminological data bases to study lexis, syntax and semantics.

2.4 Proliferation of technical work

So prolific and various has technical intellectual work now become, as compared with previous centuries, that natural and uncontrolled evolution of technical terms can no longer be relied on to ensure unambiguity and efficiency in use of language (Opitz 1983a). A remarkably systematic approach has been taken by the IEC (IEC 2010) which prepares and publishes its “International Electrotechnical Vocabulary” (see Appendix).

As technical areas touch, branch out and overlap, they graft on the store of common language, giving rise to multiple meaning in words and phrases that are easily confused and used in a haphazard if not even indeed faulty manner (Maillot 1981). It is the proper task of technical dictionaries to help reduce this danger, but this in turn has made the lexicographer’s task that much harder, demanding more precise information and more circumspect work methods than are customary in much general lexicography, in order to do justice to the profusion of technical-scientific details.

Finally, the possible impact of *geography and politics* should not be overlooked: All major languages which are important in science, technology and commerce are used not only in a *single country*, but in *several countries* or even in *varied geographical areas.* Examples are German in Germany, Switzerland and Austria; as well as Portuguese in Portugal, Brazil and several African countries. Obviously, this fact gives rise to the creation of separate and diverging terminologies which tend to make *accurate information exchange* between the entities concerned impossible (Gong 2006). The development of a common and comprehensive terminology *in the common language* is therefore essential.

3. Basic issues in technical-scientific terminology work

This chapter considers basic issues required as underpinning in assessing different methodologies. These issues include, besides general aspects of linguistic standardization, related user requirements and qualitative aspects.

3.1 General remarks

Most general dictionaries which have been published in the major world languages deal predominantly or exclusively with the so-called *standard norms* of usage, i.e. the cultivated, educated, literary norms, rather than the broad, common, illiterary norms. It has been stated that all human thinking and communication occur in two different worlds (Galinski and Hjulstad 1998): (a) the real world ("worldscape" of *existing objects*), and (b) the world of ideas ("mindscape" with *conceived objects*). This action takes place at three different levels: (a) the level of *objects,* (b) the level of *concepts,* and (c) the level of *representation.* Representations are necessary to communicate the concepts that correspond to the objects. *Objects* are either things, such as organisms, creatures, processes, phenomena of the *real world,* or they are *conceived* objects. *Concepts* are mental abstractions that correspond to objects; they are produced by the human mind and have characteristics that correspond *to properties* of objects (and can be classified according to various criteria); the concepts are units of thought (in the process of abstraction), units of knowledge (if agreed upon by a subject-field community), or units of communication (when used in written or spoken communication); and finally concepts have relations to other concepts and can form concept systems.

Representations are verbal and non-verbal representations of concepts (e.g. terms or other kinds of designations for denoting concepts, definitions or other kinds of explanations for describing concepts, graphical symbols, pictures and diagrams). These representations must be "physical" in order to make them communicable; they actually represent concepts in a perceivable form; and they may have different physical forms, e.g. linguistic symbols, formalized codes, as well as graphical symbols.

Differences in extension between the words of two given languages constitute the most elementary lexicological distinction. In point of fact, there is no reason why two equivalents should have identical extension, i.e. why they should cover the same semantic area.

3.2 User requirements

It should not be overlooked that, besides the different types of monolingual and interlingual dictionaries which are relevant in the given context, further dictionary types serving numerous other and sometimes highly specialized applications do exist (Wüster 1991). However, dictionaries used in technical and scientific work are *monolingual* or *interlingual.* Both types differ in several respects, according to the users they intend to serve, the needs they cater for, and to the methods of their compilation. The morpho-phonemic, syntactic and semantic problems involved in dictionaries for translation are different from and more complicated, in many ways, than those in dictionaries for definitions or synonyms (Al-Kasimi 1983). One major source of difficulty in dictionaries for translation is that they deal not only with different kinds of *cultural and linguistic behaviour,* but also with two different systems of *concept formation.*

Terminology may be presented in *glossaries* or *vocabularies* (see Subclause 4.4). "Technical Dictionaries" serve for the most part specific trades or occupations from brewery to road construction, production engineering or computer software, and are intended as an aid in communication between people working in a given field and outsiders, or between specialists in the field speaking one language and their counterparts speaking a different language (Opitz 1983b). Accordingly, technical dictionaries may be conceived as either monolingual or bilingual reference works stressing either the *information aspect* through definition, explication or example, or the *translation aspect* through equivalent expressions in one or more different languages. Sciences and occupations all constitute valid areas of concern displaying their particular linguistic frameworks or "registers," i.e. lexical, stylistic and idiomatic patterns.

The first and foremost of the users' required skills is obviously the ability to find and identify lexical items in a total word-list. In practically all cultures and at almost all levels of activity *the alphabet* as established by the language community in question serves to forge a reliable link of communication between individuals and groups of different intellectual or occupational levels. It is therefore also best suited to organize the lexical content of a dictionary that will be used by an occupational as well as educational cross-section of the society.

Technical talk is often more or less incomprehensible to the lay person. Assuming that its "jargon" is meant to exclude outsiders from the dealings of specialists, the lay public will occasionally get angry at this apparent abuse of language for purposes of social competition. Such suspicion may not be altogether unfounded: people have indeed always been fond of secrets that help to establish their particular position in society. The compelling reason for the continued or even increased application of highly specialised language is, however, that scientists, scholars and technicians, in pursuing their work, have no use for words that might be ambiguous and open to varying interpretations.

3.3 *Qualitative aspects*

Unfortunately, certain multilingual vocabularies present as "terms" for a given concept in different languages merely *ad hoc translations* of the source language terms, rather than the terms which would actually be used by native speakers. As Maillot (1981) points out, other possible pitfalls are polysemy, "faux amis" and paronyms. *Polysemy* means that a language uses a given term for several distinct notions. - "Faux amis" are terms of different languages and of *common origin* which have different meanings but may be taken for equivalent. This problem is especially frequent where a great deal of borrowing has occurred between the two languages concerned (for instance, between English and French). - Unlike "faux amis," *paronyms* do not belong to the same language but to a different language. They are terms based on the *same root*, i.e. they have the same derivation. Therefore, paronyms are sometimes taken as equivalents although they do have *different meanings.*

There is an important difference between *technical* and *scientific* terminology development: whilst *scientific* terminology work is based on the knowledge of the relevant scientific field, the preparation of *technical* terminology work requires in addition detailed knowledge of the *professional practice* involved. Rather practical aspects should not be overlooked either: the distinction between dictionaries for *production* and dictionaries for *comprehension* determines the choice of the respective source language (SL) and target language (TL). In compiling for instance an English-Arabic dictionary for English speaking users, English should be the SL if the dictionary is intended for production, whereas Arabic should be the SL if it is meant as a tool for comprehension. Asked to make two dictionaries of the same size, one for *comprehension* and one for *production*, the lexicographer should include more entries with more senses in the former than in the latter. On the other hand, the entry words in the dictionary *for production* should be of productive nature, and their treatment should provide the translator with all the morphological and syntactic information that enables him to use the words correctly.

Note: It is a well-known fact that computer technology based on English conquered the world by storm. Unsurprisingly, countries which at a later stage translated relevant concepts into their own language as *a conscious and deliberate linguistic exercise* may have a more coherent set of terms than the original set. For instance, the French terms "logiciel" and "matériel" are semantically more satisfactory than the original English terms "software" and "hardware."

4. Lexicographical aspects

This review of lexicographical aspects provides an underpinning for the assessment of the compilations of technical-scientific dictionaries. Hartmann (1983) defines the *dictionary* as a "reference book or list of words (usually in alphabetical order) together with a guide to their meanings, pronunciations, spelling or equivalents in another language." This means that the lexicographer is concerned with the job of describing all or some of the words of one or more languages in terms of their characteristic features, notably of their meaning. This is in most cases a *descriptive* activity, recording existing usage rather than laying down *prescriptive* or *normative* rules about how words should be used or which words are to be avoided. In practice, however, a lexicographer will often find himself in a situation in which he must also decide on whether an expression is current or deviant, appropriate or inappropriate, typical or abnormal for the variety of the language which he has set out to describe.

In contrast to such an essentially descriptive activity, the experts in international standardization of *technical-scientific* terminology usually have to lay down *prescriptive* rules. Terminology work differs from *lexicography. Terminology* consists of vocabularies related to a given domain. It is organized and defined with regard to specific subject matters (the so-called semantic criterion), and with regard to the methodology used (the socio-cultural criterion). According to Rey (1979), this may be the reason why terminology is sometimes mistakenly considered as lexicography in specialized technical-scientific domains.

4.1 Keeping technical-scientific dictionaries up to date

Gradual changes to accommodate the written to the spoken language are not only proper, but indispensable. In this context, particular problems resulted for domain specific languages: they tend to be more transitory than common speech or literary language, due to the rate of change in the material basis underlying their linguistic manifestation. Such areas are for instance electronic engineering, the chemistry of polymers and computer technology (Opitz 1983a).

It is obvious that dictionaries covering such fields easily suffer from two kinds of inadequacy: On the one hand, they often lack *quite recent lexical material*, which is after all most strongly in need of comment and clarification and one of the chief reasons for the user to turn to the specialized dictionary. Considering the time it normally takes to publish a revised edition of a dictionary, this is an almost insoluble task. The second shortcoming lies in the opposite direction: *lexical material that has lost currency* may not be eliminated but may stay on contributing eventually to a sizeable portion of terminological deadwood which under the most favourable of circumstances merely represents a nuisance, making the dictionary unnecessarily bulky and its handling tedious and time-consuming, and in the worst possible case produces direct mistakes. The weeding out of superseded items can be one of the most unpleasant albeit extremely responsible tasks. This is because it involves not only an estimate of the items' technical validity, but also an appraisal of the needs they are actually fulfilling.

4.2 Compilation of specialist dictionaries

The "technical" dictionary is compiled on the basis of criteria provided by particular target groups and their professional or special-interest needs. Neither its content nor its structure and methods can predominantly be determined by purely linguistic considerations. Therefore, the technical dictionary is usually "segmental," focussing on a distinctly limited language area circumscribed by a non-linguistic situation.

Almost all technical dictionaries profess to present, within the chosen technical domain, a full lexical representation of the underlying domain. Any successful limitation of size in the segmental dictionary must thus be achieved *through* a *limitation* of the technical domain. This in turn raises problems of practical nature. How closely, the lexicographer must ask himself, can I reasonably draw the limits of a technical register without leaving too many of the user's question unanswered because they might happen to originate in a different, though related field? Insofar as a segmental dictionary is intended to isolate a distinct register from the total language for precision and ease of language, it will try to avoid polysemy within its own partial lexicon. Its aim will therefore be to gloss no entry with more than one denotation. The likelihood of reaching that aim is the greater the more specialized the treated activity is and the more exclusive it tends to be in its use of language (Opitz 1983b).

Most authors of specialist dictionaries are neither linguists nor professional lexicographers, but *specialists in the particular discipline*, whether it is international law, psychology, or pipeline technology. Confronted with the irritating terminological problems of their respective fields, these specialists tend to get down to business of creating what they regard as an adequate communication tool (Moulin 1983). It is felt from many prefaces of specialist dictionaries that their authors considered that they had a kind of law-giving mission.

4.3 Coining new technical terms

Technical terms may enter a language rather abruptly. Word formation by use of prefixes, suffixes or other systematic variations of existing morphology is rather more usual than the invention of totally new lexemes. Another way of creating new technical terms is by adopting expressions from foreign languages, fitting them as best as possible into one's own language system. A third method consists in arbitrarily assigning to an existing lexical item a new semantic change: it is given another "meaning" which should, however, be discernible from the form of the lexeme. The result of this operation would otherwise be polysemy, bane of laymen and specialist, translator and lexicographer. Terms arrived at through polysemy are easily the most confusing of all technical coinages since they work only in a "marked" linguistic environment with speakers who are fully aware of the polysemous quality of such terms; in the typical confrontation of specialist versus layman they are the most frequent source of communication failure (Opitz 1983b). Therefore, theoretical work is being undertaken which investigates in a systematic manner the elements which determine the quality of new technical-scientific terms (Schnieder 2010).

4.4 Glossaries versus vocabularies

A glossary is an alphabetical list of terms in a particular domain of knowledge with the definitions for those terms. Traditionally, a glossary appears at the end of a book and includes terms within that book which are specialized. A bilingual (multilingual) glossary is a list of terms in one language which are defined in a second language (or several languages). In the *domain of international standardization*, a glossary may be included by the TC concerned as (a) part of the "terms and definitions" clause of standard, (b) in an independent Standard or (c) in a Technical report. According to Wright (1997), individual committees tend to have strong feelings about how they want their standards look like, which results in some degree of stylistic variability. Therefore, terminology standardization requires *uniform methods* to efficiently pursue practical and applied terminology management and to produce *coherent and consistent* terminology.

Potential users of standardized terminology sometimes search in vain for multilingual standardized terminology resources, i.e. vocabularies: preferably as a single, readily accessible online terminology resource. The precondition for providing this service is the availability of *consistent data from multiple sources* that can be successfully merged into a coherent data base. Accepted rules for the preparation and layout of terminology standards are required to overcome impending incompatibility. The International Electrotechnical Vocabulary (IEV) of the International Electrotechnical Commission (IEC) is an example of such a single terminology resource.

5. Conclusions

The following conclusions concern, besides general aspects, international terminology standardization's role and impact, and the specific challenges in terminology development. These conclusions may serve *as starting point* for the assessment and comparison of competing methodologies.

It should be clear at this stage that, contrary to popular belief, international terminology work is not merely an obscure pastime performed by a small minority of introverted word collectors, but a professional activity with its own established practices and strong international contacts. Where and whenever specialized information and specialized knowledge are prepared, presented, processed, transformed and transferred, *terminology* should be accorded a crucial role. There is, in fact, hardly any area in a company or other specialized organization where terminology is *not used.*

Terminology standardization cannot be concerned with isolated terms but must create systems that are open to new developments on the *conceptual level* and consequently also on the *linguistic level* of term creation. If it has been decided to prepare a *bilingual* terminology, it is obviously necessary to choose the SL and the TL. Better results will be achieved if *both languages involved* serve in turn as SL and as TL. The main disadvantage of this option is naturally the higher cost. Similar conditions apply to the preparation of terminology in more than two languages.

Special languages are based on natural languages, but in order to serve their more limited functions they reduce polysemy and ambiguity by process of regularisation, standardization and de-contextualisation, and thereby develop properties which may be associated in some way to artificial languages. Standardization is a deliberate and planned activity, and attributable to individuals. A *norm* makes creativity possible, but *standardization* restricts it when the topic of the message takes precedence over situational factors. New terms should *not be translations* from other languages: they should be *"coined"* – but definitely always *by native speakers.*

The terminological vocabulary related to the "mindscape" consists of concepts (and their interrelations) represented by terms and definitions (or other kinds of determinations) and should be characterized by *completeness* as regards terminological information and at the same time by *lack of redundant information.* In other words, clarity, simplicity and brevity are the virtues which are highly prized by most users of technical-scientific dictionaries. If *attention to detail* is one cornerstone of technical lexicography, *standardization* is another. All dictionaries wittingly or unwittingly contribute to the codification of language use by their mere existence. Their listing of certain words or phrases as having a defined sense, however tenuous or dubious that definition may turn out to be, seems to confer an uncontested authority upon those listed items. It is therefore essential that terminology in any language is developed by *qualified native speakers*, or at least *with their participation.*

Standardization in a *technical-scientific dictionary* works well beyond the common range of natural respect paid to the printed page. It extends to the methods proper by which language elements are denoted, representing an effort on the part of the lexicographer to present definitions, or equivalents that will permit the universal use of the underlying lexical material in full accordance with the needs and claims of those branches of skill and knowledge in which it took its origin, and which in turn it helps to shape further. Appreciation for terminology should emanate from the *language users themselves* since one could never succeed *by forcing* terminology, a language or language variety into use. Irrespective of how well trained and resourceful terminologists may be, and irrespective of how elegant and sophisticated the set of terms they create, large scale term creation will remain a wasteful endeavour unless the end-product is going to be appreciated and utilized fully by the community of subject specialists and language practitioners – the end users. The success of a dictionary is largely determined by the right degree and method of subject specialisation, which lies in a sound balance of exclusiveness and inclusiveness.

Sociolinguists are for the time being unable to formulate laws on the *acceptance or rejection of new terms:* these laws are terribly complex because they involve not only linguistic, psychological and social factors, but also the relationship between a huge number of practicing technicians, engineers and scientists, on the one hand, and a very small number of terminology standardizers, on the other hand.

With regard to *subject specialization*, an important question to be answered is what the practical scope of a technical field is and where the limits of the lexicon of the corresponding technical dictionary are hence to be drawn. What makes the answer difficult is not only the well-established fact that modern technological processes share as many concepts as there are to separate them: the result is an ever-expanding basic technical vocabulary that forms an integral part of its specialized branches. In practice, technical dictionaries are always under great strain *to stay up to date*, particularly if they deal with subject areas marked by particularly rapid or thorough development.

International terminology work involves necessarily varied cultures and therefore comprises a double process: transfer of *elements of knowledge* to the different cultures, and transfer of an *appropriate terminology structure* to the vocabulary of the dominant language of these cultures. A particular difficulty may be observed in the following situation: Languages which extend over a number of countries will naturally tend to develop competing regional varieties. Sub-languages may be liable to different kinds of lexical codification in the form of dictionaries.

Even when composed by native speakers, standards *written in world languages* may not be universally useful in *all countries* where these languages are spoken. In fact, some standards (for instance of the ISO 9000 family of quality assurance standards) have actually been "translated" from ISO English into American English for use in the United States because subject specialists working there did not comprehend or accept the original. Similarly, European Spanish standards or ISO standards *in European Spanish* must sometimes be retranslated for South American audiences. These examples *do not mean* that international terminology work is a futile endeavour – they stress on the contrary its importance.

Acknowledgements

The author wishes to thank Ms. Kara Warburton, Chair of ISO/TC 37, Manfred J. Holler, (University of Hamburg and editor of Homo Oeconomicus) and several anonymous reviewers for their helpful comments and suggestions.

References

Alberts, M. (2006), Standardisation, Modernisation and Harmonisation: A Sociolinguistic Perspective, in: Y. Wang, Y. Wang and C. Zhou (eds.), *International Conference on Terminology, Standardization and Terminology Transfer*, Beijing: Ecyclopedia of China Publishing House.

Al-Kasimi, A.M. (1983), The Interlingual/Translation Dictionary, in: R.R.K. Hartmann (ed.), *Lexicography: Principles and Practice*, London: Academic Press.

APEC (2010), D.G. Choi (ed.), *Standardization: Fundamentals, Impact, and Business Strategy*, Seoul: APEC.

Delbridge, A. (1983), On National Variants of the English Dictionary, in: R.R.K. Hartmann (ed.), *Lexicography: Principles and Practice*, London: Academic Press.

Drame, A. (2010), Verbesserte Kommunikation durch Terminologiestrategien in Unternehmen, *DIN Mitteilungen* 9: 19-23.

Galinski, C. and Budin, G. (1993), New Trends in Terminology-Oriented Management, in: S.E. Wright and L.D. Wright (eds.), *Scientific and Technical Translation*, Amsterdam/Philadelphia: John Benjamins.

Galinski, C. and Hjulstad, H. (1998), ISO/TC 37, Terminology (principles and coordination), in: A. Munteanu (ed.), *Terminology Work and Knowledge Transfer: Best Practice in Terminology Management and Terminography*, Vienna: Infoterm.

Gong, L. (2006), Terminology Standardisation and Modern Lexicography, in: Y. Wang, Y. Wang and C. Zhou (eds.), *International Conference on Terminology, Standardization and Terminology Transfer*, Beijing: Encyclopedia of China Publishing House.

Hahn, W. von (1983), *Fachkommunikation: Entwicklung, Linguistische Konzepte, Betriebliche Beispiele*, Berlin: De Gruyter.

Hartmann, R.R.K. (1983), Theory and Practice in Dictionary-Making, in: R.R.K. Hartmann (ed.), *Lexicography: Principles and Practice*, London: Academic Press.

IEC (1992), *IEC Multilingual Dictionary of Electricity, Electronics and Telecommunications*, Amsterdam: Elsevier.

IEC (2008), *IEC Guide 108: Guidelines for ensuring the coherency of IEC publications – Application of horizontal standards*, Geneva: IEC.

IEC (2010), *Electropedia: The World's Online Electrotechnical Vocabulary*, www.electropedia.org.

ISO/IEC (2008), *ISO/IEC Directives–Supplement–Procedures specific to IEC*, Geneva: IEC.

Kocourec, R. (1982), *La Langue Française de la Technique et de la Science*, Wiesbaden: Brandstetter.

Maillot, J. (1981), *La Traduction Scientifique & Technique*, Technique & Documentation: Paris

Moulin, A. (1983), The LSP Learner's Lexicographical Needs, in: R.R.K. Hartmann (ed.), *Lexicography: Principles and Practice*, London: Academic Press.

Niedziella, W. (2007), Wie *funktioniert die Normung?*, Berlin/Offenbach: VDE.

Opitz, K. (1983a), Special-purpose Lexicography: Dictionaries for Technical Use, in: R.R.K. Hartmann (ed.), *Lexicography: Principles and Practice*, London: Academic Press.

Opitz, K. (1983b), The Segmental Dictionary, in: R.R.K. Hartmann (ed.), *Lexicography: Principles and Practice*, London: Academic Press.

Pinchuck, I. (1977), *Scientific and Technical Translation*, London: André Deutsch.

Rahmsdorf, G. (1993), Role and Representation of Terminological Definitions, in: K.-D. Schmitz (ed.), *Terminology and Knowledge Engineering*, Frankfurt: Indeks.

Rey, A. (1979), *La Terminologie: Noms et Notions*, Paris: Presse Universitaire de France.

Sager, J., Dungworth, D. and McDonald, P. (1980), *English Special Languages: Principles and Practice in Science and Technology*, Wiesbaden: Brandstetter.

Schnieder, L. (2010), Innovative Terminologiearbeit als Grundlage sprachlicher Konvergenz, *DIN Mitteilungen* 5: 10-14.

Teichmann, H. (2010a), *Global Standardization: Coping with Multilingualism*, Aachen: Mainz.

Teichmann, H. (2010b), Effectiveness of Technical Experts in International Standardization, in: J.C. Graz and K. Jakobs (eds), *EURAS Proceedings 2010*, Aachen: Mainz.

Tomaszczyk, J. (1983), The Case for Bilingual Dictionaries for Foreign Language Learners, in: R.R.K. Hartmann (ed.), *Lexicography: Principles and Practice*, London: Academic Press

Winckler, R. (1994), *Electrotechnical Standardization in Europe: A Tool for the Common Market*, Brussels: CENELEC.

Wright, S.E. (1997), Terminology Standardization: Management Strategies, in: S.E. Wright and G. Budin (eds.), *Basic Aspects of Terminology Management*, Amsterdam/Philadelphia: John Benjamins.

Wright, S.E. (2004), *The Creation and Application of Language Industry Standards*, Terminology, Computing and Translation: Swansea.

Wüster, E. (1931), *Internationale Sprachnormung in der Technik, besonders in der Elektrotechnik*, Berlin: VDI.

Wüster, E. (1991), *Einführung in die Allgemeine Terminologielehre und Terminologische Lexikographie*, Bonn: Romanistischer Verlag.

Appendix: The International Electrotechnical Vocabulary (IEV) of the International Electrotechnical Commission (IEC)

In addition to providing a unique multilingual reference work, the IEV is intended to facilitate understanding between electrical engineers of all countries and assist in eliminating a certain laxity in technical language, the source of potential misunderstandings, costly in terms of both time and money. Noteworthy aspects in the development of the IEV are the following: (a) In IEC's TC 1 a broad and truly international consensus has to be reached. (b) Working documents are prepared in principle by a Working Group (WG) of the *TC concerned.* (c) NCs consult their experts of TC 1 and of any other interested committee and submit their *collated comments* in a single document. (d) The entries of the IEV are selected by *experts in the relevant technical field* rather than lexicographers. (e) Drafts are circulated to *all parties concerned* (including other international organizations). - Further details are laid down in Appendix I of the ISO/IEC Directives (2008).

Since the first years of its existence, questions of international nomenclature have engaged IEC's attention. An alphabetical list of electrotechnical terms, together with their definitions, proposed by IEC's first Technical Committee "Nomenclature" was approved in 1913. From the early twenties onwards, the Commission prepared the first edition of its "International Electrotechnical Vocabulary" which was published in 1938. That edition contained some *2000 terms* accompanied by the definitions of the concepts represented.

In 1983, the “IEC Multilingual Dictionary of Electricity” was published. It was based on *40 IEV chapters*, defined more than *7 500 terms* in French and English, and gave the equivalent terms in seven other languages: Russian (the third official language of the IEC), as well as German, Spanish, Italian, Dutch, Polish and Swedish. In the 1983 edition, terms relating to *telecommunications* were excluded. - The title of the dictionary’s second edition, (IEC 1992), was “IEC Multilingual Dictionary of Electricity, Electronics and Telecommunications,” reflecting both the ever-increasing role of *electronics* in the activities of the Commission as well as the inclusion of terms relating to *telecommunications*. - The IEV chapters of the 700 series have been prepared by *joint groups of experts* from the TCs of the ITU, the International Consultative Radiocommunication Committee (CCIR), the International Consultative Telegraph and Telephone Committee (CCITT), and of course from IEC. – The 1992 edition of the dictionary was based on nearly *70 IEV chapters* and contained *18 000 terms and synonyms*.

At present, the IEV contains *82 chapters* with more than *20 000 terms* and definitions in English and French, organized by subject area (IEC 2010). Equivalent terms are given in no fewer than *ten languages*: Arabic, Chinese, German, Italian, Japanese, Portuguese, Polish, Russian, Spanish and Swedish (with the coverage varying by subject area). The IEV gives its stakeholders in general satisfaction.

Homo Oeconomicus 27(4): 545–573 (2011)

www.accedoverlag.de

Supranational Agency: A Solution for Conflict in International Mergers?

Poonam Mehra
National Institute of Securities Markets, Mumbai, India
(eMail: poonammehraster@gmail.com, poonam.mehra@nism.ac.in)

Abstract Conflicts among antitrust authorities in different countries are likely to increase with globalization. This paper develops a two-country, three-firm model to analyze the possibilities of conflict between national antitrust authorities. It is shown that if countries maximize their national welfare there is a possibility of conflict that blocks welfare-enhancing mergers. It is also shown that convergence to a reference standard based on global welfare or consumer surplus resolves conflicts but may not always lead to an efficient outcome. Efficiency can be ensured through transfer payments coupled with the total welfare standard. In light of the above it is argued that there is scope for institutions like WTO to assume the role of supranational authority to ensure conflict-free, efficient outcomes.

JEL Classifications D74, F51, F53, L4
Keywords conflict, cross border merger, efficiency, standards, welfare

1. Introduction

Cross-border mergers and acquisitions have been a source of conflict between various antitrust/competition authorities across countries.[1] Any international merger or acquisition is subject to review in all the countries affected by the deal. For instance, the Gillette and Wilkinson merger was reviewed and approved by as many as 14 different jurisdictions in the early 1990s (Sarah 2008). The regulatory authorities in different countries are guided by different legal systems, giving rise sometimes to potentially

[1] Antitrust is a term used in US, while competition is used in other countries, particularly in Europe. In this study, we use these two terms interchangeably.

ISBN 978-3-89265-075-1 ISSN 0943-0180

conflicting decisions. However, firms require concurrent approval from the national regulatory agencies involved.

Conflicting outcomes, in general, have been attributed to either procedural or substantive differences. Procedural standards set up a legal framework for substantive standard setting, decision making and enforcement. Venit and Kolasky (2000) point out the procedural differences between EU (European Union) and US (United States) antitrust agencies over notification deadlines, review thresholds, level of information required for initial filing, regulatory burden, time limit for review, etc. For instance, in US the threshold for the pre-merger notification to the Department of Justice and Federal Trade Commission stands at $15 million in assets or voting securities. However, the threshold for notification in the EU is much higher and "captures only those large enough to justify the burdens imposed on the parties and Commission." On the other hand, substantive standard generally contains a right or obligation to proceed or not to proceed in a particular manner. Dissonance in substantive standard was observed, for instance, in General Electric and Honeywell proposed merger case where the market definition adopted by authorities in US was relatively narrow as compared to that adopted by the European Commission.[2]

According to Evenett and Hijzen (2006), conflict in cross-border mergers often arise due to the fact that while the externality of a merger transcends national border, its review by competition authorities remains a national affair. This gets starkly reflected in the $60 billion merger of the two Swiss firms Ciba-Geigy and Sandoz (1996). By confining their interests solely to national markets while the European Commission found no member state market to be sufficiently concentrated so as to require any remedial enforcement action, authorities in US found a more anti-competitive situation in the US market and demanded divestitures.

Moreover, as Dixit (1984) argues when there are monopoly profits to be attained, each country has an interest to "annex them for their own benefits." In particular, as Guzman (2007) argues that since the cost and benefit of regulation falls on different countries, domestic competition authorities have an incentive to alter their domestic laws in favour of their own residents at the cost of foreigners. This was one of the important issues raised in the context of the potential conflict in case of Boeing and McDonnell Douglas merger (1996). This case involved the merger of the world's largest producer of commercial aircraft manufacturer (Boeing) with the world's

---

[2] In the GE/Honeywell case, European Union's definition of market included markets for aerospace and power systems, large commercial aircraft engines, large regional jet aircraft engines and corporate jet engines and avionics and non-avionics products while US concerned itself only with helicopter engine market (Schnell 2004).

third largest producer (McDonnell Douglas), both American firms, in a highly concentrated market thereby disadvantaging the second largest manufacturer Airbus, a European firm. This merger was approved by antitrust authorities in United States. However, the European Commission initially blocked the merger and approved it only after Boeing accepted some remedial measures allegedly beneficial to Airbus (Harrison 2003).

Irrespective of the root cause, conflicts between jurisdictions over merger review add to transaction costs and uncertainty in international business. Inter-jurisdictional conflicts also undermine the confidence in antitrust laws and raise efficiency concerns in terms of its impact on the different stakeholders involved. Consequently, conflict resolution mechanisms deserve special attention, particularly, because a conflict free outcome need not be efficient.

This paper attempts to address two issues. Firstly, it focuses on the possibilities of potential conflict between jurisdictions, arising out of divergent national interests over the review of an international merger. One of the ways in which conflicts between competition authorities from different countries over review of a proposed merger can be resolved is by developing standards (Blumenthal 2004, Fugina 2006, Schnell 2004 etc). This study focuses on developing standards within the welfare framework where the objective of standardization is to define a common code or principle which does not vary across nations, thereby leading to a conflict free outcome. In particular, a two-country, three-firm model is developed, where the firms produce a single homogeneous product. The paper attempts to analyze the decision of antitrust authorities in case two firms propose to merge and examines the potential for conflict. The review of the proposed merger by antitrust authority in a particular country is based on the change in the welfare of the respective country due to merger. The study assumes that antitrust authority in each country takes into account only domestic welfare, thereby ignoring the impact of merger on the foreign countries affected by the deal.

The second issue pertains to the efficiency of the outcome. Efficiency, in this context, is defined in terms of the domestic welfare of the respective countries, i.e. an outcome following a common standard would be termed efficient only if it leaves each of the countries at least as well off as they were by adopting their domestic welfare standards. The paper proposes that the common code or standard which would be able to ensure a conflict free efficient outcome is consumer welfare or world welfare standard coupled with transfer payment from the country whose domestic welfare increases after merger to the country whose domestic welfare decreases after merger.

Rest of the paper is organized as follows. In Section 2.0, we discuss standards and develop the general model in the following section. In

Section 4.0, we analyze the possibilities of conflict under different standards. Section 5.0 briefly discusses the role of a supranational agency in implementing standards. Concluding remarks follow in Section 6.0. All the technical details and proofs of all propositions are given in a technical appendix in Mehra (2010).

2. Standards

In common parlance, standard refers to "the way things should be" (David 1987). Any standard has some well defined characteristics and its economic function is to reduce transaction costs (David and Steinmueller 1994). In this paper, we are concerned with two issues related to standards. One pertains to the definition of standards. The other is concerned with ways to achieve standardization. In Section 2.1, we introduce different standards within the welfare frame-work that can be applied to merger review. The different possible ways in which the different countries can reach a common standard are discussed in Section 2.2.

2.1 Definition of standards

This section analyzes the nature of standards that should be adopted by competition authorities in reviewing mergers so as to ensure a conflict free efficient outcome. In this paper we focus on welfare standards. Following David (1987), standards can be divided into three categories, namely, standard as a definition or reference, standard as a minimal admissible attribute and standards as means of ensuring interface compatibility. Welfare standards, according to David's taxonomy, fall under the category of reference standards.

According to Motta (2004), "economic welfare is the standard concept used in economics to measure how well an industry performs. It is a measure which aggregates the welfare (or surplus) of different groups in the economy." Following this definition of welfare, Reckens (2007) defines welfare standard "as a rule defining how the welfare of different groups in the economy is taken into account." Alternatively, De la Mano (2002) defines welfare standard in the context of mergers as follows: "The welfare standard is a rule to assign weights to the welfare of different groups of market participants. The chosen welfare standard is determined by whose welfare the merger enforcement agency seeks to maximize." There are different types of welfare standards depending on the weights given to the interests of different parties involved.[3]

This paper focuses on two forms of welfare standard: consumer surplus standard and total welfare standard. According to the consumer surplus standard, if the overall consumer surplus after merger increases the merger would be approved by authorities. On the other hand, under the total welfare standard a merger is approved if "the unweighted sum of consumer and producer surplus is positive," or in other words, "if the amount of cost savings is greater than the deadweight loss." This welfare standard is mostly favored by economists and is often referred to as Williamson's standard. Total welfare standard can be defined in terms of nation or world. The national welfare standard as introduced by Gifford and Kudrle (2005) characterizes the gainers and losers by nationality. The only criterion is that only gains and losses to resident (national) consumers and producers are taken into account. For world/global[4] welfare standard, the focus is on all gainers and losers, irrespective of their nationality. In this paper, we consider the effect of merger on merging firms, rival firms and consumers.[5]

Economists for long have been engaged in a debate on what should be the appropriate standard for antitrust authorities to review mergers. Farrell and Katz (2006) argue the ultimate goal of antitrust policy should be to maximize total welfare following "efficiency-oriented policies." In this context, Heyer (2006) also argues in favour of total welfare standard as being theoretically the best possible standard and "one that can be employed with no significant increase in administrative costs."

If the antitrust authorities maximize consumer welfare, as Farrell and Shapiro (1990) argues, then only price reducing mergers would be approved. However, if the objective of the antitrust authorities is to maximize aggregate welfare then efficiency requirements, measured by cost savings for a merger to be approved, are less restrictive. In particular, they calculate the external effect of a merger which comprises of the profit of the competitors and the consumer surplus. They argue that information about the market share and output responsiveness of the non-participants is enough to determine whether the merger benefits or harms the rivals. Farrell and Shapiro also claim that this approach of reviewing a merger is

---

[3] In most papers the following welfare standards are distinguished: price standard, consumer surplus standard, Hillsdown standard, weighted surplus standard and total surplus standard. For a detailed discussion see Reckens (2007).

[4] In the paper, world and global mean the same thing and have been used interchangeably.

[5] Studies also include the effect of merging firms on upstream or downstream firms and stakeholders of the firms which include shareholders, investors and employees.

consistent with the market policy analysis and it also assists antitrust authorities to provide a larger role to cost savings.

Extending the idea of Farrell and Shapiro (1990) to an open economy and using the concept of external effect of a merger, Barros and Cabral (1994), argue that in case of cross-border mergers, the regulators take into account only the domestic welfare. They apply their analysis to cross-border mergers in case of a "single market" characterized by consumers and producers in different countries. They find that in case of mergers between firms of two countries if the external effect is opposite on the two countries then the decision by a supranational authority reduces the possibility of a welfare reducing merger proposal being approved. However, in this situation, the chances of rejection of welfare enhancing merger proposals also increase. Further, when we consider only the external effect of a merger, we would be ruling out mergers where the gains from merging firms offset the loss of the rival firm and consumers, which in turn can be approved subject to the possibility of redistribution of gains from beneficiaries to the losers to the extent that all parties are better off.

Distinction between fixed and marginal cost turns out to be an important factor in determining the choice between consumer and total welfare standard. While changes in marginal cost generally do alter the firm's profit-maximizing price and output, changes in fixed cost do not have any such effect unless they affect "the firm's very viability." As a result, changes in fixed cost may have no effect at all on the welfare of consumers in the relevant market (Heyer 2006).

This paper considers mergers affecting firm's marginal cost which in turn affects both consumer surplus and total welfare. Further the analysis considers both the consumer surplus and total welfare standards defined at the national and world/global level. However, when dealing with transfer payment, the paper would focus exclusively on total welfare.

2.2 *Ways to achieve standardization*

Standardization of competition policy, as discussed in the literature, can be attained in different ways, broadly categorized as cooperation, convergence and devising an international framework which could act as a "transnational regime for the global economy." Cooperation involves bilateral or multilateral agreements between countries. There are a number of bilateral agreements reached between US and Australia,[6] Canada[7] and European

[6] A cooperation agreement on antitrust matters was signed between the Government of the United States of America and the Government of Australia on June 29, 1982.

[7] Memorandum of Understanding between the Government of the United States of

Union.[8] In fact the OECD has been issuing recommendation for cooperation in antitrust law since 1960s (Gorinson and Pambianco 2002). Cooperative agreements between countries, however, have been usually confined to information sharing over issues related to procedural standard (Guzman 2001). Moreover, cooperation alone is being universally regarded as an inadequate response to the more substantive problems of international antitrust law (Gerber 2002).

Gerber (2002) defines convergence as an increase in the characteristics shared by competition regimes and a reduction in non-shared characteristics. Convergence could be of two different types, viz. formal and functional. A formal convergence involves changes in the institutional structure with the objective of attaining conformity. But sometimes such formal forms of convergence are neither desirable nor feasible. In that case, one alternative form of convergence that is adopted is functional convergence. This is directed by efficiency parameters measured by performance indicators. Often it is observed that functional convergence is the first response, particularly if competitive pressures are involved because changing the form of the existing institution is time consuming.

The third alternative suggested in the literature focuses on developing an international legal framework or regime for competition law with a dispute settlement mechanism in place. At the extreme, such a framework is expected to replace the domestic legal regimes of different countries in matters of competition policy. Head and Reis (1997) examine the welfare consequences of a horizontal merger under decentralized antitrust policy and compare it with the outcome under supranational agency. In particular they show that when mergers are associated with no cost savings then national agencies are sufficient to review mergers. However, when mergers are associated with cost savings national authorities cannot be relied upon to prevent world welfare reducing mergers and hence in that case the role of a supranational antitrust agency becomes crucial.

Gerber (2002) argues that the policies of cooperation and convergence are fostered either through negotiations among the parties involved or through soft law institutions, like UNCTAD, ICN and OECD. International framework, on the other hand, is associated with hard law institutions, like the WTO. Further, the same policy or objective might not be suited for all types of conflicts. It is often argued that convergence and cooperation are better suited to deal with conflicts arising out of procedural

---

America and the Government of Canada as to Notification, Consultation and Cooperation with respect to the application of National Antitrust Laws, March9, 1984.

[8] In 1991, the US and European Union adopted cooperation agreement aimed at minimizing the impact of differences in their respective competition laws.

and interpretational differences. On the other hand, supranational agencies or international frameworks act better as substitutes for national agencies, in cases where national agencies fail to reach efficient outcomes. However, Gerber (2002), in this context, argues that the formation of an international frame work is not an alternative to either cooperation or convergence rather they can complement each other. For instance, convergence of the "content of law" of different countries under the monitoring of some international or supranational authority can be a possible way to resolve conflicts.

This paper shows that if the national competition authorities adopt a standard which yields the same outcome, irrespective of nationalities, then conflicts over merger review can be resolved. This can be interpreted as convergence to a common code or standard. Convergence, as Gerber (2002) argues can be attained voluntarily or via binding agreements. We show that convergence between national authorities, as discussed in this paper can be achieved under the supervision of supranational agency. Such a supranational agency can enforce binding agreements, act as a dispute settlement mechanism and provide a platform for negotiations over transfer payments in order to achieve an efficient outcome. In particular, we argue that an international agency like World Trade Organization (WTO) could ensure a conflict free efficient outcome of the nature discussed in this paper.

3. General model

Consider two identical countries $j=A,B$ with N_A and N_B number of firms, respectively. A Firm i belonging to Country j sells an amount h_{ij} in the home country and exports an amount e_{ij} to the other country. Then the demand function for Firm i in Country j is given by

$$P=a\text{-}bQ_j \tag{1}$$

where $Q_j=\left(\sum_{i=1}^{N_i} h_{ij}+\sum_{i=1}^{N_k} e_{ik}\right) \quad j,k=A,B, \quad j\neq k$

The profit of Firm i belonging to Country j, is given by

$$\pi_{ij}=(P_j-c)h_{ij}+(P_k-c)e_{ij} \tag{2}$$

where P_j is the price that the firm charges in its home Country j. P_k is the price that the firm charges on its exportable to Country k.

National welfare of Country j is given by

$$W_j = \frac{1}{2}Q_j^2 + \sum_{i=1}^{N_j} \pi_{ij} \tag{3}$$

where consumer surplus in Country j is

$$CS_j = \frac{1}{2}Q_j^2 \tag{4}$$

and Q_j is the total quantity demanded in Country j.

World/global welfare is given by

$$W_W = \frac{1}{2}Q_W^2 + \sum_j \sum_{i=1}^{N_j} \pi_{ij} \tag{5}$$

where $w = A+B$ i.e. world in this model consists of two countries A and B. Q_W is the total quantity demanded in both countries A and B together.

Assume that the firms choose their quantities simultaneously. Then the optimal quantities under Cournot competition is given by

$$e_{ij}^* = h_{ij}^* = \frac{a-c}{N+1} \quad \forall i,j \quad \text{where } N = N_A + N_B \tag{6}$$

Suppose now two firms want to merge. The paper then examines the conditions under which a merger is desirable for the merging firms and acceptable to the two countries with the jurisdiction to review the merger. The incentive to merge arises from cost savings in terms of a decrease in post-merger marginal cost for the merging firms, which is the efficiency argument.[9] Assume that the marginal cost in the competitive fringe remains unchanged after the merger between two firms.

In this model, merger has two effects. Firstly, it has an anticompetitive effect since the number of firms in the industry is reduced after merger.

[9] Cost savings in merger can arise due to increasing returns to scale, economies of scale and/or scope or fixed cost savings.

Secondly, the merger leads to an increase in efficiency through cost savings as discussed above. There are two possible cases in which two firms in this model can merge:

Case (i) Firms belonging to the same country merge

In particular, suppose two firms in Country A merge to form Firm M. Then the demand function can be written as follows

$$P_A = a - b\left(\sum_{i=1}^{N_A - 2} h_{iA} + h_M + \sum_{i=1}^{N_B} e_{iB}\right) \tag{7}$$

$$P_B = a - b\left(\sum_{i=1}^{N_B} h_{iB} + \sum_{i=1}^{N_A - 2} e_{iA} + e_M\right) \tag{8}$$

where h_M, e_M represent the production for the domestic market and export share of the merged firm's output, respectively.

The post-merger marginal cost of the merged firm is given by $c_M < c$. The profit of the merged firm is given by

$$\pi^M = (P_A - c_M)h_M + (P_A - c_M)e_M \tag{9}$$

The profit of a representative non-merged Firm i in Country j after merger of the two firms is given by

$$\pi_{ij}^M = \left(P_j - c\right)h_{ij} + \left(P_k - c\right)e_{ij}, \quad i \neq M \tag{10}$$

The welfare of Country A and B will then be

$$W_A^M = \frac{1}{2} Q_A^{M^2} + \sum_{i=1}^{N_A - 2} \pi_{iA}^M + \pi^M \tag{11}$$

$$W_B^M = \frac{1}{2} Q_B^{M^2} + \sum_{i=1}^{N_B} \pi_{iB}^M \tag{12}$$

The consumer surplus being

$$CS^M = \frac{1}{2} Q_j^{M^2} \tag{13}$$

World/global welfare is

$$W_w^M = \frac{1}{2} Q_W^{M^2} + \sum_j \sum_{i=1}^{N_j - 1} \pi_{ij}^M + \pi^M, \quad j \neq M \tag{14}$$

Case (ii) Firms belonging to two different countries merge

In this case, the demand function for each country would be

$$P_A = a - b\left(\sum_{i=1}^{N_A - 1} h_{iA} + h_{MA} + \sum_{i=1}^{N_B - 1} e_{iB} \right) \tag{15}$$

$$P_B = a - b\left(\sum_{i=1}^{N_B - 1} h_{iB} + h_{MB} + \sum_{i=1}^{N_A - 1} e_{iA} \right) \tag{16}$$

where the total output of the merged firm is

$$h_{MA} + h_{MB} = h_M \tag{17}$$

Here it is assumed that when firms from two different countries merge, the merged firm operates as a domestic firm in both countries, implying $e_M = 0$.[10]

The profit of the merged firm is given as

$$\pi^M = (P_A - c_M) h_{MA} + (P_A - c_M) h_{MB} \tag{18}$$

The profit of the non-merged firms and consumer surplus remain same as given by (10) and (13) respectively.

[10] This assumption is made for the ease of calculation. However, relaxing this assumption would not affect our results since we assume the countries to be identical and the firms to be symmetric.

The welfare of Country j will then be

$$W_j^M = \frac{1}{2} Q_j^{M^2} + \sum_{i=1}^{N_j - 1} \pi_{ij}^M + \frac{1}{2} \pi^M \tag{19}$$

World/global welfare is

$$W_w^M = \frac{1}{2} Q_W^{M^2} + \sum_j \sum_{i=1}^{N_j - 1} \pi_{ij}^M + \pi^M, \quad j \neq M \tag{20}$$

Again assuming that the merged and rival firms choose their quantities simultaneously after firms merge, the optimal quantities under Cournot competition can be obtained as follows:

$$e_{ij}^{M*} = h_{ij}^{M*} = \frac{a - 2c + c_M}{N}, \quad \forall i,j, \quad i \neq M \tag{21}$$

And the output of the merged firm is given as

$$\text{Under Case (i), } h_M = e_M = \frac{a - 2c_M + c}{N} \tag{22}$$

$$\text{Under Case (ii), } h_{MA} = e_{MB} = \frac{a - 2c_M + c}{N} \tag{23}$$

Substituting these values in the expression for profit, welfare and consumer surplus for the pre and post-merger cases, the corresponding optimized values are obtained. Next, define a variable

$$X^* = X^M - X \quad \text{where } X = \pi, CS, W \tag{24}$$

At $X^* = 0$ the value of the post-merger marginal cost (C_M) corresponds to the point of indifference between the pre and post-merger.

In this section the general Cournot model with $(N+1)$ firms has been derived and profits, consumer surplus and domestic and world welfare have been obtained. Following this, merger between two firms belonging to same country or different countries has been introduced. Finally, this section defines a variable which is the difference between the pre and post-merger welfare levels and obtains the threshold marginal cost which makes the firms, consumers and regulatory authorities of both countries indifferent between the pre and post-merger levels.

4. Welfare standards

This section discusses the possibilities of conflict in a merger between two firms under three different standards, namely, national welfare standard, consumer efficiency standard and world welfare standard (defined below). As mentioned earlier, following David (1987) these are referred to as reference standards.

In order to simplify our analysis, the paper considers the case of three firms variously distributed between two countries. For each of the cases, we get a value of the threshold post-merger marginal cost of the merging firms, at which the merging firms and the authorities are indifferent between the pre and post-merger situation under national, global or consumer surplus standard. Each of the parties concerned (i.e. merging firms or the authorities in the respective countries) would be interested in those mergers for which the post-merger marginal cost of the merged firm is lower than the respective critical levels, if the curve is negatively sloped at the threshold level. In case the curve is positively sloped at the threshold interest would lie on points which are higher than the threshold. The values are summarized in Table 1. First, the paper considers the possibility of conflict when the countries adopt a national welfare standard in Section 4.1. Next the paper allows the national competition authorities to converge to the global welfare and consumer surplus standard respectively in Section 4.2 and 4.3 respectively and analyze its effect on conflict and efficiency.

Table 1 Critical level of post-merger marginal cost of merged firms

X^*	C_M^X (Post merger marginal cost)		
	4.1.1	4.1.2	4.1.3
Country A Welfare	$1.07c$-$0.07a$	$0.984c$+$0.016a$	$1.1c$-$0.1a$
Country B Welfare	$1.55c$-$0.55a$ $1.25c$-$0.25a$	$1.25c$-$0.25a$	$1.03c$-$0.03a^+$
Global Welfare	$1.05c$-$0.05a$	$1.05c$-$0.05a$	$1.05c$-$0.05a$
Consumer Surplus	$1.25c$-$0.25a$	$1.25c$-$0.25a$	$1.25c$-$0.25a$

[+] Threshold corresponding to the effective welfare difference curve.

4.1 National welfare standard

National welfare of a country i is defined as the sum of the profit of the domestic firms and the consumer surplus. Here each country is only concerned with the welfare consequence of the merger on their own country, irrespective of its effect on the other country.

4.1.1 Both the merging firms belong to Country A and the rival firm belongs to Country B $(N_A = 2, N_B = 1)$

Country A is interested in maximizing the sum of consumer surplus and profit of the merging firms. Country B, on the other hand, is interested in maximizing the sum of consumer surplus and profit of rival firm. The results are given in Table 2. We analyze the results in terms of a diagram as given by Figure 1.

Table 2 Possibilities of conflict when both the merging firms belong to Country A and the rival firm belongs to Country B

	National Welfare			
Region	Left of E	Between E and F	Between F and G	Between G and H
Country A	Allows Merger	Allows	Allows	Does Not Allow
Country B	Allows Merger	Does Not Allow	Allows	Allows
Points of Conflict	No Conflict	Conflict	No Conflict	Conflict
Efficiency of Mergers	Efficient	Inefficient	Efficient by Global Standard/ Inefficient by Consumer Surplus Standard	Inefficient by Global Standard/Efficient by Consumer Surplus Standard

In Figure 1, the horizontal axis measures post-merger marginal cost of the merged firm, the vertical axis measures the post and pre-merger welfare difference curves of country A $\left(W_A^*\right)$ and B $\left(W_B^*\right)$ and the post and pre-merger profit difference curve of the merging firm π_M^*. In the figure, E and F correspond to the threshold level at which Country B is indifferent between pre and post-merger level of domestic welfare of Country B, while G corresponds to the threshold level at which Country A is indifferent between pre and post-merger level of domestic welfare of Country A. As evident from Figure 1, the welfare curve of Country B, in the relevant region, is a U-shaped curve, where both the roots are less than the pre-merger marginal cost level. In this case, there would be some possibilities of conflict. The zone of conflict is given by the region between E and F and the region to the right of G. Merger proposals to the left of E and in the region between F and G do not involve any conflict i.e. these are the "no conflict zone."

Figure 1 Possibilities of conflict when merging Firms 1 and 2 belong to Country A and the competing Firm 3 belongs to Country B

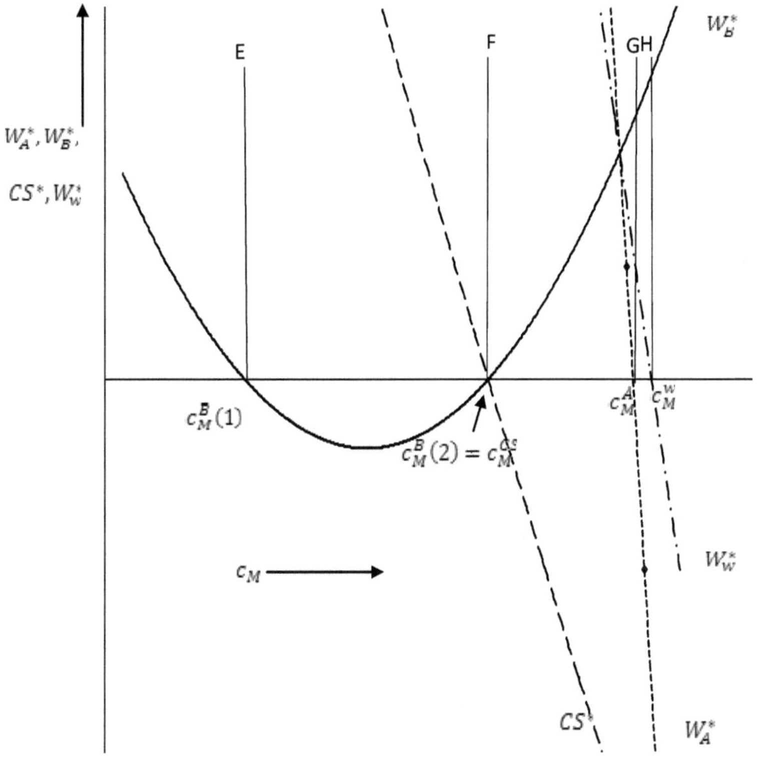

The salient features of Figure 1 are listed in Table 2.

4.1.2 *All firms belong to Country A* $\left(N_A = 2,\ N_B = 0\right)$

In this case, the only interest Country B has is the welfare of the consumers since there are no firms located in Country B, its welfare difference curve is given by CS^* and that of Country A is given by W_A^* in Figure 2. In Figure 2, I corresponds to the threshold level at which Country B is indifferent between the pre and post-merger level of domestic welfare of Country B, while K corresponds to the threshold level at which Country A is indifferent between the pre and post-merger level of domestic welfare of Country A.

Figure 2 Possibilities of merger when all firms belong to Country A

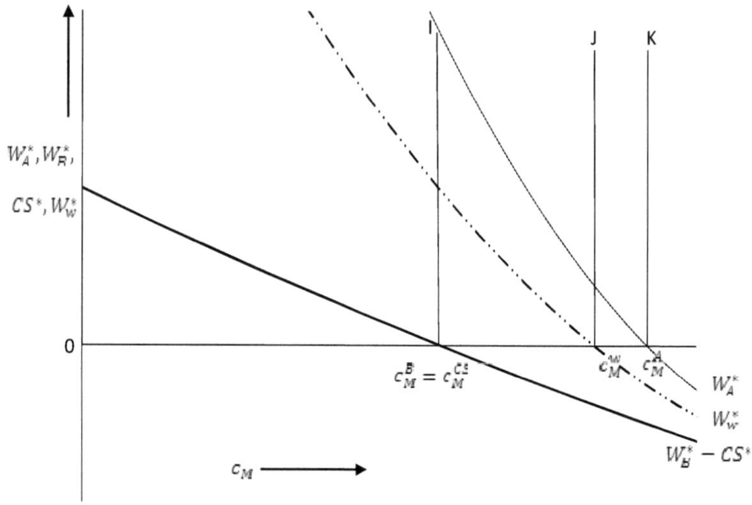

The salient features of Figures 2 are listed in Table3.

The threshold level of post-merger marginal cost of the merged firm corresponding to the welfare difference curve of Country A is greater than the pre-merger marginal cost of firms. However, no merger would be proposed to the right of K, the profit difference curve of the merging firms can be considered as the effective welfare difference curve of Country B. Here we observe that the zone of conflict, given by the region between I and K in Figure 2 shrinks as compared to Case 4.1.1, considering both the actual and effective welfare difference curve of Country A. The results are summarized in Table 3.

4.1.3 Firm 1 belongs to Country A, Firm 2 and 3 belongs to Country B $(N_A = 2,\ N_B = 2)$

When the merging firms belong to two different countries, we assume that the merged firms simply divide their profits into two equal shares, since cost is symmetric. This is shown in Figure 3. In Figure 3, N and P correspond to the threshold levels at which Country A and B are indifferent between pre and post-merger levels of their respective country's domestic welfare levels.

Table 3 Possibilities of conflict when all firms belong to Country A

	National Welfare			
Region	Left of I	Between I and J	Between J and K	To the Right of K
Country A	Allows Merger	Allows Merger	Allows	No Merger Proposed
Country B	Allows Merger	Does Not Allow	Does Not Allow	No Merger Proposed
Points of Conflict	No Conflict	Conflict	Conflict	-
Efficiency of Mergers	Efficient	Efficient from Welfare Standard/ Inefficient from Consumer Standard	Not Efficient by Global and Consumer Welfare Standard	Efficient

Figure 3 Possibilities of merger when merging Firms 1 and 2 belong to two different Countries A and B respectively, rival Firm 3 belongs to Country B

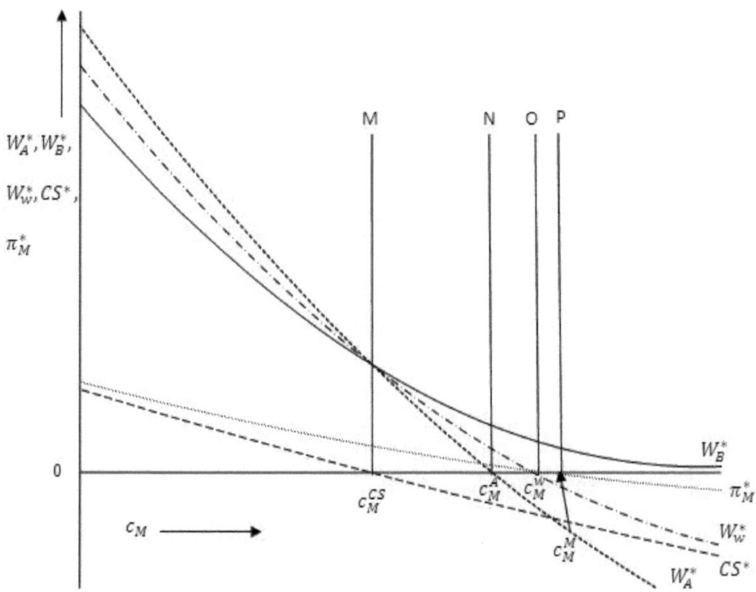

The salient features of Figure 3 are listed in Table 4.

Again, W_A^* and W_B^* are the welfare difference curves of Country A and B respectively. The zone of conflict is undefined, since Country B always lies on the positive quadrant. This implies that any point to the right of N would result in a conflict between the two countries. However, there would not be any merger proposed by the merging firms in the region to the right of P. Hence, this can be considered as the effective welfare difference curve of Country B. Thus the effective zone of conflict lies between N and P, while the region to the left of N is the zone of no conflict. The results are given in Table 4.

Table 4 Firm 1 belongs to Country A, Firm 2 and 3 belong to Country B

	National Welfare				
Region	Left of M	Between M and N	Between N and O	Between O and P	Right of P
Country A	Allows	Allows	Does not Allow	Does not Allow	No Merger Proposed
Country B	Allows	Allows	Allows	Allows	No Merger Proposed
Points of Conflict	No Conflict	No Conflict	Conflict	Conflict	-
Efficiency of Mergers	Efficient	Inefficient by Consumer Standard/ Efficient by Welfare Standard	Inefficient in World Welfare Terms/ Efficient by Consumer Standard	Efficient by Both Global and Consumer Standard	Efficient

The results of Section 4.1.1, 4.1.2 and 4.1.3 can be summarized in terms of the following proposition:

Proposition 1 When consumer preferences and distributions are identical across both countries,

a. Conflict between national antitrust authorities is less when the rival firm and the two merging firms belong to the same country as compared to when the rival firm belongs to a different country.

b. Conflict between national authorities is less when the two merging firms lie in different countries as compared to when they lie in the same country.

Thus the zone of conflict is lesser when merging firms and the rival firm lie in the same country than when they lie in a different country. This result holds even when the effective welfare difference curve for Country A, i.e. the profit difference curve of the merging firms is considered.

4.2 *World/global welfare standard*

Suppose, we assume that the two countries A and B adopt a world/global welfare standard as defined by the sum of profit of all firms, irrespective of their nationality and consumers' surplus. In that case both countries would converge to the same standard and hence there would not be any conflict. When the countries adopt a global welfare standard, the outcome of the review process is no longer affected by the distribution of firms across the countries. We examine the effect of the shift from the national welfare curve to the world welfare curve for both countries, for each of the cases discussed in the previous section. In this context, we consider whether the shift from national welfare to global welfare standard is efficient for the individual countries. In this study, efficiency is measured in terms of national welfare. As mentioned earlier, an outcome under the global welfare standard would be considered efficient for a particular country, if the welfare of the country is at least as much as it were if the country adopted its national welfare standard to review the merger. The value of post-merger marginal cost of the merged firm $\left(W_A^*\right)$ which makes one country indifferent between the pre and post-merger global welfare levels is given by

$$c_M^W = 1.05c - 0.05a \tag{25}$$

Plotting this as point H in Figure 1, we observe, for Case 4.1.1, that the national welfare difference curve for Country A lies to the left of the global welfare difference curve, implying that Country A would be approving more mergers if it adopts a global welfare standard i.e. Country A would have to approve some mergers which are welfare decreasing in terms of its national welfare. However, so far as Country B is concerned, it will approve lesser number of mergers if it shifts to the world welfare standard.

For Case 4.1.2, the global welfare difference curve lies to the left of the welfare difference curve for Country A. This is given in Figure 2, where point J gives the threshold level corresponding to the global welfare difference curve. This in turn implies that for Country A, adopting a global welfare standard would imply approving lesser number of mergers as compared to their national welfare standard. However, the global welfare difference curve of Country B lies to the left of the global welfare difference curve and hence for Country B adopting a global welfare standard would mean approving some mergers which the countries would not have approved under national welfare standard. This means that some of the mergers approved by adopting the global welfare standard may not be welfare increasing for Country B.

Finally, we consider, Case 4.1.3. If we incorporate the global welfare difference curve in Figure 3, we observe that it lies to the right of the country welfare difference curve of Country A (the threshold level being given by point O), but to the left of the effective welfare difference curve of Country B. Thus, when Country A and B adopt a global welfare standard, it would imply a rightward shift for A and a leftward shift for Country B, which in turn implies Country A would be approving more mergers than when they adopt a national welfare standard, while Country B would approve less mergers.

Proposition 2 Global welfare standard resolves conflicts between countries over merger but does not always yield an efficient outcome. Thus, when the countries adopt a global welfare standard, the outcome turns out to be inefficient for at least one country.

4.3 Consumer surplus standard

If both countries adopt a consumer surplus standard, then there would not be any conflict irrespective of the distribution of the firms across the countries. This would imply that only mergers with substantial cost savings would be approved. This, in turn, would lead to an efficient outcome for Country A and partially efficient outcome for Country B in Case 4.1.1 as evident from Figure 1. If the post-merger marginal cost of the merging firm lies between $C_M^B(1)$ and $C_M^B(2)$, then by consumer welfare standard (threshold level given by F where $C_M^B(2) = C_M^{CS}$) the mergers would be approved but it would be welfare reducing for Country B. Hence in this range, shifting from the national welfare standard to consumer welfare standard would be inefficient for Country B. In Case 4.1.2 and Case 4.1.3, the shift from national welfare to consumer welfare standard would lead to an efficient outcome, since in these cases the consumer surplus difference curve lies to the extreme left (the corresponding threshold levels being given by J in Figure 2 and M in Figure 3 respectively), implying that consumer surplus standard would involve maximum cost savings.

Proposition 3 When consumers are homogeneous across countries, adopting a consumer surplus standard resolves any conflict between countries. The outcome is efficient, in general but may turn out to be inefficient when the two merging firms and the rival firm belong to two different countries.

Thus, we observe that in general a shift from the national welfare standard to consumer welfare standard leads to an increase in efficiency as measured in national welfare terms and at the same time resolves conflict. The only exception to it is the region given by $C_M^B(1) < C_M < C_M^B(2)$ in Case 4.1.1 as shown in Figure 1.

So far we have assumed that the two countries are identical and the firms are homogeneous. Relaxing these assumptions would have an impact on the extent of conflict. This involves a case by case analysis, involving the interaction of firm distribution and asymmetry in firm and market characteristics, which is beyond the scope of this paper and has been dealt in a companion paper Mehra (2008). Mehra (2008) shows that when the firms are asymmetric (where asymmetry is captured by differences in the cost structure), merger between firms belonging to the same country involves greater possibilities of conflicts, with the increase in the cost asymmetry across the firms. However, if the merger occurs between firms belonging to different countries, then the results are ambiguous and depend on the initial cost structure of the merging firms. Further, Mehra (2008) also shows that when the country or market sizes of the two countries differ, the greater the difference between the markets of the two countries with jurisdiction, higher is the possibility of conflict, irrespective of the distribution of the firms across the countries.

Thus, we observe that differences in the firm and country characteristics have an impact on the magnitude of the possibilities of conflict. However, this does not affect the implications of the results for standardization, which we discuss in the next section.

5. Implications for standardization

This paper, as seen in Section 4.2, proposes convergence to a common standard namely a world/global welfare standard and consumer surplus standard as a means to resolve conflict between jurisdictions. The next question that arises is how this convergence can be achieved. This section attempts to address this question.

Convergence, as Gerber (2002) argues, can be achieved either through independent choices i.e. voluntarily or through international agreements. This paper shows that when both countries with jurisdiction to review mergers converge to similar standards, namely, global welfare or the consumer surplus standard, conflicts over mergers do not occur. However, the problem in such a case is that it may not always be individually rational for any country to adopt these standards as they might be welfare reducing for it as shown in Proposition 2 and 3 in Section 4.2 and 4.3 respectively. Thus, it is difficult to expect a country to adopt the global welfare or consumer surplus standard voluntarily. Hence, convergence of rules and procedures may not resolve the problem unless they are enforced. In such cases the role of a supranational agency becomes crucial. Particularly, it becomes important to define the nature and function of the supranational authority in such a way that it suits the need of the problem and is able to discharge its functions on grounds of non-discrimination and efficiency.

The literature discusses various possibilities. Most important among them being the development of competition forums based on voluntary principles, such as the International Competition Network (ICN) and the inclusion of competition policy within the WTO framework (Bode and Budzinski 2005). The paper argues that of the two existing institutions, World Trade Organization (WTO) is the one that can be entrusted with the responsibility of acting as a supranational agency to govern international antitrust pertaining to conflicts discussed in the paper. WTO being an organization based on the principle of non-discrimination makes it difficult for countries to pursue their national interest at the expense of other countries. This significantly reduces the scope of the kind of divergent and conflicting decisions in international cases as discussed in the paper. Overtime WTO has proved to be competent in dealing with conflicts in international trade issues and also has a reliable dispute settlement body that can be used to handle international competition related conflicts. Further, the experience in guiding negotiations and enforcing binding rules allows WTO to assure protection of competition worldwide.

The key issues involved in the role of WTO as a supranational agency, as pertaining to the issues discussed in this paper, are enforcement of binding rules and the provision of a dispute resolution mechanism. As discussed earlier, it is difficult to ensure voluntary adoption of the consumer or world welfare standard by nations. In this context, informal networks like ICN based on principles of voluntary acceptance of policies, as argued by Budzinski (2004), may not be able to shift the focus of countries from their national markets and welfare towards a more global approach. On the other hand, the competition policy under the WTO approach can ensure the adoption of global welfare through its binding rules.

Given WTO's involvement in trade related issues over the years, it has its own dispute settlement body. Further, its reliability and competence in handling issues of international conflict has been well-established on grounds of fairness and legitimacy (Bode and Budzinski 2005). Thus, conditions of non-compliance or alleged violation of the terms of agreement or non adoption of the agreed substantive standard can be handled effectively under the WTO approach. On the other hand, although ICN can reduce the possibilities of conflict resulting out of interpretational difference because of its cooperative arrangements, it would not be able to handle serious conflicts arising out of national interests as dealt in this paper.

Moreover, even if a merger is welfare increasing under the global welfare or consumer surplus standard, it adversely affects some groups. For instance, in Case 4.1.1, when the post-merger marginal cost lies in the region between G and H in Figure 1, the conflict leads to an outcome which would otherwise have been efficient from the global welfare perspective but turns out to be detrimental for consumers. Similarly, the consumer surplus standard might allow mergers which are global welfare reducing, but are welfare increasing for consumers. Such a case however does not arise in the context of this paper.

One of the ways in which a globally efficient outcome can be ensured is transfer payments from the countries benefiting from the merger to the losers. Global welfare standard with the provision of transfer payments is an interface compatibility standard (David 1987) in the sense that decision made in accordance with this standard leads to identical outcomes in both the jurisdictions. Thus, inclusion of transfer payment to the global standards shifts the paradigm of standards from reference or definition to interface compatibility. Here it bears noting that in the presence of transfer payments the national welfare standard includes firm profits, consumer surplus and transfer payments. The quantum of transfer payments can be arrived at through various ways. One alternative is to allow Nash bargaining between the two jurisdictions over the division of the total welfare after merger.[11] We adopt the symmetric Nash bargaining solution to determine transfer payment, since both the countries are identical. Here the total surplus obtained after merger following the world/global welfare standard is split between the two jurisdictions.

The global welfare attained after a merger is denoted by Π.

$$\begin{aligned}\Pi &= \frac{(a-2c_M+c)^2}{9}+\frac{(a-2c+c_M)^2}{9}+\frac{(2a-c-c_M)^2}{18} \\ &= \frac{8(a-c)^2+11(c-c_M)^2+8(a-c)(c-c_M)}{18}\end{aligned} \tag{26}$$

The disagreement points of the two jurisdictions are their pre-merger welfare levels. For Case 4.1.1, these are given by

[11] There are other norms that can be applied to allow bargaining between parties. For a detailed discussion see Anbarci, et. al. (2002).

$$d_A = \frac{2(a-c)^2}{16} + \frac{9(a-c)^2}{16} = \frac{17(a-c)^2}{64} \tag{27}$$

$$d_B = \frac{(a-c)^2}{16} + \frac{9(a-c)^2}{64} = \frac{13(a-c)^2}{64} \tag{28}$$

Following the Nash bargaining solution, the post-bargaining shares S_i^W of each of the jurisdictions is given by,

$$S_i^W = d_i + \frac{1}{2}\left[\Pi - d_i - d_j\right], \quad i,j = A,B, \quad i \neq j \tag{29}$$

At $C_M = C_M^W, [\Pi - d_A - d_B] = 0$

Hence, both the countries get their pre-merger welfare levels.

At any $0 < C_M < C_M^W, [\Pi - d_A - d_B] > 0$

Therefore, $S_A^W > d_A$ and $S_B^W > d_B$

The amount of transfer in general is $S_i^W - W_i^M, \quad i = A,B$.

For instance for Case 4.1.1, the amount of transfer is $W_B^W - S_B^M$ which in turn is equal to $S_A^W - W_A^M$.

Above, we saw that a simple transfer of payment is possible from the country whose post-merger national welfare is higher as compared to the pre-merger level to the country whose post-merger national welfare level is less than the pre-merger level under the global welfare standard. The level of transfer varies with the level of cost savings. In the context of consumer surplus standard, except for a particular range in Case 4.1.1, a shift from national to the consumer welfare standard yields a conflict free efficient outcome. Hence, in this case there is no transfer payment required.

Given that transfer payments are possible, it is important that the negotiations associated with the transfer are carried out at low cost. Agencies like WTO, as Guzman (2001) argues, provide a forum for these agreements to be carried out at minimum costs. Moreover, the dispute settlement mechanism also ensures that the countries involved would credibly commit to a standard competition policy. In this context, since ICN deals exclusively with competition issues, it cannot facilitate transfer payments and concessions in other areas.

However, it has been argued by some that WTO is structurally incapable of handling the 'unique body of antitrust law' (Schnell 2004). This concern is reciprocated by Tarullo (2000) who argues that WTO being a trade organization involves norms which do not conform to the regulatory role of competition policy. Further, Davison (2002) argues, due to strategic bargaining, WTO negotiations might not lead to preferential outcome. These criticisms against the WTO stand merit. A solution to this would involve a change in the institutional design of WTO to suit the needs of competition policy on one hand and introduction of more transparent procedures on the other. However this argument does not provide a convincing reason to avoid introducing competition policy in the WTO as a solution to the potential conflicts discussed in this paper.

Thus, the issue of conflict resolution arising from differences in the way an international merger affects national welfare of different countries, as discussed in this paper, can be handled effectively by WTO with its superior ability in implementing binding international rules and the existence of a dispute settlement body, combined with the possibilities of arranging for transfer payments or concessions. Further, despite the imperfections in WTO, it can still be considered as the best available platform to ensure compliance in competition policy pertaining to review of international mergers as it has "universal representation, is relatively transparent and is experienced in handling international negotiations and agreements" (Guzman 2001).

This paper, as mentioned earlier, focuses on the role of the supranational agency vis-à-vis inter-jurisdictional conflicts. However, competition policy involves many more complex issues which have not been dealt in this paper and in those cases the role of WTO needs to be examined and compared with that of ICN and other forms of cooperation and convergence which are beyond the scope of this paper.[12]

6. Conclusion

In this paper, we analyze the welfare implication of a horizontal merger between two firms in a two country, three firm oligopoly framework characterized by Cournot competition. We find that when there are marginal cost savings involved in a merger, then if both countries with

[12] For discussion on these issues, see Gerber (2002), Hoekman and Mavroidis (2002), and Bode and Budzinski (2005).

jurisdiction, adopt a consumer welfare standard or global welfare, there would be no conflict. In case of international mergers, however, countries are often assumed to maximize their national welfare. We show that under national welfare standards, conflicts between jurisdictions of different countries can occur. Particularly, in such cases, there is a possibility that the authorities might ban a global welfare increasing merger, as seen in this paper. Further, conflicts also depend on the distribution of firms and consumers across the two countries.

To resolve conflicts adoption of a uniform standard is essential. This calls for adoption of consumer surplus standard and/or a global welfare standard, which is a definition or reference standard. However, adopting a global welfare and consumer surplus standard alone does not always ensure an efficient outcome. This brings the issue of transfer payment from the countries which experience an increase in welfare from the merger to the countries which experience a reduction in welfare to ensure overall efficiency in a merger on one hand. On the other, it also implies that since adopting such standards may not be advantageous to both countries simultaneously, one or more countries may not agree to adopt such standards voluntarily. These issues together suggest that national authorities cannot be relied upon to implement standards to ensure a conflict free efficient outcome in the context of international merger. Hence there arises the need of a supranational authority to enforce such standards on the individual countries.

Thus, we observe that international antitrust encompasses two issues. On the one hand, there is the issue of conflict in the decisions. On the other, there is a question of efficiency which can be ensured through transfer of gains from gainers to losers. We show that such transfer payments are possible through Nash bargaining. In such a case the standards adopted become standards of interface compatibility. In this context, we find that institutions like, WTO, provide an avenue for resolving conflicts that arise due to national antitrust agencies adopting practices which protect their domestic market, without taking into consideration the effect of their policies on foreign economies. Simultaneously, they can also facilitate negotiations to ensure transfer or redistribution of the gain since WTO as an organization provides a platform to deal with many issues through which such transfers can be ensured. While a lot many criticisms against the WTO approach need consideration, none of them are strong enough to rule out the possibility of WTO assuming the role of a supranational authority in international merger cases pertaining to the issues discussed in this paper.

One limitation of this study is that its analysis is based on the distribution of three firms, for computational ease, rather than a continuum of firms. Moreover, this study is based on assumptions of homogenous consumers across countries and identical firms. This, however, may not be the case. This criticism is resolved in the companion paper Mehra (2008) where we examine the implication of differences in firm and market size on the possibilities of conflict in cross-border mergers and acquisitions. One further limitation of this study is that it does not provide a direct link between the issues of conflict and the choice of institutions to resolve such conflicts; rather it draws implications about the kind of institutions which can discharge such functions. This can be a subject matter of future research in this area.

Acknowledgements

I would like to thank all participants of the Dresden SCR Conference 2007, seminar participants at the University of Bath, January 2008 and two anonymous referees for their valuable comments and suggestions. I owe special thanks to Ajit Mishra, P. G Babu, Manfred Holler and Vikas Kumar for their comments and support. I am grateful to Institute of Law and Economics, University of Hamburg and Indira Gandhi Institute of Development Research, India for their financial assistance.

References

Anbarci, N., Skaperdas S. and Syropoulos, C. (2000), Comparing Bargaining Solutions in the Shadow of Conflict: How Norms against Threats Can Have Real Effects, *Journal of Economic Theory* 1-16.

Barros, P.P. and Cabral, L. (1994), Merger Policy in Open Economies, *European Economic Review* 38: 1041-1055.

Blumenthal, W. (2004), The Challenge of Sovereignty and the Mechanisms of Convergence, *Antitrust Law Journal* 72: 267-278.

Bode, M. and Budzinski, O. (2005), *Competing Ways towards International Antitrust: The WTO Versus ICN*, Marburg Economics Working Paper No. 03-2005.

Budzinski, O. (2004), The International Competition Network: Prospects and Limits on the Road towards International Competition Governance, *Competition and Change* 8: 223-242.

David, P.A. (1987), Some New Standards for the Economics of Standardization in the Information Age, in: P. Dasgupta and P. Stoneman (eds.), *Economic Policy and Technical Performance*, Cambridge: Cambridge University Press.

David, P.A. and Steinmueller, W.-E. (1994), Economics of Compatibility Standards and Competition in Telecommunication Networks, *Information Economics and Policy* 6(3-4): 217-241.

De la Mano, M. (2002), For the Customer's Sake: The Competitive Effects of Efficiencies in European Merger Control, *EC Enterprise Papers No. 11.*

Dixit, A. (1984), International Trade Policy for Oligopolistic Industries, *The Economic Journal* 94: 1-16.

Evenett, S.J. and Hijzen, A. (2006), *Conformity with International Recommendations on Merger Reviews: An Economic Perspective on "Soft Law,"* University of Nottingham Research Paper No. 2006/04.

Farrell, J. and Katz, M.-L. (2006), The Economics of Welfare Standards in Antitrust, *Competition Policy International* 2(2): 3-39.

Farrell, J. and Shapiro, C. (1990), Horizontal Mergers: An Equilibrium Analysis, *American Economic Review* 80: 107-126.

Fugina, K. (2006), Merger Control Review in the United States and the European Union: Working towards Conflict Resolution, *Northwestern Journal of International Law and Business* 26: 471-489.

Gerber, D.J. (2002), The U.S. Europe Conflict over the Globalization of Antitrust Law: A Legal Experience Perspective, *New England Law Review* 34: 123-143.

Gifford, D.J. and Kudrle, R.-T. (2005), Rhetoric and Reality in the Merger Standard of the United States, Canada and the European Union, *ANTITRUST Law Journal* 72(2) :423-470.

Gorinson, S.M. and Pambianco, R. (2002), U.S and European Merger Policies Move towards Convergence, *Washington Legal Foundation* 17(30):1-4.

Guzman, A. (2001), Antitrust and International Federalism, *New York University Law Review* 76: 1142-1163.

Harrison, M.J. (2003), *U.S. versus EU Competition Policy: The Boeing-McDonnell Douglas Merger*, American Consortium on European Union Studies (ACES) Cases on Transatlantic Relations, No. 2. Manuscript.

Head, K. and Reis, J. (1997), International Mergers and Welfare under Decentralized Competition Policy, *Canadian Journal of Economics* XXX: 1104-1123.

Heyer, K. (2006), *Welfare Standards and Merger Analysis: Why Not the Best?*, EAG Discussion Paper 06-8.

Mehra, P. (2010), *Technical Appendix to Supranational Agency: A Solution for Conflict in International Mergers?*, available at: http://works.bepress.com/poonam_mehra/16.

Mehra, P. (2008), *Conflicts in Cross-border Mergers: Effect of Firm and Market Size*, IGIDR Working Paper No. WP-2008-030.

Motta, M. (2004), *Competition Policy: Theory and Practice*, Cambridge: Cambridge University Press.

Reckens, A. (2007), Welfare Standards, Substantive Tests, and Efficiency Considerations in Merger Policy: Defining the Efficiency Defense, *Journal of Competition Law and Economics* 3(2): 149–179.

Sarah, G.T. (2008), *Cross-border Mergers and the Experience of Developing Countries*, CUTS CCIER Briefing Paper No. 11/2008.

Schnell, D.K. (2004), All Bundled up: Bringing the Failed GE/Honeywell Merger in from the Cold, *Cornell International Law Journal* 37: 217-261.

Tarullo, D.K. (2000), Norms and Institutions in Global Competition Policy, *American Journal of International Law* 94: 478-504.

Venit, J.S. and Kolasky, W.-J. (2000), Substantive Convergence and Procedural Dissonance in Merger Review, in: S.J. Evenett, A. Lehmann and B. Steil (eds.),

Antitrust Goes Global: What Future for Transatlantic Cooperation?, London: Royal Institute of International Affairs, Brookings Institution.

Homo Oeconomicus 27(4): 575–595 (2011)

www.accedoverlag.de

Standardization of Real Property Rights and Public Regulations: A Terminological Approach

Jesper M. Paasch
KTH Royal Institute of Technology, Stockholm, Sweden, and, Lantmäteriet [Swedish mapping, cadastral and land registration authority], Gävle, Sweden
(eMail: jesper.paasch@lm.se)

Abstract This article discusses a standardized, terminological approach for describing real property rights and public regulations. Real property rights are e.g. the right to perform some activities on another's real property such as rights of way or to take water from a well. Public regulations are officially imposed burdens like planning regulations, etc. Real property rights and regulations are an important part of the legal domain and function as instruments of conflict resolution regulating the use of real property. The outcome of the approach is a classification of rights and regulations in order to further cross-border transfer of real property information.

JEL Classifications H89, K11, K39, N79, Z00
Keywords legal standardization, terminology, real property rights, public regulations, legal modelling, land administration

1. Introduction

This article is a revised version of an article previously published by this author in the EURAS Yearbook of Standardization in 2008 (Paasch 2008). The aim of this article is to describe the theoretical basis for a standardized approach named the Legal Cadastral Domain Model, LCDM, previously published by this author (Paasch 2005). The model allows the classification of real property rights and public regulations without any regard to the jurisdiction they are valid in. It is therefore possible to compare seemingly different rights and regulations on a pan-national basis. Real property rights are e.g. the right to perform some activities on another's real property such as rights of way or to take water from a well. Public regulations are officially imposed burdens like planning regulations, etc. Real property rights and regulations are an important part of the legal domain and func-

ISBN 978-3-89265-075-1 ISSN 0943-0180

tion as instruments of conflict resolution regulating the use of real property. The model is described in Section 5.

The model is a contribution to the ongoing research towards achieving cost-effective cross border information services, focussing on a terminological approach describing real property rights and public regulations. The purpose is to contribute to the research on real property transactions by producing a terminological framework which can be used for grouping existing real property rights and regulations. A "neutral" terminological framework would not interfere with the different legal systems in existence, but make it possible to create a standardized terminology for classification.

The cadastral domain is a common term for maps, databases and other registers managing cartographic and legal information regulating the ownership and use of real property, private and public access rights, public regulations, land registration systems, etc. These rights and regulations are fundamental instruments for effective land use, land management and conflict resolution. However, the means of conflict solutions are not standardized internationally since they originate from different legal traditions and cultural backgrounds.

The article is aimed for readers with different backgrounds. Primary target groups are land surveyors, real property lawyers, knowledge engineers and other professions dealing with research in real property legislation and classification in connection with cross-border transfer of real property information. However, this author hopes the article also will be of interest to others who study the concept of standardization and related issues. Some parts may seem obvious to some readers, but the aim is to introduce a categorization of real property rights and regulations to a broad academic and professional audience.

The article does not deal with any organizational aspects or the resources needed or the normative power to achieve the intended classification. The history and development of the different systems of law is also outside the scope of the article.

2. The legal domain

Law is an instrument stating what is allowed or not allowed in society, i.e. what is legal or illegal, thus commanding citizens how to behave. These "commands"[1] issued by a recognised authority provide a framework in which a society and individuals can operate. They also decide who has the

---

[1] In this article, "command" used as a general expression and does not refer to any specific type of legislation or legal rule.

right to act or not to act according to the law and their interpretation influences all sectors of our daily life, from how we behave towards each other in traffic to e.g. how to regulate ownership of material and immaterial things.

Without the security of a legal framework to ensure individual rights, organised society as we know it, and perhaps taken for granted, would not be able to function. In any large group of people, general rules and principles must be the main instrument of social control, and not particular directions given to each individual separately, as mentioned by Hart (1961: 124), and, as correctly pointed out by Watson (2004: 2), must be authoritative. Thomas Hobbes pointed out that life would be "solitary, poor, nasty, brutish and short" without a common power to regulate the activities within society. In order to avoid this depressing situation it is necessary to have instruments of government to secure the rights granted by society and resolve any conflict(s) of interest which may occur.

The internationalisation of law is an old dream, leading to visions of legal integration or even unification (Delmas-Marty 2004). For example, the French legal scholar Eugéne Lerminier (1803-1857) expressed that "we may say that there will be a world State, and say it, not simply a chimera, or utopia, but as a real and powerful fact" (Delmas-Marty 2004: 247). However, as Delmas-Marty (2004: 246) correctly has pointed out, Lerminier was undoubtedly a little quick of the mark and there is today no genuine attempt aiming at the creation of a "world State."

There is no given structure in law helping us to achieve any standardization. Numerous theories regarding the nature, structure and content of law exist and different theories have been presented and discussed by legal scholars during the last two and a half centuries. Some of the more recent contributors to the discussion are Wahlgren (1992), Susskind (1987), Harris (1979) and Peczenik (1974). The legal domain has been described as being a "well of legislative source materials with conceptually-shaped buckets of many kinds, and we will then bring up rules, standards, and laws of any favoured pattern" (Harris 1979: 92).[2] These "buckets of law" must be described in one way or another in order to bring structure and order to the domain. One attempt to structure the legal domain is to divide the legal domain into smaller parts, starting with the fundamental question regarding what law is and to the development of different legal "families" or other systems of classification. It must be stressed that there are no official legal "families" or classification of legal systems. Any classification is made on the conditions and principles made up and used by the classifier, and are therefore to some extent subjective. Examples of such families are the

[2] Cited in Susskind (1987: 118).

Common Law family on the British Isles and the Civil Law families in Continental Europe.[3] The dividing of law into distinct and more manageable components has been - and still is - subject for discussion among legal scholars, such as Hoecke (2004), Zweigert and Kötz (1995), Susskind (1987) and Hart (1961).

No legal framework is however effective without communication. The use of words and their correct interpretation has always played a central role for communication and thus for culture, and the legal domain is no exception (Glenn 2004). A thorough and correct understanding of the specific legal terms we use when working on mutual tasks and projects are therefore of vital importance for the success of our enterprises. Any description must be understandable by all parties involved and any success is based on the achievement of understanding. However, understanding requires a defined and accepted terminology; otherwise we will not be able to understand correctly what is meant. There are a multitude of different terms used in the legal domain. As a result, terminology and semantics has been subject for much research among legal scholars and philosophers, e.g. Hoecke (2004) and Nuopponen (1994).

However, the problem of furthering a correct understanding has not newly arisen. For example, Ogden and Richards have as early as 1923 eloquently described the problems of understanding as:

> There is no doubt an Art in saying something when there is nothing to be said, but it is equally certain that there is an Art no less important of saying clearly what one wishes to say when there is an abundance of material; and conversation will seldom attain even the level of an intellectual pastime if adequate methods of interpretation are not also available (Ogden and Richards 1923: 8-9).

One of these methods of interpretation of the world around us, consisting of a countless number of objects, allowing us to rise to and above the level of an intellectual pastime is to apply the principles of terminology to the domain which has to be discussed. Without any agreement, it is impossible to achieve any communication or comparison. This has been noted by e.g. Ekelöf who stated that "it is even of rather huge practical importance that certain and clear-cut terms are commonly accepted as representatives for different elements in the process of legal deduction" (Ekelöf 1945: 221).[4]

---

[3] Common law is "the unwritten law based originally on common customs and precedent but now administered by the courts" (UNECE 2004: 56). Civil law is "the law laid down by the State regarding the rights of inhabitants" (UNECE 2004: 56).

[4] Author's translation from Swedish.

The common nominator for all legal families is that they are expressed in natural languages. With natural languages there is always the risk of misunderstanding, since natural languages are not predefined and clear systems of communication. Words might mean one thing in one legal (sub-)domain and another thing in another legal (sub-) domain. Therefore, any comparison of legal systems must include a study of to what extent the words used in the legal systems which are subject for comparison bear the same meaning (Hoecke 2004: 175). Without a defined terminology describing the subject or domain that is being researched, every attempt to further a common terminological approach will forever be shrouded into mystery.

Legal reasoning is a complex process and diversity might be explained by that researchers have concentrated on different areas of the legal domain and "at a number of things that initially stand out as dissimilarities might be explained by the lack of inconsistency in the use of terminology" (Wahlgren 1992: 43). Nevertheless, without an established terminology, nothing can be compared or harmonized. There are several factors to take into account when applying terminology in the legal domain. A law is not always easy to understand and the use of words in the legal domain is surrounded by the same semantic problems of interpretation of words in other domains. Peczenik (1974) illustrates this by using the word "house" as an example, and notes that "cabin" or "hut" under some conditions can be called a house and sometimes not. Even if a word or expression is ambivalent or vague, it is not interesting to describe every possible interpretation and focus is made on the specific case where the word or expression is used (Peczenik 1974: 61f). A problem is that the legislator cannot foresee all possible future use of a law and vague words and expressions might leave room for different interpretations, sometimes due to situations that were not present when the law was made. However, legal institutions are obligated to follow the intentions of the law, even if it might result in words and legal practices differing from each other within a legal system, or even worse, within a single law (Peczenik 1974). Strömberg has stated that knowledge in conceptual analysis can be of help in research regarding the use of legal tools. However, such knowledge does not "completely scatter the existing obscurity of how laws and precedents shall be interpreted and how the existing legal body shall be used" (Peczenik 1974: 19).[5]

The semantic problems of the legal domain described above are complicated even further, when concepts originating from different legal systems might describe the same thing, but are called different names, or worse, when terms originating from different legal systems are used to describe

[5] Strömberg, T., cited in Peczenik, (1974: 19). Author's translation from Swedish.

more or less the same legal concept. For example, a specific type of right regulating the (partial) use of another real property, "easement," is, according to Hoecke (2004: 174), rather similar to another real property right, "servitude," but is not the same. However, recent guidelines on real property units, published by the United Nations, describes a servitude as an easement or right of one real property over another (UNECE 2004: 61).

The, in this author's eyes, more or less fruitless initiatives of different legal movements to solve the problems of semantics and terminology within the legal domain have been reported by several authors, e.g. Zweigert and Kötz (1995), Wahlgren (1992) and Susskind (1987). However, the legal movement of conceptualism has gone further than most others, claiming that everything could be described and defined by applying methods originating in the natural sciences. German legal scholars were in the second half of the 19th century much in favour of the ideas described in conceptualism (in German: *Begriffsjurisprudenz*), admiring the achievement of exact results in the realms of natural science and striving at such exact results in their own, legal field, as reported by several legal scholars, e.g. Wahlgren (1992), Susskind (1987), Strömholm (1981) and Peczenik (1974).

The aim of conceptualism was to find legal concepts without any faults and every legal interpretation should have only one, right solution. In other words, law was in those circles seen as a standardized system of rules allowing only one, and correct, answer, trusting in the emerging principles of the natural sciences, where everything seems possible to be understood and explained. An example is the structure of the above mentioned, servitude. Puchta (1798-1846) produced a "conceptual pyramid" of the "logical components" of an "easement" (i.e. a property's right in another property). An easement is, according to Puchta, first of all a right, then a property right, then a property right belonging to a person, then a property right regulating a "thing" belonging to another person, then a property right over a property belonging to another person, then a right to in some way use a real property belonging to another person.[6] The concept is shown in Figure 1.

This logical method would, according to the conceptualists, bring order and structure to the complex and unstructured legal world. However, conceptualism has been the subject of much criticism during the 19th and 20th centuries, stating that it is impossible to structure the legal domain, based on traditions, history and culture as if they were components of the

[6] Referenced in Peczenik (1974: 145). Author's translation from Swedish.

Figure 1 Puchta's conceptual pyramid illustrating the "logical components" of a right (Paasch 113)

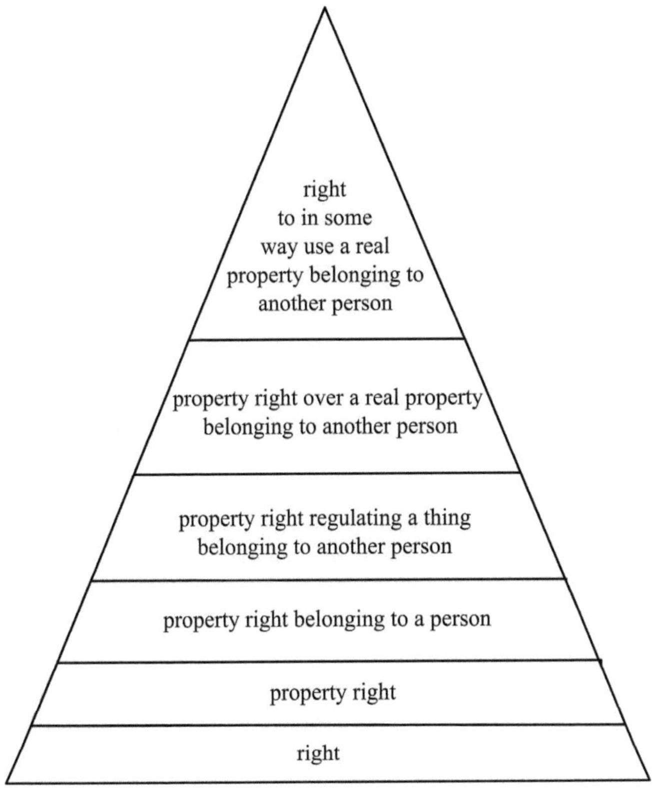

natural sciences. Conceptualism has during the years maintained a rather bad reputation among legal scholars. To call the working methods of a legal scholar conceptualism today is, according to Peczenik (1974: 148), actually regarded as almost insulting! The downfall of conceptualism was due to the too rigorous formulation of legal principles, unclear and unmotivated definitions without any relation to how legal work was carried out in real life. Rudolf von Jhering, who earlier had been much in favour of conceptualism, wrote a very satiric book stating that conceptualists after their death would ascend to a "conceptual heaven," where they after their death, without intervention from social life, could reflect on concepts like "right to a right." There would even be a "hair-splitting machine," to which you could only get access by breaking down a wall with your head! (Jhering 1884: 245-334).

However, even if conceptualism is regarded as almost insulting today, we might use some of the principles incorporated in this method without getting a headache, e.g. the appliance of logic and structure on selected areas of the legal domain to achieve a standardized approach, without going back to the extreme wish to standardize "everything," which reduced the movement to only an intellectual pastime and a curiosity in legal history. Even if conceptualism is reduced to a historical curiosity today, the movement has had a strong influence on the establishment of the modern German legal system in the 19th century (Peczenik 1974).

Even if we consider contraptions such as a "hair-splitting machine" as an amusing fictional anecdote, it does not take away the need for a common language for communication. This has become even more important during the computer age, where e.g. correct registration of e.g. a real property right can be of vital importance for processing and analysis of information and the settling of land related conflicts. An example is the use of standards and an accepted vocabulary when storing information regarding real property rights and regulations in a nation's real property management system. The importance of a standardized approach to real property information was e.g. noticed as early as 1966 in connection with the establishment of the digital Swedish real property register and that "[t]he aim has to be the fitting of the separate registers into a uniform flexible net of information systems. This uniformity implies that the different registrations within the net must be able to fit in an integrated information processing" (SOU 1966: 310).

It might be argued that the legal domain is neither sufficiently structured nor formal enough to be described into a pan-national computerized knowledge base since the domain involves the complexities of both syntax and semantics which makes it difficult to be incorporated into legal expert systems and other databases. Furthermore, the short-comings and inconsistent use of our natural languages has led to the development of a domain related specific language with its specific vocabulary, terms and synonyms.

However, a domain specific terminological approach, focussing on the characteristics of rights and regulations regulating ownership and interests in land might be a way to bring structure to this selected part of the legal domain. Real property rights and regulations are regulating and influencing the ownership and use of real property. Applying standardized principles from the field of terminology will help to structure this part of the legal domain. However, Paasch and Paulsson (2011) argues that it is difficult, if not even impossible, to create a general terminology applicable to society as a whole. For example a "person" may be regarded as something very different in the cadastral domain (e.g. a person who is allowed to own a real property) than a person in e.g. the health domain, which may be seen a patient (e.g. in need of care). The basic qualities of both persons are the same (i.e. they are e.g. both living individuals), but the specialisation is different in each domain due to the role the person plays. The narrower a domain becomes, so the need for a specialised terminology increases. However, the specialised definitions must build on broader, common definitions shared by two or more general domains.

3. The cadastral domain

The cadastral domain is part of both the legal domain (i.e. real property legislation) and what can be called the technical domain (i.e. the creation and management of land registration systems). However, this article focuses only on the legal part and not the technical aspects.

Real property rights and public regulations (e.g. the right to travel over another property or a public planning permission) are important parts of the cadastral domain. The cadastral domain has however been subject to a standardized approach for a number of years conducted by both the scientific community and professional organisations, e.g. Hespanha et al. (2009), Ottens (2004), Paasch (2011, 2008, 2007, 2006, 2005, 2004), Paasch and Paulsson (2011), Zevenbergen (2004a, 2004b, 2002) and Zevenbergen and Stubkjær (2005), who focus on the non-technical aspects of the domain. Examples illustrating the achievements and visions done in recent years to increase uniformity in the cadastral domain are e.g. the presentation of the FIG (International Federation of Surveyors) Cadastre 2014 statement for a vision for a future cadastral system (Kaufman and Steudler 1998), the presentation of a Core Cadastral Domain Model, describing the content of the central parts of the cadastral domain (Oosterom et al. 2006), the ongoing work creating an international standard for land administration, LADM (ISO/TC211 2011),[7] and the EULIS (European Land Information Service) initiative, providing a facility for reaching on-line and up-dated information about land across European borders (Laarakker and Gustafsson 2004, Ploeger and Loenen 2004). EULIS is focusing on mortgaging and conveying of real property, in order to improve the possibilities of cross-border transfer and to compare national practices. However, even if these initiatives are aiming at describing the cadastral domain and making comparison easier for the users, they do not provide a fully standardized description of real property rights and regulations. The author is of the opinion that standardized vocabularies or descriptions based on the legal content of rights and regulations are important tools in avoiding land and

[7] The standard is currently in its draft stage (DIS) and is expected to be accepted as an ISO standard in July 2012.

tenure conflicts and even being a tool for furthering cross-border real property transactions.

However, in order to achieve a thorough understanding of a fact, a problem or a semantic network of events, we must understand not only what the case is and what it consists of, but we must also understand how and why it is the case. We are even limited by our own thoughts, as the symbolism we employ when we speak is partly caused by the reference we are making and partly by social and psychological factors (Ogden and Richards 1923: 10). A standardized classification would contribute to the "matching" of real property rights and regulations existing in national legal systems with their corresponding counterparts existing in other national legal systems, even if they are not created by the same legal process or are named in different ways. It would be able to compare a right in country "A" with the corresponding right (i.e. a right having the same characteristics) in country "B," since both rights have the same impact on ownership. The principle is illustrated in Figure 2.

Figure 2 The principles of a terminological framework for comparison of real property rights and public regulations. Based on Paasch (2007: 177)

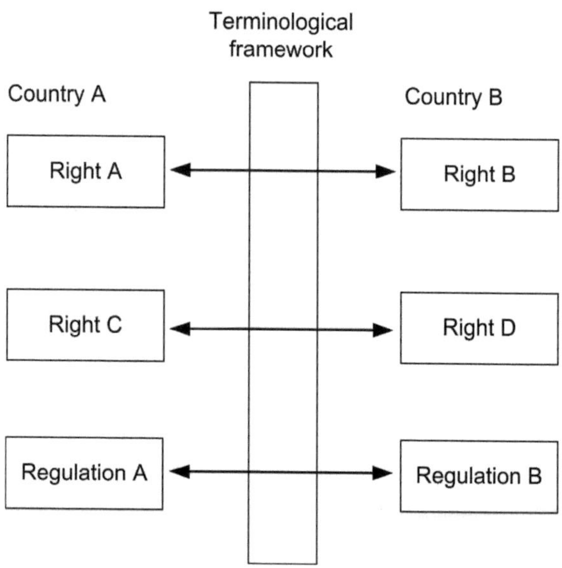

It might be argued that an approach focussing only on a very limited part of the legal domain might not be cost effective. However, in order to achieve a scientific depth the research is limited to real property rights and regulations. The field still covers a significant legal sub-domain which is important for settling of land conflicts and furthering economic development. Assuring access to land is a vital part of a nation's legal infra-structure and economy. Furthermore, any attempt to bring any logic structure into the legal domain must, in this author's opinion, be tested on limited areas of the domain. If the results of this research are positive it must be considered to expand the terminological approach to other parts of the legal domain by further research activities.

4. Terminological approach

Terminology is a methodology to describe and order the use of terms and language in a number of fields. This advanced method of furthering understanding has a vital role in not only the traditional IT-community. One example is the development of ontological models describing parts of the legal domain, e.g. the management of Intellectual Property Rights (Gangemi et al. 2005, Sagri et al. 2004), and the development of new ways of terminology descriptions in a socio-cognitive approach (Temmerman 2000).

The theoretical ideal for normative terminology is to have *one* expression describing *one* concept, but for the achievement of effective communication within specialist domains the use of synonyms cannot be excluded (Pilke 2000: 281). For example, a "cat" is not only a four legged, furry creature (*Felis silvestris catus*) which we all are familiar with, but can also be a whip or a part of a ships equipment, depending on our own preferences. A "cat-of-nine-tales" is an expression for a whip. However, a "cat" is also a sort of tackle used on ships (Paasch 1885: 150). We are, in order to communicate with each other, forced to establish mutual preferences which we all agree too. We must, in other words, standardize our vocabulary in order to improve communication.

In order to apply a terminological approach we must first take a look at the basic components used in terminology: concept, object, characteristic, definition and term. These components are closely related and one is either the result or basis of another. The content of this section is based on the international standards ISO 704 (2000), ISO 860 (1996) and ISO 1087-1 (2000) unless otherwise noted.

Object An object is anything that is perceivable or conceivable. Some objects are material, (e.g. a piece of land), immaterial (e.g. an urban planning zone) or imagined (e.g. a unicorn). However, we cannot speak of objects in the real world, since we do not have the ability to see the world with neutral and non-biased eyes. We have our own understanding or perception, i.e. a mental picture, a concept (see below), of what we see. It might be a house, chair, horse or, focussing on the legal domain, a right to use a real property.

Concept A concept is a mental construction of the real world formed in our own mind. A concept does not stand alone, but is part of a concept system, where concepts are put in relation to each other according to specific rules. Concepts are based on a selected number of characteristics (see below) that we think best describe the object we see (Suonuuti 1997). Concepts are in a terminological approach to be considered mental representations of objects within a specialised context or field.

Characteristics It is the characteristics which make us identify the "real world" when we create our vision of it in our mind as a concept. If we, theoretically, never have seen a "house," we still are able to produce the concept based on characteristics like walls, roof and windows and the fact that the building is intended to be used for dwelling or industry. However, we would not call it a "house," but something else since a "house" does not exist in our mental view of the world.

Definition We cannot use objects, concepts or characteristics to communicate effectively. In order to communicate precisely we need to define the concept as a unit. To define means to describe the concept by a descriptive statement which serves to differentiate it from other, related concepts. Producing definitions is producing "true" statements or statements as near to "truth" as possible, delimiting the concept from other concepts.

A definition must be as precise as possible to avoid misunderstandings and confusions. Ambiguity of words makes it difficult to express precisely what is meant. A general, methodological problem is the use of words. It is a major task for any standardization project to apply the correct terminology and ensure the correct understanding of the texts and diagrams describing the content of the standard. However, it would be rather complicated to always use definitions when we communicate. We therefore need *terms* to express them.

Term Terms are the instruments we use for communication. A term must have a specific meaning, based on the definition delimiting and describing a concept. Otherwise it would mean different things to different people. A term is a verbal designation, i.e. representation of a concept by a sign which denotes it within a specific subject field. A term might exactly describe the object in question, but it might also be a commonly accepted word. For example, the use of the English term "Parcel" does not only mean (a part of) land belonging to a real property, but also does also mean a small container used for sending postal goods. The English term "Lot," does, among other things, also mean a part of land. The problem becomes even greater when communicating in different languages. Communicating with other communities we are forced to use other terms based on the same concept described by the same characteristics, e.g. "Katasterparzelle" (Germany), or "Fastighetsområde" (Sweden), which equates to the English real property term "Parcel." Terms may not only consist of words, but also symbols, e.g. ©, @ or $. They are also considered terms as they describe real or imaginary objects.

However, applying terms is not simply a matter of using one word or another for describing something. Any term must be based on the discussion of our mental pictures of real world objects, delimited by a number of characteristics which are mandatory for the object in question. The characteristics are the basis for how we identify, describe and name an object. It is the relations between the terminological elements that are the basis for any description.

5. A legal cadastral domain model, LCDM

Bearing the principles of terminology in mind, we are now able to illustrate our understanding of parts of the real world and communicate the result using terms based on certain characteristics and definitions. The model described below is, as already mentioned, a hypothesis classifying rights and regulations regulating real property. A part of the model has been tested through case studies, which have been conducted by this author and others in order to verify or develop the LCDM. Case studies have been conducted on the German, Dutch, Irish and Swedish real property legislations (Paasch 2011), the Portuguese real property legislation (Hespanha et al. 2009), and the Danish, Norwegian, Swedish, Icelandic and Finnish real property legislations (Pålsson and Svensson 2007). The results of the case-studies show that the model is suitable for classifying real property rights. However, the model has to undergo minor changes in regard to e.g. some specific characteristics and the use of the English legal terminology (Paasch 2011). An updated version of the LCDM is shown in Figure 3. A case study on Swedish public regulations is currently being conducted by this author and the results are intended to be published during 2012.

The LCDM approach is based on the hypothesis that it is possible, in contrast to what Jhering believed only could be done in a conceptual heaven, to structure "rights to rights." The numerous real property rights and public regulations influencing the ownership of real property can be systemised as belonging to a few numbers of "classes." "Class" is in this article used as a synonym for a group and presented as a box in the illustrations. Furthermore, they are “connections” between real property and the one’s who are executing them, e.g. a person who has been given the right to harvest fruits from the land. The connections do not have to exist, but there might even exist one or more rights or regulations influencing the same ownership right. These connections can be expressed as being either beneficial or burdening to ownership, based on their characteristics, i.e. you may be restricted to do specific actions on your own land or you are allowed to do something on another person’s land.

Figure 3 The legal cadastral domain model in Paasch (2011)

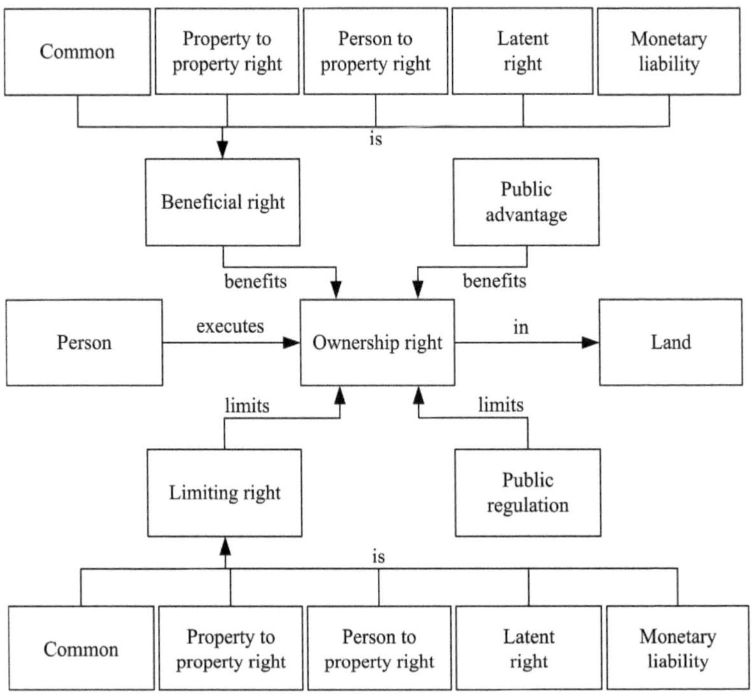

The class names and definitions are taken from Paasch (2011), except the Public advantage and Public regulation definitions, which are taken from Paasch (2008: 127). The definitions of the classes are shown in Table 1.

Table 1 Class names and definitions (based on Paasch 2011, 2008)

Class name	Definition
Beneficial right	rights beneficial for the use and enjoyment of real property
Common	part right in a part of common land owned and shared by several real properties
Land	part of earth which is regulated through ownership. Land is the surface of the Earth and the materials beneath. Note: Water and the air above land might also be considered land in some legislation.
Latent right	right which is not yet executed on a real property
Limiting right	rights limiting the use and enjoyment of real property
Monetary liability	latent, financial security for payment
Ownership right	right to own real property according to legislation
Person	human being or legal person, state, municipality and other private or governmental authority who owns real property according to legislation
Person to property right	right executed by a person to use, harvest the fruits/material of, rent or lease the real property in whole or in part, including the claim against a person
Property to property right	right executed by the owner of a real property in another real property, due to his ownership right
Public advantage	publicly imposed advantage which is beneficial to ownership and use of real property
Public regulation	legally imposed burden by an official organisation

It must however be noted that the concept of "to own" has not been properly defined by any author and is somewhat unclear in this author's opinion. Black (1891: 933) describes ownership as a "bundle of rights" allowing one to use, manage, and enjoy property, including the right to convey it to others. Friedman et al. (1984: 193) describes real property ownership as methods of owning real estate, which affect income tax, estate tax, continuity, liability, survivorship, transferability, disposition at death and at bankruptcy. Gifis (1984: 331) describes ownership as one's exclusive right of possessing, enjoying, and disposing of a thing. In this paper ownership is regarded as the right to sell, transfer or in other way use a piece of land. To "own" is, in its outmost consequence, the "ultimate" right to a piece of land. The concept of ownership has been discussed by several scholars, e.g. MacCarty (2002), Honoré (1987), Snare (1972) and Hohfeld (1913, 1917).

The rights and regulations have relations to and from the *ownership right* class, since they are benefiting or limiting ownership and thereby, according to the definition used in this paper, regulating the real property as such. They are divided into four main sections: *beneficial right* (i.e. rights beneficial to ownership), *limiting right* (i.e. rights burdening to ownership), *public advantage* (i.e. public regulations beneficial to ownership) and *public regulation* (i.e. public regulations burdening to ownership, e.g. a municipal zoning plan).

The beneficial right and limiting right classes are divided into specific types of rights which are labelled "common," "property to property right," "person to property right," "latent right' and 'monetary liability." The classes appear in "two places" in the model mirroring each for pedagogic reasons, being either beneficial or limiting to ownership. Examples are a right of way that the owner of one property has on another real property. The right is limiting for one property but beneficial for the other property. Another example is a person's right to collect fruits, etc. from a property in exchange of a fee. The right is limiting the owner's use of the property, but is at the same time beneficial for him since he receives compensation.

6. Interaction between the legal domain and standardization

This paper has so far been focussing on the legal domain, terminology, the cadastral domain, and a description of the LCDM. However, it is necessary to describe the interaction between the legal domain and standardization in order to analyse if in fact it is realistic to apply the terms on the legal domain and if the approach described in this paper in fact is a standardized approach.

Legislation is the oldest way of standardization we know (Jørgensen 1997). However, these legal instruments are traditionally normally not regarded as formal standards. Legal rules and standards are not substitutes, but they interact. They are the result of different processes. Formal standardization differs from legalisation in the way that standards are private agreements based on voluntary implementation and legislations are officially imposed rules. However, it is possible to talk about e.g. the standardization of legal rules and procedures as long as we keep in mind that we do not mean the process of formal standardization by a national or international standardization institute. The legal domain can be seen as a "standardized" framework in which a society and individuals can operate. See e.g. Adams (1994), who discusses the "standardization" of legal norms and regulations within the European Union.

During the last decades the increased use of computers and the establishing of databases on a national level have forced a standardization of terms within numerous fields in order to communicate effectively between e.g. governmental and municipal organisations. Furthermore, there are situations where standards are used as legislative references. A governmental body may issue legislation based on the implementation of certain standards or actions fulfilling the intentions of certain standards. If legislation is referring to a standard, the use of the standard might become mandatory in the fields which are covered by the standard. Examples are the so-called New Approach and the Global Approach initiatives which are regulated in EC Directive 98/34/EC and its amendments (EC 1998a, 1998b, 2000). The principle is based on the use of standards in order to reach the essential requirements allowing a product free movement on the European market. Furthermore, the EC does also have the possibility of inviting the European standards organizations to elaborate European standards and enabling the free movement of goods (EC 2000). However, the application of standards is voluntary and a manufacturer may use other means than standards to meet the technical requirements laid out in a standard, thus fulfilling the requirements. Legislative harmonisation is limited to essential requirements that products placed on the Community market must meet, if they are to benefit from free movement within the Community.

There are also several glossaries describing land tenure (i.e. rights of others in a land owner's resource) and other land and ownership related terms in existence throughout the world today, aiming at improving the correct use of terms applied in the cadastral domain, e.g. UNECE (2004), Leonard and Longbottom (2000) and Bruce (1998). These glossaries are important tools when communicating within the real property field, but they are, in this author's opinion, to be seen as a rather limited tool for structuring a common terminology due to the fact that they are based on the principles of different legal families or legal traditions, regardless of their good intentions. They can therefore not be seen as an efficient way of furthering any standardized approach towards the structuring of real property rights and public regulations on a pan-national level.

7. Conclusion

The aim of this article has been to describe a terminological framework for classification of real property rights and public regulations on a pan-national basis. The author has in this paper argued that it is necessary to develop a terminological framework for real property rights and public regulations, the Legal Cadastral Domain Model. A terminological framework would make it easier to compare rights and regulations existing in different legislations, thus reducing transactions costs in pan-national real property transactions. the part of the model describing real property rights has been tested through case-studies. The result is that this part of model is valid, but the model has to be updated with minor changes, .e.g. has some of the terms used to be revised to further understanding of the model and some descriptions had to be revised to allow the model to described all investigated rights.

This article has illustrated that it is possible to apply the principles derived from traditional terminology on a limited part of the legal domain. However, more research is needed to confirm or falsify the Legal Cadastral Domain Model outlined in this paper, especially by testing the proposed terms, characteristics and definitions by conducting case studies on real property rights and regulations originating from different legal families.

References

Adams, M. (1994), Rechte und Normen als Standards [Rights and Norms as Standards], *Homo Oeconomicus* 11: 501-552.

Black (1891), *Black's Law Dictionary*, St. Paul, MN: Thomson West.

Bruce, J. (1998), Review of Tenure Terminology, *Tenure Brief* 1 (July), Madison, WI: University of Wisconsin at Madison.

Delmas-Marty, M. (2004), Comparative Law and the Internationalisation of Law in Europe, in: M. van Hoecke (ed.), *Epistemology and Methodology of Comparative Law*, Portland: Hart Publishing.

EC (1998a), Directive 98/34/EC of the European Parliament and of the Council of 22 June 1998 Laying Down a Procedure for the Provision of Information in the Field of Technical Standards and Regulations, *Official Journal of the European Communities L 204*, 21/07/1998.

EC (1998b), Directive 98/48/EC of the European Parliament and of the Council of 20 July Amending Directive 98/34/EC Laying Down a Procedure for the Provision of Information in the Field of Technical Standards and Regulations, *Official Journal of the European Communities L 217*, 05/08/1998.

EC (2000), *Guide to the Implementation of Directives Based on the New Approach and the Global Approach*, European Communites.

Ekelöf, P. (1945), Juridisk slutledning och terminology [Legal Interference and Terminology], *Tidsskrift for rettsvitenskap* 1945: 211-272.

Friedman, J., Harris, J. and Lindeman, J. (1984), *Dictionary of Real Estate Terms*, New York: Barron's.

Gangemi, A., Sagri, M.-T. and Tiscornia, D. (2005), A Constructive Framework for Legal Ontologies, in: V. Benjamins et al. (eds.), *Law and the Semantic Web*, Berlin: Springer-Verlag.

Gifis, S. (1984), *Law Directory*, New York: Barron's.

Glenn H. (2004), Legal Cultures and Legal Traditions, in: M. van Hoecke (ed.), *Epistemology and Methodology of Comparative Law*, Portland: Hart Publishing.

Harris, J. (1979), *Law and Legal Science*, Oxford: Clarendon Press.

Hart, H. (1961), *The Concept of Law*, Oxford: Clarendon Press.

Hespanha, J., Jardim, M., Paasch, J. and Zevenbergen, J. (2009), Modelling Legal and Administrative Cadastral Domain: Implementing into the Portuguese Legal Framework, *Journal of Comparative Law* 4: 140-169.

Hoecke, M. van (2004), Deep Level Comparative Law, in: M. van Hoecke (ed.) *Epistemology and Methodology of Comparative Law*, Portland: Hart Publishing.

Hohfeld, W. (1913), Fundamental Legal Conceptions as Applied in Judicial Reasoning, *Yale Law Journal* 23: 16-59.

Hohfeld, W. (1917), Fundamental Legal Conceptions as Applied in Judicial Reasoning, *Yale Law Journal* 26: 710-770.

Honoré, T. (1987), *Making Law Bind*, Oxford: Clarendon Press.

ISO 704 (2000), *Terminology Work: Principles and Methods*, International Organisation for Standardization (ISO).

ISO 860 (1996), *Terminology Work: Harmonization of Concepts and Terms*, International Organisation for Standardization (ISO).

ISO 1087-1 (2000), *Terminology Work: Vocabulary - Part 1: Theory and Application*, International Organisation for Standardization (ISO).

ISO/TC211 (2011), ISO 19152, *Draft International Standard (DIS), Geographic Information: Land administration domain model (LADM)*, International Organization for Standardization, non-public ISO document.

Jhering, R. von (1884), *Scherz und Ernst in der Jurisprudenz* [Jokes and Seriousness in Jurisprudence], Leipzig: Breitkopf & Härtel.

Jørgensen, S. (1997), Law as a Standardizing System, *EURAS Yearbook of Standardization* 1: 411-416.

Kaufman, J. and Steudler, D. (1998), *Cadastre 2014: A Vision for a Future Cadastral System*, Copenhagen: The International Federation of Surveyors (FIG).

Laarakker, P. and Gustafsson, S. (2004), European Land Information Service (EULIS), in: B. van Loenen and B. Kok (eds.), *Spatial Data Infrastructure and Policy Development in Europe and the United States*, Delft University of Technology.

Leonard, R. and Longbottom, J. (2000), *Land Tenure Lexico: A Glossary of Terms from English and French Speaking West Africa*, London: International Institute of Environment and Development.

MacCarty, T. (2002), Ownership: A Case Study in the Representation of Legal Concepts, *Artificial Intelligence and Law* 10: 135-161.

Nuopponen, A. (1994), *Begreppssystem för terminologisk analys* [Concept Systems for Terminological Analysis], Vasa University, Finland.

Ogden, C. and Richards, I. (1923), *The Meaning of Meaning*, London: Ark Paperbacks.

Oosterom, P. van, Lemmen, C., Ingvarsson, P., Molen, P. van der, Ploeger, H., Quak, C., Stoter, J. and Zevenbergen, J. (2006), The Core Cadastral Domain Model, *Computers, Environment and Urban Systems* 30: 627-668.

Ottens, M. (2004), The Cadastral System as a Socio-technical System, *Proceedings of the Workshop Standardization in the Cadastral Domain*, Bamberg, Germany,

9-10 December 2004, Copenhagen: The International Federation of Surveyors (FIG).

Paasch, H. (1885), *Paasch's Illustrated Marine Dictionary*, New York: Lyons and Burford Publishers.

Paasch, J. (2004), A Legal Cadastral Domain Model, *Proceedings of the Workshop Standardization in the Cadastral Domain*, Bamberg, Germany, 9-10 December 2004, Copenhagen: The International Federation of Surveyors (FIG).

Paasch, J. (2005), Legal Cadastral Domain Model: An Object-orientated Approach, *Nordic Journal of Surveying and Real Estate Research* 2: 117-136.

Paasch, J. (2006), Standardization of Real Property Rights and Restrictions: A Fool's Task?, *Proceedings of the XXIII International FIG Congress*, Munich, 8-13 October 2006, Copenhagen: The International Federation of Surveyors (FIG).

Paasch, J. (2007), Real Property Transactions: An Approach Towards Standardisation of Legal Issues, in: J. Zevenbergen, A. Frank and E. Stubkjær (eds.), *Real Property Transactions; Procedures, Transaction Costs and Models*, Amsterdam: IOS Press.

Paasch, J. (2008), Standardization within the Legal Domain: A Terminological Approach, *EURAS Yearbook of Standardization* 6: 105-130.

Paasch, J. (2011), *Classification of Real Property Rights: A Comparative Study of Real Property Rights in Germany, Ireland, the Netherlands and Sweden*, forthcoming publication, expected to be published 2011 at KTH Royal Institute of Technology, Stockholm.

Paasch, J. and Paulsson, J. (2011), Terminological Aspects on Three-dimensional Real Property, forthcoming publication, submitted for review to *Nordic Journal of Surveying and Real Estate Research.*

Peczenik, A. (1974), *Juridikens metodproblem* [Methodological Problems of the Doctrinal Study of Law], Stockholm: Almqvist & Wiksell Förlag.

Pilke, N. (2000), *Dynamiska fackbegrepp: Att strukturera vetande om handlingar och händelser inom teknik, medicin och juridik* [Dynamic Specialist Concepts. To Structure Knowledge about Actions and Events within the Fields of Technology, Medicine and Law], Acta Wasaensia (81), University of Vasa.

Ploeger, H. and Loenen, B. (2004), EULIS: At the Beginning of the Road to Harmonization of Land Registry in Europe, *European Review of Private Law* 3: 379-387.

Pålsson, H. and Svensson, M. (2007), *Kategorisering av rättigheter i Norden: Är det möjligt att genomföra?* [Classification of Rights in the Nordic Countries: Is it possible?], master thesis, Stockholm: KTH Royal Institute of Technology.

Sagri, M.-S., Tiscornia, D. and Gangemi, A. (2004), An Ontology-based Model for Representing "Bundle-of-Rights", in: R. Meersman, et al. (eds.), *OTM Workshops*, Berlin: Springer-Verlag.

Snare, F. (1972), The Concept of Property, *America Philosophical Quarterly* 9: 200-206.

SOU (1966), *Fastighetsregistrering* [Real Property Registration], Statens Offentliga Utredningar, 1966: 63, Stockholm: Ministry of Justice.

Suonuuti, H. (1997), *Guide to Terminology*, Helsinki: Tekniikan Sanastokeskus ry.

Strömholm, S. (1981), *Rätt, rättskällor och rättstillämpning* [Law, legal sources and the application of law], Stockholm: Norstedts Juridik.

Susskind, R. (1987), *Expert Systems in Law,* Oxford: Clarendon Press.

Temmerman, R. (2000), *Towards New Ways of Terminology Description: The Sociocognitive Approach,* Amsterdam: John Benjamin Publishing Co.

Wahlgren, P. (1992), *Automation of Legal Reasonin:. A Study on Artificial Intelligence and Law,* Stockholm: Juristförlaget and Deventer-Boston: Kluwer Publishers.

Watson, A. (2004), Legal Culture v Legal Tradition, in: M. van Hoecke (ed.), *Epistemology and Methodology of Comparative Law,* Portland: Hart Publishing.

UNECE (2004), *Guidelines on Real Property Units and Identifiers,* Working Party on Land Administration (WPLA), United Nations Economic Commission for Europe (UNECE), ECE/HBP/135.

Zevenbergen, J. (2002), *Systems of Land Registration: Aspects and Effects,* Delft: Delft University of Technology.

Zevenbergen, J. (2004a), A Systems Approach to Land Registration and Cadastre, *Nordic Journal of Surveying and Real Estate Research* 1: 11-24.

Zevenbergen, J. (2004b), Expanding the Legal/Administrative Package of the Cadastral Domain Model: From Grey to Yellow?, *Proceedings of the Workshop Standardization in the Cadastral Domain,* Bamberg, Germany, 9-10 December 2004, Copenhagen: The International Federation of Surveyors (FIG).

Zevenbergen, J. and Stubkjær, E. (2005), Real Property Transactions: Challenges of Modelling and Comparing, *Proceedings of From Pharaohs to Geoinformatics,* FIG Working Week 2005 and GSDI-8, Copenhagen: The International Federation of Surveyors (FIG).

Zweigert, K. and Kötz, H. (1995), *Introduction to Comparative Law,* Oxford: Clarendon Press.

The *electronic archive* of HOMO OECONOMICUS (full text since volume 17, 2000) is retrievable via www.gbi.de

See also: www.accedoverlag.de and www.DeutschesFachbuch.de.

Orders for back issues and subscriptions should be sent to the publisher: ACCEDO, Gnesener Str. 1, D-81929 München (Germany), FAX: +49 89 929 4109 or eMail: accedoverlag@web.de

HOMO OECONOMICUS 27(3), 2010
ISBN 978-3-89265-074-4, 153 pages, EUR 24.00

Articles: Non-instrumental Behavior in an Environmental Public Good Game, *Leif Helland and Jon Hovi*; On Making Full Sense of Adam Smith, *Richard Sturn*; Strategy in the Kautiliya Arthasastra, *Vikas Kuma*; Freedom, Opportunity and Uncertainty: A Critical Review, *Ruvin Gekker and Ashley Piggins*.

Symposium: Letter to the Queen, edited by *Manfred J. Holler*

"The Letter" and "A Response," The Great Detour, *Peter Skott*; Why no one Foresaw the Economic Crisis?, *John Hudson*; A Letter Reminding the Profession of its True Tasks, *Andreas Freytag*; "... so that you Never Need to Ask your Question Again," *Leif Helland*; Is the Economic Crisis a Crisis of Economics as well?, *Gebhard Kirchgässner*; Economics, Political Economy and Social Philosophy: A Reaction to the Letter to the Queen, *Alain Marciano*; On the Dismal State of a Dismal Science?, *Heinz D. Kurz.*

HOMO OECONOMICUS 27(1/2), 2010
Schumpeter for Our Century, edited by
Horst Hanusch, Heinz D. Kurz and Christian Seidl
ISBN 978-3-89265-073-7, 227 pages, EUR 24,00

ISBN 978-3-89265-075-1 ISSN 0943-0180

Articles: Thoughts on Socialism Seventy Years after Schumpeter, *John E. Roemer*; Neo-Schumpeterian Flexicurity Capitalism: Heterogeneous Skills and the Formation of Elites, *Peter Flaschel; Alfred Greiner and Sigrid Luchtenberg*; Schumpeter on Queen Elizabeth's Stockings and the Co-evolutionary Nature of Innovation, *Kanak Patel and Kirill Zavodov*; Fighting the Crisis: Public Sector Governance in a Comprehensive Neo-Schumpeterian System, *Horst Hanusch*; Beyond the Third Pillar: Neo-Schumpeterian Economics and Stakeholder Theory, *John Donohue*; Governing Finance and Knowledge: An Evolutionary Perspective, *Leonardo Burlamaqui*; Evolutionary Economics and the Disappearing NAIRU and Phillips Curve, *Richard G. Lipsey*; Overcoming the Next Crisis: Some Preliminary Thoughts, *Christian Seidl.*

HOMO OECONOMICUS 26(3/4), 2009

Essays in Honor of Hannu Nurmi: Vol. I, edited by
Manfred J. Holler and Mika Widgrén
ISBN 978-3-89265-072-0, 276 pages, EUR 36.00

Articles: Introduction, *Manfred J. Holler*; **On Power**: Strategic A Priori Power in the European Union's Codecision Procedure, *Stefan Napel and Mika Widgrén*; The QM Rule in the Nice and Lisbon Treaties: Future Projections, *Dan S. Felsenthal and Moshé Machover*; A Priori Voting Power and the U.S. Electoral College, *Nicholas R. Miller*; A New Family of Power Indices for Voting Games, *Vito Fragnelli, Stefania Ottone and Roberto Sattanino*; The Public Good Index with Threats in A Priori Unions, *Manfred J. Holler and Andreas Nohn*; The Banzhaf Value When Some Players are Incompatible, *José Maria Alonso-Meijide, Mikel Alvares-Mozos and Maria Gloria Fiestras-Janeiro*; Power Indices in Politics: Some Results and Open Problems, *Gianfranco Gambarelli and Izabella Stach*; A Preliminary Simulative Assessment of Disproportionality Indices, *Matteo Migheli, Guido Ortona and Ferruccio Ponzano*; **On Voting**: Voting and Power, *Annick Laruelle and Federico Valenciano*; A Geometric Approach to Paradoxes of Majority Voting: From Anscombe's Paradox to the Discursive Dilemma with Saari and Nurmi, *Daniel Eckert and Christian Klamler*; List Apparentements in Local Elections: A Lottery, *Peter Leutgäb and Friedrich Pukelsheim*; The Core with Positional Spatial Voting, *Donald G. Saari*; **Truth and Chance**: Can Students Evaluate Teaching Quality?, *Matti Wiberg*; 'Objectivity' in Parliamentary and Scholarly Disputes: On Max Weber's Rhetorical Redescription of a Concept, *Kari Palonen*; Why Theory Choosing is Better than Hypothesis Testing, *Donald Wittman*; Fortune is a Woman: Machiavelli on Luck and Virtue, *Timo Airaksinen.*

HOMO OECONOMICUS 26(2), 2009

ISBN 978-3-89265-071-3, 111 pages, EUR 16.00

Articles: Interative Reasoning in an Experimental Lemon Market, *Annette Kirstein and Roland Kirstein*; On Procedural Freedom of Choice, *Ritxar Arlegi and Dinko Dimitrov*; Freedom and Unanticipated Consequences, *Frank A. Hindriks*; Necessary and Sufficient Conditions to Make the Numbers Count, *Marlies Ahlert and Hartmut Kliemt*; A Note on Measuring Voters' Responsibility, *Dan S. Felsenthal and Moshé Machover*; Why Private Events are Associative: Automatic Chaining and Associationism, *Robert Epstein*.

HOMO OECONOMICUS 26(1), 2009

The Secrets of Secrets, edited by
Timo Airaksinen and Manfred J. Holler

ISBN 978-3-89265-070-6, 174 pages, EUR 22.00

Articles: Editorial Introduction, *Timo Airaksinen and Manfred J. Holler*; Masking and Revealing Secrets: Encryption, Competitive Intelligence and Spy Games, *Rupert A. Brandmeier and Florian Rupp*; The Zimmermann Telegram: How to Make Use of Secrets?, *Manfred J. Holler*; The Secret Partnership and the Dynamics of Art, *Barbara Klose-Ullmann*; Don't Tell Us: The Demand for Secretive Behavior, *Pierre Salmon*; The Strategic Use of Secrets: Doubts about a Proposal of Schelling, *Friedel Bolle and Yves Breitmoser;* Secrets, Mysteries and Art, *Leonidas Donskis*; Conspiracy as a Dirty Secret: The Case of 9/11, *Timo Airaksinen*; Conservativism and Secrecy, *Heta Aleksandra Gylling*; Secrets and Lies: The Neighbourhood of No-Truth, *Patrick A. McNutt*.

HOMO OECONOMICUS 25(3/4), 2008

ISBN 978-3-89265-069-0, 208 pages, EUR 28.00

A Festival Issue: 25 volumes of HOMO OECONOMICUS

Articles: Approximate Truth in Economic Modelling, *Geoffrey Brennan, Werner Güth and Hartmut Kliemt*; Choosing Guilt, *Luciano Andreozzi*; Aggregation of Lexicographic Orderings, *Marlies Ahlert*; The Majority Judgement Voting Procedure; A Critical Evaluation, *Dan S. Felsenthal and Moshé Machover*; The Efficiency of Fairness in Voting Systems, Frantisek Turnovec; Modelling Political Economy, *Norman Schofield*; Neo-Conservatives or Neo-Liberal?, *Shanti P. Chakravarty*; Presupposition in Empirical Ethics, *Timo Airaksinen*; TV, Time and Happiness, *Bruno S. Frey and*

Christine Benesch; Trying to Understand Nothing, *Friedel Bolle*; Re-Defining Arts, Readymades and Secrets, *Manfred J. Holler*; Waves, Spectra, Sounds: Fourier Analysis, *Florian Rupp*.

The DessertSection: Beigli, *George Frankfurter*.

HOMO OECONOMICUS 25(2), 2008

ISBN 978-3-89265-068-3, 123 pages, EUR 20.00

Articles: Do Voting Power Considerations Explain the Formation of Political Coalitions?, *Vincent C.H. Chua and Dan S. Felsenthal*; Peace and the Sharing of Power: Contrasting Conquest and Non-Conquest Settings, *Martin Leroch*; Straffin Meets Condorcet: What can a Voting Power Theorist Learn from a Jury Theorist?, *Serguei Kaniovski*; Negotiating European Economic and Monetary Union, *Madeleine O. Hosli*; On Power and Punishment: Buddhism and Statecraft in Ancient India, *Michael Zimmermann*.

The ArtsSection: The Container Manifesto: Why Boxes Must Remain Closed, *Alex Close*.

HOMO OECONOMICUS 25(1), 2008

ISBN 978-3-89265-067-5, 134 pages, EUR 22.00

Articles: Adam Smith's Intuition Pump: The Impartial Spectator, *Martin Leroch*; Three Versions of Impartiality: An Experimental Investigation, *Kaisa Herne and Tarja Mård*; Religion, Politics and Luck: Explaining the Rise of Sustained Innovation, *Leonard Dudley*; Who Votes for Ecologist Parties? Evidence from Suburban France, *Yves Egal, Raphaël Franck, Nicolay Getchev, Bruno Jérôme, Betrand Lemencier and Nicolas Vaillant*; Wealth In duced Multiple Equilibria in Small Open Economy Versions of the Ramsey Model, *Franz X. Hof and Franz Wirl*.

HOMO OECONOMICUS 24(3/4), 2007

Power Measures IV, edited by
Gianfranco Gambarelli

ISBN 3-89265-066-9, 168 pages, EUR 28.00

Articles: Minimax Multi-District Apportionments, *Gianfranco Gambarelli and Arsen Palestini*; On Penrose's Square-Root Law and Beyond, *Werner Kirsch*; From a Toy Model to the Double Square-Root Voting System, *Wojciech Slomiczynski and Karol Zyczkowski*; Voting Operators and Weak

Dictatorship, *Massimiliano Ferrara*; Worth-Sharing through Möbius Inversion, *Giovanni Rossi*; Discovering Electorate Preferences in Voting Procedures, *Jerzy Holubiec, Grazyna Szkatula and Darius Wagner*; The Public Good Index when Some Voters are Incompatible, *J.M. Alonso-Meijide and B. Casas-Mendez*; Partnership in Politics: A Case Study, Francesc Carreras, *Maria Dolores Llongueras and Maria Albina Puente*; The Best Represented Voters in Europe: An a priori Voting Power Analysis of the 2004 Elections for the European Parliament, *Hannu Nurmi, Tapio Raunio and Julia Helin.*

HOMO OECONOMICUS 24(2), 2007

ISBN 3-89265-065-0, 165 pages, EUR 28.00

Articles: A Formal Classification of Power, *Mario Stoppino*; Mario Stoppino – A Bio-Bibliographical Note, *Ian Carter*; Social Power and Negative Freedom, *Ian Carter*; Conceptions of Freedom and Ranking Opportunity Sets: A Typology, *Antoinette Bbaujard*; The Potential of the Holler-Packel Value and Index: A New Characterization, *Ruxandra Haradau and Stefan Napel*; Public and Private Choice in Organ Donation, *Marlies Ahlert*; Regret and Retroaction, *Jeanne Peijnenburg.*

Book Review: Moral und Ökonomie by Birger Priddat, *Martin Leroch.*

HOMO OECONOMICUS 24(1), 2007

ISBN 3-89265-064-0, 145 pages, EUR 24.00

Articles: Speeding up Bureaucrats by Greasing Them: An Experimental Study, *Luis C. González, Werner Güth and M. Vittoria Levati*; Tax Morale and the Legitimacy of Economic Policy, *Jan Schnellenbach;* Plotting the Consequences of Electoral Change: Causes, Outcomes and Visualisation, *Maria Suojanen*; The Ruin and Redemption of Homo Oeconomicus, *Jan-Willem van der Rijt*; Market Efficiency cum Anomalies or Behavioral Finance, *George M. Frankfurter*; Comparing Games: Go versus Chess, Remarks on the Methodology of Games Research, *Ernst Strouhal*; European Culture Capitals and Local Development Strategies: Comparing the Genoa and Lille 2004 Cases, *Pier Luigi Sacco and Giorgio Tavano Blessi.*

Notes from the Profession: Why Doesn't Britain Trust its Academics?, *Susanne Kord, Leonard Olscher, Robert Weniger and W. Daniel Wilson.*

www.accedoverlag.de

Instructions to Contributors

1. Papers must be in English.
2. Manuscripts should be around 7000 words. Longer manuscripts will be accepted for review following consultation with the Managing Editor. Manuscripts should be at least 12pt type, 1.5 line spaced throughout (including footnotes), with 3cm margins. All pages should be numbered consecutively. Titles and subtitles should be short.
3. The *first page* of the manuscript should contain the title, the name(s), institutional affiliation(s), postal address and e-mail address of the author(s), a list of JEL codes, a list of five key words, and an abstract of not more than 150 words. For multiple authored papers, the corresponding author to whom proofs and the reprint order form should be sent should be clearly indicated. Acknowledgements and information on grants received can be given in a section headed 'Acknowledgements' at the end of the paper but before the list of references.
4. *Important formulae* (displayed) should be numbered consecutively throughout the manuscript as (1), (2), etc. on the right-hand side of the page.
5. *Footnotes* should be kept to a minimum and numbered consecutively throughout the text. Footnotes should preferably not include formulae.
6. *References* should include the most relevant papers. In the text, references to publications should appear as follows: 'Farrell (1986: 68) reported that …' or 'This problem has been a subject in literature before (e.g. Farrell 1986: 68)'. The author should make sure that there is a strict 'one-to-one correspondence' between the names (years) in the text and those on the list. At the end of the manuscript (after any appendices), the complete references should be listed as:

   For monographs:

   Tirole, J. (1988), *The Theory of Industrial Organization*, Cambridge, Mass.: MIT Press.

ISBN 978-3-89265-075-1 ISSN 0943-0180

For contributions to collective works:

Shaked, A. and Sutton, J. (1984), Natural Oligopolies and International Trade, in: H. Kierzkowski (ed.), *Monopolistic Competition and International Trade*, Oxford: Clarendon Press.

For periodicals:

Gabszewicz, J.J. and Thisse, J.-F. (1979), Price Competition, Quality, and Income Disparities, *Journal of Economic Theory* 20: 340–359.

7. All mathematical expressions, either in-line or set-off, should be entered using an equation editor.

8. If illustrations, graphs, and figures are not provided electronically they should be sent in triplicate and should be marked on the back with figure numbers, title of paper, and name of author. If not inserted in text, a location in the text should be indicated drawings should not be inserted in the text. All graphs and diagrams should be referred to as *figures* and should be numbered consecutively in the text in Arabic numerals. Care should be taken that lettering and symbols are of a comparable size.

9. All unessential tables should be eliminated from the manuscript. Tables should be numbered consecutively in the text in Arabic numerals. If not inserted in the text, insertion points should be indicated.

Please note that manuscripts that do not conform to the above instructions may be returned for the necessary revision *before publication.* Page proofs will be sent to the corresponding author.

Submissions are to be sent electronically (preferably in PDF format) to the *Managing Editor*:

Manfred J. Holler, e-mail: holler@econ.uni-hamburg.de

Institute of SocioEconomics (IAW)
University of Hamburg
Von-Melle-Park 5
D-20146 Hamburg, Germany

Submission of a paper will be held to imply that it contains original unpublished work and is not being submitted for publication elsewhere. The editors do not accept responsibility for damage or loss of submissions.

A copy of the printed volume is supplied free to the author.

*J*ournal *of* Universal Rejection

About the Journal | Instructions for Authors | Subscriptions | Archives

Editor-in-Chief: Caleb Emmons

About the Journal

The founding principle of the Journal of Universal Rejection (JofUR) is rejection. Universal rejection. That is to say, all submissions, regardless of quality, will be rejected. Despite that apparent drawback, here are a number of reasons you may choose to submit to the JofUR:

- You can send your manuscript here without suffering waves of anxiety regarding the eventual fate of your submission. You know with 100% certainty that it will not be accepted for publication.
- There are no page-fees.
- You may claim to have submitted to the most prestigious journal (judged by acceptance rate).
- The JofUR is one-of-a-kind. Merely submitting work to it may be considered a badge of honor.
- You retain complete rights to your work, and are free to resubmit to other journals *even before our review process is complete.*
- Decisions are often (though not always) rendered within hours of submission.

Instructions to Authors

The JofUR solicits any and all types of manuscript: poetry, prose, visual art, and research articles. You name it, we take it, and reject it. Your manuscript may be formatted however you wish. Frankly, we don't care.

After submitting your work, the decision process varies. Often the Editor-in-Chief will reject your work out-of-hand, without even reading it!

However, he might read it. Probably he'll skim it. At other times your manuscript may be sent to anonymous referees. Unless they are the Editor-in-Chief's wife or graduate school buddies, it is unlikely that the referees will even understand what is going on. Rejection will follow as swiftly as a bird dropping from a great height after being struck by a stone. At other times, rejection may languish like your email buried in the Editor-in-Chief's inbox. But it will come, swift or slow, as surely as death. Rejection.

Submissions should be emailed to *J.Universal.Rejection@gmail.com*. Small files only, please. Why not just send the first couple pages if it is long?

Subscriptions

An individual subscription may be secured for £120 per year (four issues). Institutional and library subscriptions are also available; prices will be provided upon enquiry. It is unknown whether the subscription will be delivered in print or as electronic content, because no one has yet ordered one.

Archives

- March 2009 (Vol 1, No 1) contents:
  (empty)
- June 2009 (Vol 1, No 2) contents:
  (empty)
- September 2009 (Vol 1, No 3) contents:
  (empty)
- December 2009 (Vol 1, No 4) contents:
  (empty - because we were on holiday)
- March 2010 (Vol 2, No 1) contents:
  (empty)
- June 2010 (Vol 2, No 2) contents:
  (empty)
- September 2010 (Vol 2, No 3) contents:
  (empty)
- December 2010 (Vol 2, No 4) contents:
  (lost when HD crashed - presumed empty)